OTTAWA
Unbuttoned

Also by Dave McIntosh:

Terror in the Starboard Seat
The Seasons of My Youth
The Collectors

OTTAWA
Unbuttoned

or who's running this country anyway? By Dave McIntosh

Stoddart

First published in 1987 by
Stoddart Publishing Co. Limited
34 Lesmill Road
Toronto, Canada
M3B 2T6

CANADIAN CATALOGUING IN PUBLICATION DATA
McIntosh, Dave
     Ottawa unbuttoned
ISBN 0-7737-2115-0
1. McIntosh, Dave. 2. Canada - Politics and government - 1935.
3. Journalists - Ontario - Ottawa - Biography. 4. Canadian Press
Association - Biography. I. Title.
FC609.M25 1987   971.064'092'4   C86-094935-4
F1034.2.M25 1987

Jacket Illustration: Graham Pilsworth

Printed and bound in the United States

CONTENTS

AUTHOR'S NOTE

I worked for twenty-six mostly joyous years for The Canadian Press (it insists on the capital T to distinguish itself from the hoi polloi Canadian press) for which my pension, unindexed, at age sixty-five, is $221 a month. I have lived in Ottawa since 1953. This book is not a rehash, to use the newspaper term for warmed-over copy. It consists mainly of heretofore unreported happenings within my personal knowledge, with a revisionist assault on accepted scripture about some reported happenings. I have always operated on the principle that governments should be changed more often than underwear. This book is therefore designed to illuminate our governance by unclothing our governors.

PART ONE

POLITICS: The Pursuit of Private Interests

Political parties once had a principle belonging to them, absurd perhaps, and indefensible, but still carrying a notion of duty, by which honest minds might easily be caught. But they are now combinations of individuals who, instead of being the sons and servants of the community, make a league for advancing their private interests.

James Boswell, *The Journal of a Tour to the Hebrides*

1

Trust Us, Bob

Winning politics depends not so much on how smart you are as on how dumb your opponent is. Lucky Pierre Trudeau had Robert Stanfield and Joe Clark for antagonists.

There was Stanfield in the catbird seat in 1968. He was a new leader for the Conservatives after the ousting of John Diefenbaker. The Liberals were in wild disarray as they fought internally and savagely over the party's leadership pending the imminent retirement of Lester Pearson.

And then the Liberals were defeated in the House of Commons on a vote of confidence, mainly because so many of them were away advancing their individual aspirations or, like Mitchell Sharp, waiting for a likely candidate to back to ensure himself a posh cabinet portfolio. Incredibly, Stanfield blew it, mostly because he never understood the difference between politics and government: politics is gaining power, government is keeping it. Poor Bob, or Boob, as Diefenbaker called him.

Pierre Elliott Trudeau announced his candidacy for the Liberal leadership February 14, 1968, but his campaign and those of the other half-dozen serious candidates were quickly eclipsed five days later when, late in the evening, the Liberals lost a Commons vote, 84 to 82, on tax legislation. The relaxed Bob Winters, acting prime minister, went to the telephone in his temporary office on the third floor of the Commons to call Pearson, on holiday in Jamaica. We reporters hung around the door until Winters came out.

"What did Pearson say?" we demanded.
"He said, 'O God'," Winters replied delightedly.

Pearson flew back from Jamaica right away to salvage the situation by persuading Stanfield to agree to a day's adjournment of the Commons while he devised a motion saying the vote on a tax measure, always considered a vote of confidence, was not really a vote of confidence and could be overtaken by a new vote. One of the persuaders Pearson used was Louis Rasminsky, governor of the Bank of Canada and already a proven political toady. (When Diefenbaker fired James Coyne as governor, Rasminsky succeeded him after signing a document declaring that in any disputes over monetary policy between the bank and the government, the government would be the automatic winner.) Rasminsky never admitted his meeting with Stanfield took place, and Stanfield himself alluded to it only in these terms: "I knew what was going on because those in charge felt I ought to know." What Pearson wanted him to know, or believe, was that the Canadian dollar was in a terrible mess and that the uncertainties surrounding a fallen government might drive it down and down. Stanfield, still naive, said as much in the Commons debate on June 1, 1970, on the unpegging of the dollar — to float up. Speaking of 1968, Stanfield said: "The government lost a vote of confidence in the House. If the Opposition had prolonged that debate, with continued uncertainty as to the life of the government, the Canadian dollar would have gone down out of sight. . . . I say that no Canadian government has been in more serious financial difficulties than . . . in 1968, and I know what I am talking about."

Stanfield after all that time (more than two years) apparently did not see that he had been had by Pearson and Rasminsky. It was true that the government had had to borrow nearly $1 billion on international markets to cover a currency exchange crisis. But did the prospect of a Stanfield government make it a likelihood that the bottom would fall out of our dollar? Hardly, but Stanfield was jigged like a squid.

Conservative MP Gordon Churchill, an able strategist who played a key part in the Tories' 1957 victory after twenty-two years out of power, told Stanfield not to go into the Commons to accept a one-day adjournment. The government had been beaten on a vote of confidence. The Liberals had no constitutional choice but to resign in favor of Stanfield or call an election. Stanfield ignored him.

Stanfield didn't seem to understand what had happened in

the Commons until it was over. He and his party answered the Commons bell for its regular sitting and quickly agreed to the adjournment. As the MPs filed out of the chamber, Jim Nelson of Canadian Press asked Mr. Stanfield whether he realized that his response to the Commons bell was an admission that the government was still governing. Stanfield's jaw dropped, as if the realization had just struck him for the first time, though Churchill had advised him to that effect. The day's adjournment gave Pearson time to sick Rasminsky onto Stanfield with his false message of dire straits for the dollar. The Liberals assembled their members for a new vote which wiped out the 84 to 82 loss and the Commons sailed on calmly, allowing the Liberals plenty of time to hold their convention in peace and quiet and elect Trudeau leader. Trudeau then immediately called an election and won in a walk. Stanfield had missed a golden opportunity to spread panic and dismay among the Liberals and to capitalize on being a new and fresh leader. Instead, he permitted the Liberals to have an even newer and fresher leader for an election which came anyway only a month or two after the one he would have had if he had brought down the government. The Liberals themselves at the time weren't keen on Trudeau. If Stanfield had forced an election or, even more in his favor, made the Liberals cling to power with an interim leader in place of Pearson, his opponent would have likely been Paul Hellyer, an easy mark.

2

Enter the Destroying Worms

Joe Clark (Joe Cluck, to Diefenbaker) by contrast blew it after he had actually gained power. He was toppled by a fatal combination of his own ineptitude and insatiable Liberal hunger for power. It took a Liberal junta only ten days — from December 3 to 13, 1979, to plot and carry out a bloodless coup based almost entirely on a single Gallup poll.

Clark won the May 22, 1979, election, but with a minority government: 136 seats out of 282. He won because the Conservatives more than doubled their strength in Ontario to fifty-seven seats from the twenty-five they held after the 1974 election.

One would have thought they would have lavished political care on Ontario.

Trudeau resigned as Liberal and opposition leader November 21 to the relief of many Canadians and especially of many Liberals, particularly Jean Chrétien, Donald MacDonald, Francis Fox and Lloyd Axworthy, all of whom wanted to succeed him. (Chrétien was nothing if not frank. I once attended a Speaker's garden party in the Gatineau Hills and Chrétien, smilingly serious, was openly saying to small groups: "Can anybody here tell me when that goddam Trudeau is going to quit?") A few days after Trudeau's resignation, the Liberal junta — Allan MacEachen, Marc Lalonde, Jim Coutts and Keith Davey — began picking up blips that western Ontario had turned sour on Clark. Sure enough, on December 3, the Gallup poll showed Liberals 47 per cent, Conservatives 28 per cent. This was up seven points for the Liberals, down eight for the Conservatives since the May election, when the Liberals had dropped in Ontario to thirty-two of ninety-five seats from fifty-five of eighty-eight in 1974. If Ontario was going back to the Liberals, the Tories were in bad trouble. But the Conservatives paid no heed. With Trudeau on the way out, the Liberals would be preoccupied with a leadership race. Plenty of time. That had been the attitude of Clark and his cabinet since the election. They had drifted along through the summer and early autumn, making some sound but not producing any real action. They swallowed themselves on Clark's ill-conceived policy to move the Canadian embassy in Israel from Tel Aviv to Jerusalem (the Arab countries were furious and threatened retaliation in the form of an oil embargo). They were all over the oil patch in policy on Petrocan. They fiddled around with their so-called "envelopes" to try to control spending. They brandished the sword at the civil service but didn't swing it and, in fact, left four former Liberal cabinet ministers in cushy government jobs. There was no sense of urgency about anything. There was no sparkle. Procrastination may be the lifeblood of majority governments, but it is the grave of minority administrations.

The Conservatives couldn't see any quicksand for them at least before the Liberals had a new leader (the convention had been set for Winnipeg March 28). Unfortunately for them, and despite all the previous examples, they didn't realize how power-hungry Liberals get after they have been away from the trough for only six months. Why should they have? The Tories were used to being out of power, for twenty-two years at one stretch, for seventeen at another. All since 1935.

The December 3 Gallup poll was sufficient proof for Senator Davey and Coutts, a management consultant who was Trudeau's chief aide, that they should go for it. Davey has long enjoyed a big reputation as an adviser on how to grab power, though his actual record since 1962 is not that hot: three majority governments, three minority governments and three losses (on the sports pages, a 3-3-3 record). Coutts, like the self-assured Dalton Camp of the Conservatives, couldn't even get elected to Parliament. No matter, that wasn't the game now. As Liberal leader Sir Wilfrid Laurier, later prime minister, said in 1893, "Principles without organization may lose; but organization without principles may often win."

While the rest of the Liberals were busy preparing for Winnipeg, (except John Turner, who opted out) Davey, Coutts, MacEachen and Lalonde began working on Trudeau to bring down the government and then withdraw his resignation.

They used an argument that went like this: Trudeau had been advised to call an election in May, 1978, when the polls showed he had a fair chance of winning. But he had shilly-shallied until the last possible moment in 1979, with defeat the result. Trudeau owed the Liberals one. The polls were propitious. He, Trudeau, could become prime minister again and erase the blot on his record put there May 22 by that "chinless wonder."

The Liberal caucus began taking the bait. So did Trudeau. After all, the December 3 Gallup poll was nothing more than the expected and customary reassurance that the Liberals are destined to govern and the Conservatives to represent the protest vote. Diefenbaker had been a six-year interregnum. Clark would be a six-months aberration.

Finance Minister John Crosbie presented his budget December 11. It didn't matter what was in it: the budget required a vote of confidence and the Liberals had determined to vote against it. The sententious New Democrats played right into the hands of Davey and Coutts, just as they had in 1972-74 in sustaining Trudeau. They presented a non-confidence motion which the Liberals could support while keeping a straight face.

The Conservatives didn't seem to sense what was going on.

They had two days to sound warnings, rally troops, halt the Liberals in their tracks. A silly story has persisted that the late Walter Baker, Conservative House leader, threw away Conservative power by miscounting the votes available to him. Baker was no more to blame than all the other Tory ministers. They were, as usual, caught asleep at the switch. Transfixed by the onrushing disaster, they couldn't even shield their eyes, let alone jump out of the way.

(One prime ministerial adviser who caught a lot of the blame internally was the Conservatives' national campaign chairman, Lowell Murray, who had been appointed to the Senate by Clark. A Cape Bretoner, Murray has spent nearly all his adult life (and a good deal of his childhood) in politics. Even after the 1980 electoral disaster, he continued to preach in caucus on how campaigns should be run. This infuriated some Conservatives and Walter Dinsdale, who had been a cabinet minister under Diefenbaker — but not under Clark — referred scornfully to Murray as the "senator for Condominium." The reference was to the fact that there was no opening except in Ontario when Clark wanted to name Murray to the Senate, where property qualifications apply. Murray had to rush out and buy an Ottawa condominium to qualify. Dinsdale had been a night fighter ace (five enemy planes destroyed) during the war and when he first ran for Parliament in a 1951 by-election, which he won, he and another Conservative, Alvin Hamilton, also a World War II flier, used a small plane to cover the Manitoba riding of Brandon-Souris. They hooked up a bullhorn and broadcast Tory advice from the air, causing a small girl to rush home and tell her parents that "God said to vote for Walter Dinsdale.")

As it turned out, the votes of Conservatives who could have been brought back from overseas would not have mattered because the separatist Social Credit group from Quebec abstained, giving silent aid to the Liberals. It would have done better to uphold the Conservatives, because Social Credit was wiped out in the 1980 election. But the Conservatives chose to try to bluff the Liberals. They could have postponed the vote on almost any trumped-out excuse but, again, they were looking at politics as some kind of knightly derring-do. The Liberals gave them plenty of warning. On Wednesday morning, December 12, the Liberal caucus began to get lathered up over the prospect of knocking off the Tories. At their Christmas party that night, Dutch courage was added to this heady brew. The Conservatives could hear the Liberals up and down the corridors celebrating a victory which wasn't to come until the next night, by vote of 139 to 133 against the government. Even the Liberal hopefuls who wanted to see Trudeau gone voted loyally with their party. They could have discreetly stayed away. But Trudeau would have noticed who was there and who was not and why jeopardize a cabinet portfolio if he were to be prime minister again? And he was, 147 seats to 103 for the Conservatives in the February 18, 1980, election. For five more years. The Tories proceeded quickly to tear down Clark, as they had Diefenbaker. This time the destroying worm was Brian Mulroney; the previous time it had been Dalton Camp.

3

Et Tu, Dalton

Mulroney's job was a lot easier than Camp's. Mulroney had to undermine a man who had blown a minority government after only half a year. But Camp pulled down Diefenbaker all the way from the biggest majority in Canadian history. (In 1958 Diefenbaker won 208 of 265 Commons seats, a percentage of 78.5. In 1984, Mulroney won 211 of 282 seats, a percentage of 74.8. Perhaps Mulroney's seat record of 211 will some day carry an asterisk, like Roger Maris' home-run record of 61 but accomplished in more games than Babe Ruth required for his 60 homers.)

People don't work for political parties for the fun of it. They want something in return, whether it be a senatorship, advertising contract, a cabinet portfolio, a judgeship, recognition by the press as an *éminence grise*, a soft job for a brother-in-law, or even the prime ministership. Camp wanted to be prime minister, even if it meant that he had to sabotage the man who had been prime minister longer than any Conservative since Borden (1911-20).

Camp made his political reputation (undeserved) for helping Robert Stanfield gain power in Nova Scotia in 1956 after twenty-three years of Liberaldom. Stanfield could have made it with the advice of a two-year-old. Camp had little or no part beyond advertising in Diefenbaker's titanic struggle to win his party's national leadership in 1956 and to beat the Liberals by a whisker in 1957. Camp showed up after Diefenbaker had coasted to his record victory in 1958. He was the campaign manager in the 1962 election when the Conservatives took 116 seats, 92 fewer than in 1958. Camp, like any advertiser, engaged in all kinds of tacky exercises. For instance, late in the campaign, near Halifax, a drunken driver wearing an old army jacket cut into the middle of the Diefenbaker cavalcade and had to be cut out by police. Camp said the Conservatives would appear oppressive if the drunk were some poor farmer, and he encouraged reporters to say the driver was a soldier. The Army vote was more expendable then the farm vote.

Diefenbaker barely survived the 1962 disaster with a minority government, but not 1963, though he prevented the Liberals from winning a majority, as he did again in 1965. We will return to those marvellous campaigns in a moment.

The search for a successor to Diefenbaker began in 1963, mostly through a whisper campaign by Camp. He was aided by others who genuinely believed that the Old Chief was a liability which the party had to shed, no matter how painfully. Generally, there were MPs, including some former cabinet ministers, who felt from their own experience under his prime ministership that he was not, or at least not any longer, a man who could make decisions and stick to them. Camp stepped up his anti-Diefenbaker campaign when he became national president of the party. In a well of bitterness, the Conservative association at Ottawa in November, 1966, decided on a leadership convention. Camp sat and watched his leader booed and hissed and made no attempt to stop it.

Camp then sounded out Conservative MPs — twice — on how many would back him for the leadership. Nothing could have shown more clearly Camp's political density. The MPs, when asked whether they would support him, stared at him in amazement — and they represented the anti-Diefenbaker faction; Camp didn't dare approach the Diefenbaker loyalists. In effect, the MPs told him: Who in hell would vote for Judas? Seventy-one Conservative MPs signed a document that Diefenbaker should remain leader. Three of the signers — George Hees, Alvin Hamilton, and Michael Starr — later became leadership candidates.

Even when Camp got on the Stanfield bandwagon he had to be quiet about it lest he further rouse the pro-Diefenbaker wing. The early pressure on Stanfield to run for the leadership came from Senator M. Grattan O'Leary, editor emeritus of the *Ottawa Journal* and long a power in federal politics, and Finlay MacDonald, a Halifax broadcaster. They were soon joined by Patrick Nowlan, Nova Scotia MP and son of the late George Nowlan, a respected member of Diefenbaker's cabinet, and Mrs. Jean Wadds, Ontario MP. Other MPs soon followed: Douglas Harkness, former defence minister; G.W. (Jed) Baldwin of Peace River who, to divorce himself from the Diefenbaker prairies, referred to himself as from northern rather than western Canada; Heath Macquarrie and David MacDonald of Prince Edward Island; Michael Forrestall of Halifax; and Gordon Fairweather from New Brunswick (Diefenbaker called him Featherweight).

Stanfield might have stood aside for Premier Duff Roblin of Manitoba, but Roblin left his declaration too late. Both went in and Stanfield beat Roblin on the fifth ballot when Davie Fulton threw to the Nova Scotian.

There was a telling little incident when the convention ended Saturday night, September 1, 1967. Camp waited in a corridor in Maple Leaf Gardens to see Stanfield. But Stanfield did not come. Camp waited half an hour, then left. Yesterday's hero, he was already the party's pariah. In 1969, Camp went to Manitoba to "help" the Conservative premier, Walter Weir, in that year's provincial election. Weir lost. In 1970, Camp offered his services to Conservative leader Richard Hatfield in New Brunswick. Hatfield asked Camp to stay away.

What Camp had done for his party was to substitute a three-time loser, Robert Stanfield (1968, 1972, 1974), for a three-time winner, John Diefenbaker (1957, 1958, 1962). In August, 1986, Mulroney appointed Camp his special adviser on re-election. Having taken Diefenbaker from 208 seats to 116, think what Camp will be able to do with Mulroney's 211.

Politically, the 1960s were as turbulent as the 1940s militarily and the 1930s and 1950s economically. Most of the turbulence was caused by Diefenbaker. Whatever he did, or didn't do, he filled the space around him. Even in his final years and at his vindictive worst, Diefenbaker could hold the House of Commons in thrall. (There were Liberals even more vindictive than Diefenbaker. J.W. Pickersgill and his wife taught their dog to defecate on Diefenbaker's lawn; I recall Pickersgill bragging one day in the National Press Club about his politically astute dog.)

Diefenbaker woke people up and kept them awake, something new for the Conservatives after the likes of Bob Manion, John Bracken and George Drew. We all liked Drew. He was an estimable man, honest, smart, and, best of all, an able teller of good jokes. But he came across in public as a stuffed shirt, which he wasn't. He just couldn't help himself. He was ruddy, a little heavy, and he looked as if he had forgotten his monocle. I remember one night leaving Stornoway, his official residence, with my wife and John and Vera Bird. We were the last out, as usual. Vera, who had met Drew for the first time that night, gave him an enormous, affectionate hug, tapped his big chest with a forefinger and declared: "George, you're not at all like people say. You're a real good shit." Drew was delighted. The Birds were invited back.

Permit me one George Drew joke. He told it at a press gallery dinner. I will shorten it. A sex therapist was conducting an all-male class and asked the participants how often they had sexual intercourse. Every night? A few hands. Twice a week? More hands. It finally came down to: once a year? One hand shot up. "My good man, why are you smiling?" the therapist asked. "Tonight's the night," was the happy reply.

4

A Stuffed Shirt in Ottawa

In contrast to Drew, Louis St. Laurent really was a bit of a stuffed shirt, a patrician who walked six blocks to work from the Roxborough apartment hotel where he lived and nodded to passers-by like a laird moving among his tenant farmers. Can you imagine him giving anybody the finger gesture, as Trudeau did later? St. Laurent's avuncular air (indeed, Norman Campbell of the *Toronto Telegram* re-christened him Uncle Louis) made him appear a good listener to (and fixer of) troubles of the common man. His biggest asset, apart from cabinet ministers like Pearson, Howe, Lesage, Martin, Claxton, Gardiner, and others, was his wife, who wanted only to live in her beloved Quebec City among her family but who pitched in loyally to help her husband discreetly at every turn in alien Ottawa. At Rideau Hall one evening, during a royal visit, Mme St. Laurent approached reporter Jim Nelson and me with a warm smile and said: "I'm going to turn and walk away from you and I want you to tell me whether my slip is showing." It wasn't and we hastily said so. St. Laurent, though a corporation lawyer turned corporate politician, did not forget his smalltown working background in the Eastern Townships of Quebec. He once opposed, for instance, a plan to beautify the parliamentary precinct by removing part of the ugly E.B. Eddy pulp and paper mill across the Ottawa River in Hull. "It is good for us politicians to be constantly reminded of where taxes come from," he said. Trudeau had the mill removed.

St. Laurent was one of the few Liberals to realize what terrible political damage had been done by the 1956 pipeline debate. He took it personally. The Liberals had plucked him out of nowhere and made him prime minister in 1948. (Mackenzie King resigned November 15, 1948. Two days earlier, King had met the Canadian Legion executive council, saying he wanted his last official business to be associated with Canada's veterans!) St. Laurent had illy repaid his party by allowing the pipeline debate to fuel itself from a simple financial issue into a full-blown fight over autocracy. Even at that, most people thought the Liberals would win the 1957 election. They had wrongly discounted the fired-up Diefenbaker, the prairie radical who had captured his party's leadership the previous year. Diefenbaker won, 112 seats to 105, and St. Laurent, broken, retired as soon as he decently could and Pearson became leader just in time to take the Liberals into an even worse disaster. Despite his 1957 minority, Diefenbaker accurately and acutely sensed that the Liberals were over-ripe for plucking. The Liberals confirmed this. Cringing abjectly at the prospect of an early election, they cravenly presented a motion (even Mrs. Pearson said it was awful) that Diefenbaker resign and turn the government back to them, without election. Diefenbaker wiped the floor with them. In the 1957 election, Quebec had given Diefenbaker only nine seats. It didn't miss the bandwagon on the second round in 1958, giving him fifty. Quebec learned from this. In 1984, it didn't wait one election to see how the wind was blowing, but leapt onto the Brian Mulroney bandwagon first chance, like the rest of the country. Who says there isn't one Canada?

5

Sod Huts and Diefendollars

It is difficult to recall now how crackerjack the Diefenbaker government was in its first year or so. The legislative mill ground swiftly and productively: national hospital insurance, higher old-age pensions, huge new outlays of mortgage money, entry into the North American Air Defence alliance, competition for CBC television and Air Canada, and a Canadian bill of rights. And there were all those measures in favor of the prairie farmer to whom Diefenbaker had made promises: a dam on the South Saskatchewan, cash advances for grain stored on the farm, acreage payments, roads to resources. Diefenbaker was fond of saying that he would be the last prime minister raised on a homestead because there was no more homestead land. He recalled how his father, William Thomas Diefenbaker, paid $250 for 121 tillable acres in 1904 by sitting on a milking stool in a queue in Prince Albert from Friday night to Monday morning when the land office opened. Young Diefenbaker had taken tea and buns to his father so that he could keep his place in the queue. "When my father got rich later on," Diefenbaker would say, "we moved into a sod hut." When the Diefenbaker home was moved to Regina as a museum, the curators tried to put a door in the north side to speed up visitor traffic. Diefenbaker had to over-rule them: "In those days nobody ever put a door on the north side of a house."

But things, as they inevitably do for prime ministers, began to go wrong. He made the right decision on the Arrow jet inter-ceptor (see chapter on defence) but bungled the handling of the cancellation, which, in turn, increased his dragging problem of unemployment. He was right in getting rid of James Coyne as governor of the Bank of Canada (it's unfortunate that every prime minister since hasn't done the same with every governor since) but so messed up the execution that some old Liberals in the Senate turned the blade on him. (Diefenbaker had one telling line in the whole affair when he scathingly described Coyne's acceptance of a fat pension increase from the bank's board of directors: "He sat, he saw, he took.") Diefenbaker never grasped the ferment of social change in Quebec and didn't have (or want) a Quebec lieutenant who could properly advise him. He danced around the nuclear warheads issue so fancifully and long that he and everybody else were exhausted and the problem lay inert at their feet, like a dead cat. There was the 1962 currency exchange crisis brought on partly by the record peacetime deficit in 1961 of $791 million. Liberals issued "Diefendollars" valued at 92½ cents American. Any federal politician today would hug Diefenbaker's deficit and dollar.

There was another problem for The Chief: he was up against a bunch of old pros on the Liberal side of the House — Pearson, Martin, Pickersgill, Lionel Chevrier, and, at the start, James Sinclair, father of the girl who was to become Trudeau's bride. Sinclair was the best needler, but the others had eternal persistence. It had been assumed that Opposition Leader Pearson, after two cozy decades in external affairs as deputy minister and minister, would be out of his political depth. But after a catastrophic start when Diefenbaker laughed him out of the House on the way to his huge majority, Pearson learned to mix it up. He never again let Diefenbaker trap him, as The Chief had in the Herbert Norman affair. Norman had been pilloried as a communist in 1951 by a U.S. Senate subcommittee though he had been given top security clearance the year before following a six-week interrogation by the RCMP. He was, said his boss, External Affairs Minister Pearson, a trusted and valuable official of his department. Nonetheless, Norman was put in the closet by External until 1956, when Pearson made him ambassador to Egypt. The U.S. Senate subcommittee again branded Norman a communist and Norman, forty-seven, committed suicide April 4, 1957, by jumping from the top floor of his nine-storey apartment building in Cairo despite stout defence from Prime Minister St. Laurent, Pearson, Parliament, and the press and public in general.

One of Diefenbaker's primary political rules was "Never ask

a question unless you know the answer." He kept prodding Pearson in the Commons for more information about Norman and Pearson finally conceded on April 12, 1957, that Norman had "as a student ideological beliefs which were close to some brand of communism" and that he "regretted these earlier associations and had voluntarily abandoned them by the time he entered the Canadian foreign service" in 1939. It has been generally assumed that Norman made American enemies when he served in Japan, where he had been born, immediately after the war and that these enemies, mainly in the military, used witch-hunting Joe McCarthyism in the United States — it slopped over into Canada — to hound him to his death. And still. Still the question remains: why would a Canadian scholar and diplomat who had the complete support and sympathy of his prime minister, minister, department, Parliament and public want to kill himself? Why, as he said at the end, did he have to "live without hope?" Did he feel guilt that he had betrayed Canada? Or was it, perhaps, that he was causing too much trouble for his government? Some day we may know.

Whatever his faults and misfortunes, Diefenbaker had fired up the political imagination of Canadians like no one else in years. The huge campaign rallies of 1962, 1963 and 1965 attested to that. Diefenbaker wasn't fully at ease in 1962 because he had a government and record to try to defend. He was at his best in 1963 and 1965 when he was the underdog and could go on the attack. In 1962, he made some campaign mistakes which he wouldn't have dreamed of making before. For instance, he told rallies in some border communities, long used to making heavy purchases in American towns, how devaluation of the dollar was going to help all Canadians. This was a set part of his speech and he seemed to forget where he was and not take that part out in communities along the U.S. boundary. And his ear for the interjection from the crowd sometimes failed him. His rule of thumb was that interjections were hostile. But sometimes he would be cheered on by an enthusiastic follower: "Go get 'em, Dief." The Chief, thinking he had been heckled with "Go home, Dief," or some such, would retort with one of his standard ripostes: "Ah, there's one voice in the wilderness," or, "There's one who stumbled into the wrong meeting." The supporter in the crowd would be deeply embarrassed while his neighbors, thinking that they had heard wrong and Diefenbaker right, would glare at him as at a viper in a nest.

Diefenbaker survived with a minority but in the 1962-63 session of Parliament forty of the sixty-one legislative items died on the order paper as the opposition waited to pounce, which it did February 5, 1963, and Pearson became prime minister, also with a minority, 129 seats to 95 for the Conservatives. Finance Minister Walter Gordon and Liberal promoter Keith Davey talked Pearson into trying for a parliamentary majority in 1965. The result was a difference of two seats — 131 Liberals and 97 Conservatives — and more minority. Gillis Purcell, the general manager of Canadian Press, was so mad at the outcome (three minority governments in three elections in four years, at great reportorial cost to CP) that he ordered me to find out who was responsible and get an explanation, if any might be had. We all knew who was responsible and at 4 a.m. I began phoning around for Gordon. He was nowhere to be found, of course. He had already gone underground.

During this time, Paul Martin was being a brilliant external affairs minister, overshadowed only because Pearson had held the portfolio.

6

Paul Martin, Christian

Paul Martin did his best in Ottawa to hide the fact that he is a practising Christian.

He talked in rotund phrases so that everybody would think he didn't believe in anything much. He dyed his hair jet black in his leadership campaign against Pearson so that everybody would think he was a bit of a faker. And he was hard on his staff to make everybody think he was unfeeling.

But as a member of the St. Laurent government, Martin used the health portfolio shamelessly to help people. He would fix a pension for somebody who didn't quite have all the necessary, red-tape qualifications. He would arrange a grant to keep some obscure but worthwhile cause or project afloat. He would dig into his own pocket for the handicapped and destitute. Evelyn Hickey, who ran a Red Cross House in downtown Ottawa, told me once: "When all else fails, I call Paul. His only question is 'What do you need?'" Those were the days when ministers took phone calls.

Granted, all these little attentions are the essence of keeping governments in office. But Martin never let on that he was the fixer and philanthropist, as minister of the crown or private citizen. His charity was carried out under the table, so to speak.

Paul Martin represented Windsor, Ontario, like no other riding was ever represented in Parliament. He once left an important NATO Council meeting in 1963 to make sure an announcement had gone out about a $25,000 bridge repair contract in Belle River, part of his constituency.

Martin knows a vast number of people by name. He seldom misses a name or face. But when he has, the gaffe has been a beaut, like this one: Martin was home, as he was every weekend for any gathering of more than one. The occasion was a large garden party and Martin was there early to shake hands all round. As he began his greetings, he ran into a man I'll call Fred Clark.

"How's your wife, Fred?"
"She died last week, Paul."

Martin offered his sympathy and moved on. He eventually arrived back at his starting point, where Fred Clark was sipping tea. Martin's internal computer blipped.

"How's your wife, Fred?"
"She's still dead, Paul."

Martin said himself that much of his constituency work was excruciatingly boring. But, if you don't get elected, and help enough of your political colleagues to get elected, and stay elected, you can never hope to see your ideas translated into government policy and implemented.

Martin's prolixity in the House of Commons became known as "Martinese," but it served his purpose. Martin was cautious, again on the grounds that if you want to have your ideas transformed into the law of the land you don't blow your chances by mouthing off or making snap statements which your constituents may hold against you.

The only time I saw an incautious Martin was in 1964 when he put a Canadian peacekeeping contingent into the air for Cyprus before he had any assurance that the United Nations was going to agree to a peacekeeping operation there. He turned out to be right, and Canada was in the field at full strength before other UN members showed up in dribs and drabs weeks and months later.

Martin loved the external affairs portfolio. He worked hard at it. By the time he finished his daily late afternoon call to Norman Hull at the *Windsor Star* to keep abreast of every newsbit in his riding, there was no time to eat before the evening round of diplomatic receptions. My wife and I one evening saw Martin perform the slickest sleight-of-hand we have ever seen.

It was the usual six-to-eight affair, this one at the Russian embassy, and Martin had arrived direct from his parliamentary office. He had a drink in his left hand and had just scooped up a right handful of tiny breaded scallops, brought around by a roving waiter.

"I'm starved," Martin said, popping a couple of warm scallops into his mouth.

At that very moment, the Russian ambassador, late for his own party, bore down on Martin, hand extended.

I must have blinked, because the next moment I saw Martin shaking hands with the ambassador. I looked down, thinking Martin must have deposited his handful of scallops quickly on the floor. The floor was as clean as a whistle. And so, apparently, was the ambassador's hand. Martin's drink was still in his left hand.

"Where did they go?" I asked Jean, meaning the scallops.

She shook her head in mystification.

The only possible explanation, we reasoned long into the night, was that Martin had plunged his hand into his right coat-pocket, dropped the scallops, and wiped his hand clean on the inside of his pocket and its flap as, in one swift, flowing movement, he purified his palm.

It was a terrible day for Martin (and Canada) when Trudeau dumped him from external affairs in favor of the obsequious Mitchell Sharp who had thrown his timorous support to Trudeau just before the Liberal leadership convention in exchange for future considerations, namely, external affairs.

I was present when Trudeau emerged from doing the dirty deed in Martin's second-floor office in the East Block in April, 1968, as the prime minister put together his first cabinet. At that time, it was still possible for a reporter to walk into the East Block, though Trudeau was soon to stop that. Already the west door was barred to the press, but I had walked in the south door and up the stairs to the second floor where Trudeau's and Martin's offices were located.

"What are you doing here?" Trudeau said as he pushed out the green baize door of Martin's office. He wasn't belligerent, just surprised.

"To ask whether Mr. Martin is still in the cabinet," I said.

"You'd better ask him," Trudeau said, and hurried down the corridor to his own office. He didn't appear upset.

Martin emerged a moment later. His eyes were full. I walked beside him down the stairs.

"Are you still in the cabinet, Mr. Martin?"

"Oh, yes", he said resignedly.

"What portfolio?"

"You know, Dave, that's up to the prime minister to announce."

"External affairs?"

"I don't feel much like talking," he said.

By this time, we had come out of the south door and he headed for the old Rideau Club less than a block away. It was a sunny day, but chilly and windy. Martin had on a topcoat which he had not buttoned and it billowed around him like a grey sail. I stopped and he stumbled on as if he weren't seeing properly, as if he had been dealt a mortal blow. He had. His new job was government leader in the Senate.

7
———

Pig Farming Days and the Election of '65

I had years of fun reporting for Candian Press. Ralph Vaughan of the *Halifax Herald* and I drove fast from Halifax to Port Mouton on the south shore to report the wreck of the *Wicklow Head*, hired a boat to get close to the scene and took the crew off the grounded freighter. I was at the sinking of the Liberal-Conservative coalition in British Columbia by W.A.C. Bennett ("come on in, boys, what can I tell you today?") There were the joyous months of hearings in the case of Montreal drug runner Lucien Rivard and the bribery attempts by crooked officials in Ottawa to spring Rivard from jail (they failed and Rivard called them, on the witness stand, an inept "gang of fuckers," causing a gulp by the rather staid female translator). There were the Con-federation debates in Newfoundland, where the switchboard oper-ator at the Newfoundland Hotel branded me a Canadian spy and wouldn't put through any of my calls, in or out, and I had to use an outdoor box down the street. I first met Joey Smallwood in a dingy room on the St. John's waterfront on a rainy Sunday afternoon. He was all alone and the room was lit by a single, unshaded low-watt bulb hanging from the ceiling on a shoelace. "Are you Mr. Smallwood?" I asked the apostle of Confederation. It was the last question I got in for two hours. Later, out at the posh Colony Club, I found Don Jamieson, Geoff Stirling and some Crosbies on the verandah telling about Joey's pig-farming days at Gander during the war and how he would slit the throat of any pig which looked sick and pack it off quickly to a military mess.

Bundled and goggled to the eyeballs against cold and snow blindness, I went into an igloo at Cambridge Bay to see how an Eskimo family lives: adults in shirtsleeves, babies naked in the toasty warmth, they all laughed until they cried at the spaceman from the south whose red face was mercifully covered.

In Tokyo in 1950, a rum and water at my hotel was three cents; a rum and coke was seven cents.

But the most fun I had was the 1965 federal election campaign. Let's begin with Richard Rohmer, bestselling author, senior officer in the militia, and amateur Conservative adviser. Somehow he got himself appointed military adviser to Diefenbaker on the campaign train, one of the last such trains in our political history. He kept churning out pages of typewritten bumf for inclusion in Diefenbaker's speeches and Diefenbaker discarded them all. He wasn't fussy about military subjects and he didn't want to remind the electorate about the Arrow and nuclear warheads and all that dreadful stuff that had helped cause his downfall. Rohmer complained to Tom Van Dusen and Greg Guthrie, two of Diefenbaker's aides, that The Chief wasn't using his carefully-crafted paragraphs on the subject of defence. How was it being overlooked? Van Dusen and Guthrie never needed more of an opening than that. They told Rohmer that Diefenbaker wanted to use his stuff but that he had to assemble his speeches out of a mass of material and didn't have time to ascertain which gems had been supplied by Rohmer. Perhaps, the terrible two suggested, Rohmer might put his thoughts down on colored paper so that it would be instantly recognizable. At the next campaign stop at a major town, Van Dusen and Guthrie looked out the train window to see Rohmer staggering down the station platform under reams of pink paper. As they later reported, this enabled Diefenbaker to spot immediately Rohmer's material and chuck it even more swiftly into the wastepaper basket.

It was an early-morning meeting in a hole-in-the-wall Liberal committee room in downtown Toronto. And it was raining. Would I get out of bed to attend Pearson at this throwaway event on a long day's schedule? Better do it. You can never tell. And the good, grey Canadian Press did them all. Dick Avery of Broadcast News, CP's radio affiliate, came with me. We were the only two reporters present. Dick stuck his mike near Pearson's face and I slouched against the wall of the tiny room to ease my hangover. Suddenly, I woke up. What in hell was Pearson saying? What he was saying was that if Canadians didn't give him a majority this time there'd be still another election. In effect, the voters had better deliver now or they'd have to bear another campaign, which would make it six in a decade. I skimmed back to the office and wrote a bulletin. I hadn't talked to Dick but he was fixing his own story elsewhere in the CP building. Then we tore to the airport to fly with Pearson to Vancouver. None of the other reporters knew about the story during the five-hour flight. Pearson himself was apparently taken aback when he was met by a press crowd at Vancouver: what was this about yet another election?

Pearson said he hadn't said it — or anything like that. Dick O'Hagan, Pearson's press secretary, a personable and reasonable man, tried to explain that it was all "cause and effect" and that Pearson had been trying to enthuse Liberal workers so that they wouldn't have to go through it all again soon. O'Hagan hadn't been at the meeting in the morning. Radio stations began playing the Pearson tapes consecutively or, as they say today, back-to-back. First Dick's tape from Toronto, then Dick's tape from Vancouver denying the first one had been said. My colleagues were sore as hell at me. What did I mean getting up in the morning like that to attend a lousy meeting of campaign workers? Surely I could judge news better than that. I asked John Dauphinee, No. 2 (later No. 1) man at Canadian Press, what would have happened if Dick hadn't had a tape of that morning meeting. "That's a very good question," he said.

CP regularly switched reporters travelling with the party leaders to show how unbiased and dispassionate it was. So this time I was on a Diefenbaker morning flight west out of Toronto, sitting beside François Morrisset of Radio-Canada, a roly-poly, happy-go-lucky man. He told me that the night before at the end of the rally he had met a tall, attractive woman who told him that Diefenbaker had the sexiest handshake she had ever felt. Just then, Mrs. Diefenbaker came down the aisle of the plane, nodding at those reporters whom she judged deserved her temporary recognition. "I'm going to tell Olive," François said. "O my God, don't," I said. François insisted. "You can't know her very well," I said. Looking up at Mrs. Diefenbaker with his cherubic smile, François told her, just like he had told me. She bristled. "Who told you a dreadful thing like that?" she demanded. "That's the very kind of story that gets started and can't be stopped. Well, we must put a stop to this one, and right now." François tried to slump as far down in his seat as I had since he had stopped her for his goddam story-telling. Mrs. Diefenbaker strode on. There was a long silence. At last, François said to me, "How did you get to know her so well?"

8

And the Ladies of the Club ... Edna, Olive & Maryon

On November 21, 1950, seventeen soldiers of the 2nd Regiment, Royal Canadian Horse Artillery, en route to the war in Korea, were killed in a CNR train wreck at Canoe River, B.C. A telegrapher was charged with negligence. At the time, Diefenbaker was returning from Australia and had arranged to meet his wife, Edna, in Hawaii for a holiday. He received a message that she couldn't go to Hawaii but would meet him in Vancouver. They met there and Diefenbaker found out why his wife couldn't make it to Hawaii: she was dying of leukemia. The telegrapher had tried to see Diefenbaker to ask him to defend him, but he was away. But Edna saw him, that being the kind of thing she would do, and promised that Diefenbaker would help him. She told Diefenbaker that she probably shouldn't have made the promise but that she felt it had to be done. Diefenbaker told his wife he would defend the telegrapher, and he did, brilliantly. He brought out how CNR officials had met to co-ordinate their testimony in the luxury of Jasper Park Lodge, travelling there in club and parlor cars while the soldiers who had been killed had been accommodated in old, wooden colonist cars. The telegrapher was acquitted and every railroader remembered. In telling the story to friends in later years, Diefenbaker said it was typical of Edna to try to help others, and that she had done so even when dying.

Maryon Pearson never made any secret of her abhorrence of politics. At a campaign meeting once at Elliott Lake, the centre of Pearson's riding, Pearson asked the crowd whether anyone had anything else to bring up. "Yes," said Maryon, not in an undertone, "that last cup of coffee." On another occasion at Elliott Lake, a prominent Liberal woman was pinning a corsage on Maryon and stuck the pin into her. "Get lost," Maryon barked.

She didn't like politics but she especially didn't like it out in the boondocks. She held Pearson to his promise not to try to stay in the prime minister's job more than five years.

Diefenbaker's second wife, Olive, was completely different. She played the political game all the way though it was difficult for her because she was a prude. But she gave marvellous support to Diefenbaker. A widowed school teacher, she took good care of Diefenbaker and puffed up his morale, something he badly needed after his 1958 majority melted away.

My most lasting impression of Mr. and Mrs. Diefenbaker is of them on the stage in the mining town of Trail, B.C., one Saturday night in the 1962 campaign, only a night after Diefenbaker had faced a lot of empty seats in Edmonton and Charlie King of Southam had written that the "Diefenbubble burst." Diefenbaker rarely lost his temper but he did about plays on his name and he chewed out King the first opportunity he got, which was after the Trail meeting. Diefenbaker was barely into his speech that Saturday night when some Doukhobor women of the Sons of Freedom sect sitting near the stage carried out their usual form of protest: they stripped. The crowd was deeply embarrassed, mostly because of the embarrassment they supposed had been caused The Chief. Any other politician might have retreated in confusion. Not Diefenbaker. "I come from the farm and I know what those things are for," he sang out above the foot-shuffling and scattered boos for the strippers. He wheezed out his high-pitched laughter. In seconds, he had the crowd laughing and applauding. Most of the reporters went racing across the hall, presumably to get names as red-faced Mounties tried to cover the women. "There they go," Diefenbaker said, "they've never seen anything like that before." Laughter and applause. He spotted me still at the press table trying to get down what he was saying. "There must be something queer about him," Diefenbaker said, still wheezing with laughter. The Doukhobor women were led out quietly by the police and the meeting resumed. Only then did Mrs. Diefenbaker change her position. The moment the incident had started, she had turned in her chair so that she was looking into the wings in the opposite direction, pretending that the whole thing simply wasn't taking place.

Mrs. Diefenbaker once received comedian Rich Little when

he went to see Diefenbaker to present him with a new record, including his impression of The Chief. She gave him tea but when Little actually tried to hand over the record, she said, "Oh, I'm afraid we can't accept anything like that." Little left, bewildered. She knew what was best for her husband.

Douglas Harkness, the defence minister whose resignation from cabinet led to the fall of the Diefenbaker government in 1963, found out what support and loyalty meant to Olive Diefenbaker. He wrote in a memoir soon after the fall:

> One other facet of the two weeks' struggle preceding my resignation was the effort made by Olive Diefenbaker to persuade my wife to put pressure on me to give way to the Prime Minister. She telephoned Fran several times, talked to her as opportunity offered, and tried to get her to spend the day with her driving to Montreal and back. These attempts to influence my wife had no success, but I resented them as a very unfair form of pressure. Olive's statements were illuminating, however, as to how Diefenbaker's mind was working and in showing the advanced state of megalomania he had reached. For example, she said he could not possibly give in to my point of view now as it would give other members of the cabinet the idea they could stand out against him and force their ideas through; also that he would appear as a weak man in history. It was quite evident from their conversations that Diefenbaker's idea was that his decisions must be accepted by everyone and that his own vanity was the overriding consideration in his mind rather than the welfare of the country or that of the party.

9
___

Renegade In and Out of Power

Harkness was too severe, I think, and blind to Diefenbaker's appealing side. When Peter Newman wrote *Renegade in Power: The Diefenbaker Years* he took a copy of the book to Diefenbaker's office. An aide took it in to the prime minister. Diefenbaker made his usual comment that he never read fiction and tossed the book into a tray. When the aide returned later, without knocking, Diefenbaker was reading the book voraciously (he was a speed reader), holding it between his knees under the desk.

On another occasion, Jim Nelson, briefly Diefenbaker's press secretary, was accompanying the prime minister to Toronto and clutching a briefcase which Diefenbaker had told him not to let out of his sight. Nelson dutifully lugged the case around all day, a little puffed up, he said, to be entrusted with vital state papers. At last, that evening, Diefenbaker called for the briefcase, opened it with a flourish and took out the only article inside — a clean shirt.

One of my favorite stories about Diefenbaker is how he handled particularly vitriolic and scurrilous letters he received. He would reply immediately, telling the sender that his (the sender's) name was being used by somebody else to write libelous letters and that he should put the matter in the hands of a lawyer. (Another former minister I know used to reply that he considered such letters tantamount to death threats and was turning them over to the RCMP). Diefenbaker handled potential conflict-of-interest cases in cabinet with these words: "Do you own any stocks? Get rid of them."

Stripped of the prime ministership and of the Conservative leadership, Diefenbaker practised some exquisite forms of torture on former colleagues who had helped to dump him. One day he ran into Paul Martineau at the Ottawa airport. Diefenbaker had made Martineau a cabinet minister (mines) in 1962 but didn't have his backing when he tried to retain his party's leadership. The conversation went something like this:

Diefenbaker: Catching a plane, Paul?
Martineau: Yes, I'm going out w---. [Too late Martineau realized his mistake].
Diefenbaker: Out west, eh? So am I. That's just fine, we can sit together all the way.
Martineau: Oh, but I'm afraid I smoke.
Diefenbaker: Oh, that never bothers me. We have a lot to talk about don't we? Why haven't you come to see me?

You know, I'm expecting all my old cabinet ministers to contribute $5,000 each to the Diefenbaker museum.
[Martineau walked disconsolately to the plane, Diefenbaker immediately behind, still talking volubly.]

10

Bye Bye, B & B

Pearson, in his comparatively short run (for Liberals) of five years as prime minister, accomplished much more than Trudeau in three times that length of time: medical care insurance, the Canada Pension Plan, the flag, the Order of Canada, the splendid Expo '67 as part of Canada's centennial, and bilingualism and biculturalism.

Trudeau is generally credited with B&B (or Bye-Bye, as some called it) but it was Pearson who got it rolling with the royal commission on the subject and introduction of bilingualism in the civil service. In the case of the latter, Pearson's policy was perfectly simple and straightforward: any member of the public was entitled to be served by government in French or English, whichever he chose. By the time the civil service finished with it, it had turned into an internal nightmare which set not rules on treating with the public but rules on how civil servants were to deal with each other on the issue of language. Along the way, the civil service rewarded itself with $40 million of public money a year ($800 each for 50,000 so-called bilingual civil servants) for the ability to speak the other official language, an ability achieved at public expense. It is entirely appropriate that the official levels of competence in the two languages are C, B and A, C being for the highest and A the lowest.

Everyone has his favorite B&B story. Here are a couple of mine. An English-speaking admiral and his family were given intensive language training for a year in Quebec City. Then he was posted to Victoria to finish his career. When I was working at the National Capital Commission, we had a summertime six-weeks, open-air nightly concert with a variety of bands, singers and instrumentalists. A bilingual master of ceremonies presided and unilingual singers were carefully balanced over the season. One day, Pierre Juneau, the chairman of the commission (one of his several Liberal patronage appointments) called me in to ask about what he said was the heavy prevalence of English-speaking acts. I said it might appear that way but if he looked carefully at the list he would see that the acts were bands or instrumentalists. He didn't seem to get my point and I had to spell it out for him: it didn't matter whether a guitar player spoke French or English or Swahili. He insisted that that wasn't good enough and the concert program (though after he left) was destroyed by a vain search for an equal number of acts by French- and English-speaking musicians.

Bilingualism reached another absurdity when Hamilton Southam, director of the National Arts Centre, interrupted a concert one evening to get the audience to its feet to observe the death of French president Georges Pompidou. He never did it for any Canadian, French- or English-speaking.

B&B will soon sort itself out, however. Before B&B, Franco-Ontarians ran nearly everything in Ottawa where both languages were needed. They are the only true bilinguals in this country, with a few exceptions in Quebec and elsewhere. The Franco-Ontarians in the federal civil service were annoyed by B&B: the government was paying for others to acquire an ability they already had at no public expense and the new flood of bilinguals was eroding their power base. But B&B is subsiding. The paid language training will soon end, impressed bilinguals will revert to unilingualism and the Franco-Ontarians will again assume their ascendancy. All's well that ends well.

Pearson said when he left office that he would need a re-training course in living: "I will have to learn to dial a telephone, cash a cheque, rake the garden, and things like that which you forget when you're spoiled and looked after as a prime minister, when you press a button and someone brings you a dollar or a jet plane." Pearson told me once that it was very difficult not to let the enormous power of the office go to the head. He was the least affected of all the politicians I have known, so much so that his orders were often ignored by members of his cabinet. Pearson had probably the leakiest cabinet in Canadian history; on occasion, a cabinet decision would reach the newspapers even before the meeting which had taken the decision concluded. The leaks were all designed to embellish the reputations of ministers who were trying to succeed to the prime ministership. One time Pearson gave an angry order that all leaks were to stop forthwith — and that was leaked. In reply to his party's farewell tribute, Pearson said, "I wish I could have done better. Perhaps I was fortunate that I have not done worse."

11

Do They Make Hats Big Enough?

Here are some examples in high contrast to Pearson's self-effacement:

Memorandum by External Affairs Minister Mark MacGuigan January 19, 1982, to Revenue Minister William Rompkey, responsible for Customs: "I am writing with regard to a letter ... concerning the attitudes of Customs officials at border crossings. I would be interested in seeing a copy of your reply, being that an examiner at the Windsor tunnel failed to recognize me after a speaking engagement in Detroit during the past year."

Finance Minister Edgar Benson in 1968 gave orders that the lights in his office in the Confederation building be left burning all night to make it appear that he was working hard. Years later, an aide at the last moment struck the postal code from the invitations to Benson's re-marriage. The code was K0K 2G0.

David Lewis when leader of the New Democratic Party kept threatening reporter Tom Earle of the CBC that he would report him to his bosses if he didn't put him on the air more often.

Sports Minister Iona Campagnolo demanded that she be put on air for the entire half-time television show at a Grey Cup game in Montreal. The show was to have been a parachute descent by the Royal 22nd Regiment but some felt the crowd would think the War Measures Act had been re-proclaimed and, instead, four paratroopers descended from the Big-O roof on ropes.

Speaker John Bosley and his wife went to a rustic lodge at Chaffey's Lock, Ontario, for a weekend. He appeared for dinner in black tie and was so angry that not another person was so dressed that he left in high dudgeon, hungry and never to return.

Robert Stanbury, minister of national revenue from 1972 to 1974, was inspecting Customs facilities at Vancouver airport. Three jets had just landed and there was a heavy crush at the Customs counters. One traveller yelled, "Who in hell is in charge here?" Stanbury stepped forward and announced, "I am the minister." The traveller kicked Stanbury in the shins.

Gen. Jacques Dextraze had been chairman of the CNR only a day or two when he ordered railway ties for his wife's garden.

Urban Affairs Minister André Ouellet sought and received this memo (June 9, 1978) from an aide, Richard Cannings: "I have contacted [Ed] Aquilina [general manager of the National Capital Commission], and have been given assurances that your name will henceforth be on the front cover of all NCC brochures and other publications."

Monique Bégin, Trudeau's health minister, could not drive herself but kept lecturing her chauffeurs — she had more than a dozen of them, serially — until one day on Highway 417, between Ottawa and Montreal, her driver pulled over onto the shoulder, turned off the ignition, got out of the car, crossed the median, and hitch-hiked back to Ottawa.

Even the photographer of prime ministers is a bighead. When Yousuf Karsh first came to Ottawa he was on his uppers and was known as Joe Karsh. The proprietor of a small eatery on Bank Street used to take pity on Karsh and give him free meals. Some years later, Karsh was walking by the restaurant and the proprietor, now an old man, rushed out: "How are you, Joe?" He got a frosty reception: "I am not Joe. I am Karsh, and I don't know you."

The biggest head, of course, belonged to Trudeau, who deserves a small section by himself.

12
_____

Trudeau in Residence: Fear & Loathing on Harrington Lake

Three long, thin lakes fill the narrow central valley of Gatineau Park whose southern wedge rests in the City of Hull, across the Ottawa River from the Parliament Buildings.

The middle one is Harrington Lake, or Lac Mousseau, to give it its French name. It is just over three miles long and a quarter-mile wide and is connected by short creeks to its two neighbors, Meach Lake, to the south, and Lac Philippe, to the north.

In 1951, the federal government bought 4,800 acres around Harrington Lake. The purchase price of $232,000 included twenty-one buildings, among them Harrington Lodge owned by the Edwards family (lumber) which had also owned 24 Sussex Drive in Ottawa whose reluctant first prime ministerial occupant in 1950 was Louis St. Laurent. The lodge was built in 1923 for $60,000, though by 1949 it was appraised at $30,000. It is surrounded by twelve acres of land at the southern tip of Harrington Lake.

Up until Mackenzie King's departure from office, the lodging of prime ministers had presented no problem. King lived in Laurier House, given to him by the widow of Sir Wilfrid, and owned a summer cottage in a 600-acre estate at Kingsmere Lake in Gatineau Park. He willed the estate to Canada which, awkwardly, made it accessible to the public and not for the private use of prime ministers. Nowadays, in summer, they serve tea in King's old cottage, sit in or take out, but recent speakers of the Commons have successfully squatted at the adjoining farmhouse, known as The Farm, at public expense. More than one speaker has tried to have a private swimming pool built at The Farm but low water pressure would require filling and refilling by tanker truck, not (so far) a politically acceptable sight. (When the film on Albert Speer, the Third Reich's economic whiz, was being made, the Ottawa producer needed a very tall and sturdy flagpole from which to fly an enormous, billowing Nazi swastika to form the backdrop for the film's title and credits. The flagpole used was the one in front of the King cottage — early in the morning, with nobody around).

With Kingsmere unavailable for prime ministerial cottaging, the purchase at Harrington Lake was made. The idea certainly didn't come from St. Laurent. He had had to be persuaded to move into 24 Sussex from the old-fashioned and comfortable Roxborough apartment hotel, which was a good deal handier to his office in the East Block. St. Laurent insisted on paying $5,000 annual rent for 24 Sussex, and so did his two immediate successors, Prime Ministers Diefenbaker and Pearson. Prime Minister Trudeau also paid the same amount — until he introduced a bill in Parliament abolishing the rent, starting with the prime minister in the next Parliament, who happened to be him. (Stornaway was not at first maintained as the opposition leader's residence at public expense. Being in opposition so long, the Conservatives bought a house in Rockcliffe Park for their leader. When they were trying to get rid of Diefenbaker after his fall, they spent little or nothing on maintenance and Diefenbaker had to stuff newspaper into window cracks to keep out winter blasts.)

Because St. Laurent took no interest at all in the Harrington Lake cottage, the National Capital Commission, the federal agency which tends the tulip beds and other public lands in the capital, rented it for $1,625 a season (May 1 to October 31). Tenants included David I. Ker, executive assistant at the *Ottawa Citizen*, Alan Jarvis, director of the National Gallery, and David Morgan of Henry Morgan and Co. Ltd., whose sub-tenant had a dog which chewed carpets and lawns with equal relish.

Diefenbaker was a keen fisherman and used the cottage on occasion as a fishing retreat, beginning in 1958. Pearson liked to go to Harrington now and then during the summer. He once gave a press reception there and I remarked to Mrs. Pearson that Harrington lacked only Kingsmere's ruins. "It doesn't lack ruins at all," she retorted. "What about Mike and me?" King's imported ruins at Kingsmere were a standing joke with the Pearsons because Pearson at the Canadian High Commission in wartime London had had to look after filling King's order in 1940 for some remnants from bombed Westminster.

The Harrington public property was still mostly public when Diefenbaker and Pearson went there. People could tramp the woods around the lake, and fish, and even drive to the lodge to gawk. Only the twelve acres around the two-and-a-half-storey cottage were regarded as private and, even then, with the prime minister away, people used to peek through the windows at the old wood stove in the kitchen and the rather meagre and bare furnishings.

All this changed when Trudeau took over in 1968. A gate, with an RCMP guard, was installed at a point long before the cottage came into view. The lakeshore and surrounding countryside were taken over by Trudeau as his private property and were patrolled by the RCMP on foot, by car and boat. One of Trudeau's favorite little tricks was to give the slip to the Mountie or Mounties detailed to follow him in the woods. A special security compound was built on the grounds and the guard detachment soon increased to twenty-six Mounties. A fair hike from the lodge, and even farther away than the caretaker's house, was the former W.D. Herridge cottage. It became the guest house where Trudeau put up old friends like Jean Marchand on weekends. (After Trudeau was married, Marchand was left alone in the guest cottage to drink by himself, and he stopped coming.)

Margaret Trudeau had a vegetable garden and a flower garden, neither of which she tended but for which she gave strict orders: only natural manure, and no spraying. In winter, the Trudeaus' two Irish setters, Farley and Fiona, frequently got loose and ran deer in Gatineau Park. Anybody else's dog was shot for killing deer but the Trudeaus' were quietly shipped to British Columbia at public expense.

On August 27, 1974, Trudeau telephoned Edgar Gallant, the chairman of the National Capital Commission, from the cottage at Harrington Lake. For twenty minutes, without a break, he complained about maintenance, or lack of it, at the lodge, and on this day specifically about noisy trucks dumping fill at the edge of the lake in front of the cottage.

The placement of the dock in the water and its retrieval in the fall had long been a matter of prime ministerial agitation. For one thing, there was a bureaucratic problem: the Department of Public Works was responsible for structures — the dock, boats, outbuildings — while the National Capital Commission looked after painting, gardening, lawnmowing and raking the beach. Each tried to shine in its small corner for the non-paying tenant, but Public Works tended to be clumsy. When it put the dock in the water, or took it out, it simply hooked it to a truck and dragged it across the front lawn, tearing the turf to shreds. The NCC was trying to fix the lawn, and was dumping some fill to make a neat little path beside the beach for placement and retrieval of the dock without creating the bi-annual grassy eyesore. Well and good, but it was making one hell of a racket.

James MacNiven, assistant general manager at the Commission, later reported to Chairman Gallant on Trudeau's complaints:

> I have been in touch with the Department of Public Works to find an easier way around the problem. I have arranged that NCC charge itself with the launching and retrieval of the Prime Minister's boat as well as the beaching of the dock in a way that will not cause a maintenance problem. I have also issued orders to remove the sand and boulders placed in the lake and to reinstate the site to its original condition.

This was part of a much longer report, as we shall see in a moment.

On August 28, Trudeau summoned Gallant to the cottage and showed him around with a new and longer list of complaints, including the wrongful removal of a rustic but dilapidated fence which Margaret had liked just as it was (or had been), poor attention to a cedar hedge, and the difficulty of paddling a canoe between Harrington and Meach Lakes because of deadfalls and weeds. Gallant promised that everything would be made shipshape. But, the next day, before he could issue the pertinent orders, disaster struck.

The NCC maintenance crew at the cottage was told it could start mowing the lawn after 2 p.m., by which time, it was assumed, Trudeau would have left for the office or 24 Sussex.

With engine start-up time for the lawn mowers approved, word was flashed that the beaver study in Harrington Lake could proceed that same afternoon. NCC frequently hands out contracts for the study of beaver, osprey, algae, deer, snow depths, trail-marking, skate-sharpening and those are just the ones I know about. In the summer of 1974, a researcher from Laval University, an unlucky Mr. Giroux, and his assistant, had been commissioned to study beaver lodges. When Howard Morris, warden of Gatineau Park, got the telephone call that lawn-mowing was sanctioned for that day, he passed the word to Giroux to launch his canoe for his beaver hunt. Morris notified the RCMP post at Lac Philippe that Giroux and his assistant had entered Harrington Lake from Lac Philippe.

Giroux paddled leisurely around the lake, and soon after taking note of a beaver lodge, spotted what he at first thought was a bald eagle but which turned out to be an osprey from a park rookery. Giroux and his assistant used their binoculars to follow the flight of the osprey across the lake.

Not far away, on the beach at Harrington Lodge, Trudeau and his wife were having a dip, apparently skinny. The prime minister peered out over the lake and saw two sets of binoculars staring at, he thought, him and Margaret. (One puts "him" first in such cases, as he invariably did himself.)

The first thing Trudeau did was to alert his RCMP guards. MacNiven's report takes up the plight of Giroux and his helper:

At a small island they were met by the RCMP security patrol in a boat. They were questioned about their presence on the lake and the work they were performing. They requested the patrol to tow them to the north end of the lake [the end farthest from the cottage] in order that they might leave the lake as soon as possible. They were questioned on their use of binoculars and stated that they had not seen anyone on the lake or along the shoreline during their entire visit. It was established that the Giroux canoe did not have any fishing or camera equipment in it.

MacNiven concluded in his report to Chairman Gallant:

There are a number of obvious improvements which suggest themselves as a result of the untoward occurrences which have prompted this report. The first is, of course, that any works within proximity of the Prime Minister's summer residence which might in any way affect the quiet enjoyment of his tenure should not be undertaken prior to clearance with him or his staff. Toward that end I will henceforth bring forward on a periodic basis a summary of proposals which the Chairman may wish to discuss with the proper authorities.

Second, it is clear that a more effective liaison must be established to ascertain when minor works may be carried out in the Prime Minister's absence to ensure that his privacy and enjoyment are not impaired. A more effective communication of this type would also have avoided the problem of the beaver survey being carried out as it was on August 29th.

The current review would also suggest that certain steps might properly be taken on lands adjacent to the creek to afford more effective visual protection to the lodge and its immediate surroundings. If the Prime Minister had no reservations, it would be possible to develop in the next short while a tree planting program in the area north of the creek which would be generally beneficial in this regard.

Once Trudeau had alerted his RCMP guard, he had his office telephone Gallant at the National Capital Commission.

Gallant was not there. He was at the hospital where his wife, Annette, had just been taken back to her room after surgery. She was still heavily sedated. Trudeau insisted that Gallant be tracked down.

Gallant was with his wife in the hospital room when the call came through from a still enraged Trudeau, who launched into a diatribe about the invasion of his privacy and the failings of the National Capital Commission, its chairman, and its entire staff. He did not ask how, or even whether, Mme Gallant had come through her operation.

Less than two years later, Trudeau appointed Gallant chairman of the Public Service Commission and issued this statement May 27, 1976:

I would have liked to be present at this session of the National Capital Commission when Ed Gallant is making his final appearance as Chairman, but my commitments will not permit it. I do, however, want to send this brief message to the Commission and to him on this special occasion. . . .

I would like to thank Ed Gallant personally for the energy, diplomacy and quiet determination he has put into a difficult job.

By October, 1974, the commission staff was busy planting maple trees on both sides of the main driveway into Harrington and near Margaret's garden, though not too near so as to put next year's unsprayed vegetables in the shade. A new entrance was installed, and a new log rail fence. Steps were taken to protect the roots of trees at the shoreline. Deadfalls were removed from the creekbed so that a canoe could make its way unimpeded between Harrington and Meach lakes. Of course, a sign had to be put up barring any public entry into the creek.

Trudeau was always extremely sensitive about his use of public funds for his private enjoyment. On May 22, 1975, in the House of Commons, he hit out wildly at former prime minister Diefenbaker: "I suppose he made the largest land grab when he was in office that was ever made by any citizen of Canada. He did so when he decided that Harrington Lake and the buildings on it should be the country residence of the prime minister."

Diefenbaker became prime minister in 1957. The land and buildings at Harrington Lake had been bought by the federal government in 1951.

Trudeau continued on that same day: "The right honorable gentleman for Prince Albert [Diefenbaker] liked fishing and had Harrington Lake stocked at public expense with fish for his enjoyment."

Diefenbaker ceased to be prime minister in 1963. The lake was stocked with speckled and rainbow trout and Atlantic salmon in 1967 and 1968 by the Canadian Wildlife Service.

Trudeau never again trusted a "pure" public servant like Gallant in the chairmanship of the National Capital Commission. Gallant's immediate successors were two former Liberal cabinet ministers, Pierre Juneau and C.M. Drury.

13
———

Smaller than a Private Beach but Bigger than a Jacuzzi

In that summer of 1974, Trudeau wanted more than his private beach at Harrington Lake. He wanted a swimming pool at 24 Sussex.

Immediately after the election in July that year, which restored the Liberals' majority following the two-year minority flotation by David Lewis of the New Democratic Party, Trudeau broached the subject of an indoor pool. Meetings were held at 24 Sussex and those in attendance included: Trudeau; Mrs. Trudeau; Drury, then minister of public works; Bill Teron, millionaire developer, head of Central Mortgage and Housing Corporation (where, it was said, he had the hottest frozen trust in Canada), and architectural adviser, though he was no architect, to Trudeau; and one or two real architects from Public Works.

During these early discussions, no mention was made about payment of the pool other than by Public Works. Teron said the pool could be built for $60,000 and Public Works sought tenders, privately, and not by the usual public tender method. Trudeau was taken aback to hear that the minimum tender was $150,000, though he had already spent $173,406 of public money for new furnishings (suede) and panelling for his office in the Centre Block of the Parliament Buildings. Instructions were given that pool expenditures were to be kept under $200,000, but there has never been a public accounting of what the final figure was. Not included in the so-called ceiling of $200,000 was $40,000 required for a new electrical system at 24 Sussex to heat the pool.

The length of the pool was decided at forty feet, the width at twenty. Trudeau insisted on a skylight, not only for natural lighting but for sufficient headroom for proper diving. The building included a sauna, change rooms, lounging area, and a tunnel to the basement of the main house. Another specification was that there must be privacy from the next-door neighbor, the French embassy. This led to some thought that the pool might be sited behind 24 Sussex instead of on the west lawn. But there were strong objections to that. It would cut off the best view of the Ottawa River and Gatineau Hills and Mrs. Trudeau said she must still be able to see the flower beds. The geologist's report finally ruled out a site behind the house: the side of the cliff might fall into the river, carrying the pool with it.

Public Works classed the plans as top secret and only the architect, Bill Thomas of Public Works, and one or two assistants were allowed to work on them. Others had to be called in for consultation, including the geologist. A photographer from the

National Capital Commission, Ian Street, took hundreds of pictures, mainly to show shady spots which would be affected by removal of trees on the west lawn. Elaborate drawings of predicted shade cast by new trees at different times of day were prepared. The patio of course had to catch the summer sun.

The Commission, which has nominal authority over the design of federal buildings in the capital, became involved because 24 Sussex is a heritage home (built in 1868) owned by the Canadian public (but which the public is never allowed to see except from the sidewalk). Any changes to the grounds would therefore be a matter of public interest. Trudeau seemed persuaded by this argument because Public Works on November 18, 1974, took its pool plans — as one method of keeping them secret the pool was never called a pool but a "swimming area" — before the Commission's advisory committee on design.

Architect Thomas of Public Works conducted the briefing of the committee. He began by saying that the delay in plans between July and November had occurred because of Trudeau's desire to put off the project until after the throne speech in the new Parliament. Trudeau had wanted the pool by Christmas, but this was no longer possible.

Members of the National Capital Commission and its various committees, including design, were all Liberal appointees. By this time there was not a single holdover from the days of the last Conservative government of 1957-63. It is not then surprising that no question was raised in the design committee about the cost, then set, ostensibly, at $185,000. Quite the contrary. One committee member asked whether there would be enough room to accommodate twenty guests at one time. The answer was yes. The minutes of the committee record:

> In response to a question, it was noted that the original design intent to line the pool with mosaic tile had to be cut out for cost reasons. The Committee expressed great concern about this aspect on the grounds that the pool lining would be comparatively permanent and that, in context, it should be of the highest possible quality. Ordinary tiling is estimated to cost $7,000 extra. Department of Public Works hopes to be able to add mosaic tile after the tender

prices come in. It was suggested that an artist could be commissioned to design the tile pattern.

The committee concluded its meeting with a motion which ended, "the design quality of the pool and ancillary building be commensurate with the dignity of the Office of the Prime Minister and which will perpetuate the heritage aspects of the residence of the Prime Minister of Canada." The committee ignored the question of what a cedar building on the lawn of 24 Sussex would do to the heritage aspect of a home of stone. One member referred to Public Works and the National Capital Commission as a firm fulfilling a contract for a client.

By this time, a lot of people were in the know and a press release was prepared. Trudeau himself inserted a paragraph in the release which said that 24 Sussex had been acquired during the St. Laurent regime and the prime ministerial summer home at Harrington Lake during the Diefenbaker ministry. Pierre O'Neil, Trudeau's press secretary, said the paragraph was included because that was the way his boss wanted it. Trudeau was wrong on both counts. The house at 24 Sussex was bought by the government in 1943, five years before St. Laurent became prime minister, and, as we have seen, the Harrington Lake property was bought in 1951, six years before Diefenbaker became prime minister.

Trudeau and his advisers, including Teron, now began to have doubts about how the public would react to paying for a private swimming pool for the prime minister, though Canadians have never begrudged their leaders the proper perquisites of office. They devised a Byzantine scheme which, in the end, caused far more embarrassment for them than if they had stuck to their original plan to take the funds from the public purse.

On December 23, 1974, one Dr. William H. Fader of Toronto announced that a group of donors would pay the costs of the pool, the money being administered by a trust fund established under his name. Dr. Fader said the idea of building a pool for the prime minister had occurred to him that fall when he had heard about American presidents having the use of such facilities for physical fitness. As a result, he had got in touch with some friends in November and had met Trudeau about the first of December. Then, he said, he had begun planning the pool. The good doctor no doubt would have been stunned to discover that Public Works had been working on plans since July.

The donors were thrown into a temporary panic when Trudeau told reporters that he didn't mind if their names were made public. Some started pulling out, and the government quickly promised them anonymity. Here's the official explanation given the House of Commons on October 28, 1975, by Mitchell Sharp, President of the Privy Council who had been demoted from External Affairs:

In 1974, after carefully considering the factors, the Prime Minister agreed to accept from a representative group of Canadians the gift of a swimming pool for the official residence at 24 Sussex Drive. In Canada, as in most other countries, the making of donations to the state is a common practice and many public buildings have been built as a result of this tradition. The group of donors was concerned that the Prime Minister and his successors have ready access to adequate physical fitness facilities without being confronted with the obvious security and privacy difficulties.

The Prime Minister agreed to be one of the contributors. He also chose not to ask for the names of the other contributors, except for their trustee, Dr. W.H. Fader, of 395 Brooks Street, Toronto, lest he be influenced or give the appearance of being influenced by them. The donations, if a properly documented tax return is filed, entitle the contributors to the deductions provided for under Section 110(1)(b) of the Income Tax Act. Given statutory provisions extant which ensure confidentiality of income tax returns, the government is not in a position to disclose the names of the contributors. The service of Hebert Brune Construction of Ottawa was engaged by the trustee for the donors to install the swimming pool at the official residence. As the costs incurred by that firm have been assumed by private donors, they are not of government record. Since these proposed fitness facilities were to be built on crown-owned land, the Department of Public Works assigned one of its architects to design the pool and related facilities to conformity with requirements of the National Capital Commission and the latter's approval at various stages of progress of work. Design costs incurred by the Department of Public Works are the responsibility of the government and are covered by Vote 10. As to the operational costs of the facilities, (and related expenditures by departments concerned), they will be included in the overall cost of the administration of the Prime Minister's residence under the relevant statutory provisions and will therefore, in the usual way, be open to the scrutiny of Parliament.

Bill Teron was believed to be the largest contributor of all: at least $60,000, his original estimate for cost of the pool. He ceased to be Trudeau's architectural adviser and soon vanished from the government scene in Ottawa. The amount of Trudeau's contribution was not known, but was believed small. As a millionaire, he never carried money on his person. When representatives of charities went to his office for the standard publicity pictures, Trudeau instructed an aide to make a donation because he didn't happen to have anything on him. The aide was never repaid. Trudeau's Christmas gifts to his staff were his own unwanted presents from foreign embassies in Ottawa. The press secretary usually got the Bulgarian vodka.

14

You've Got the Brains; I've Got the Brawn

During his prime ministership, and before and after as well, Pierre Trudeau always gave the impression — and insisted on giving the impression — of physical prowess. And he was fit. He swam, dived, skied, and, certainly, paddled his own canoe.

Despite appearances, he was not robust, and had little stamina. He was fagged out by 11 p.m., or earlier, and he rarely reached his office before 9:30 a.m. He became annoyed and angry with me more than once for seeming to suggest — no suggestion was intended — that he was not up to the mark physically every minute. For instance, when he became prime minister, I wrote that he had had to give up driving his Mercedes. This is a perfectly normal procedure because no one wants to see a driver-prime minister involved in a car acccident, whether or not his fault. Trudeau took it, and so informed me through his press secretary, Roméo LeBlanc, that I was insinuating some new-found physical disability which prevented him from driving. On another occasion, he was furious with me for reporting that he had gone to a doctor to be treated for sunburn.

Trudeau was also, how shall I put it, physically apprehensive. On a trip down the Nahanni River, he was badly frightened by the white water. He was careful and took good care of himself. (During World War II, Prime Minister Mackenzie King flew home in a converted bomber after being booed by Canadian troops. When he visited the cockpit before takeoff, he asked the purpose of a certain lever. To open the bomb bay doors, he was told. King ordered the lever tied down, and stayed there until it was firmly in the "shut" position.) Trudeau feared wilful harm, as so many leaders do in terrorist times, and with reason. But he feared harm from Canadians — even in Saskatchewan. On July 16, 1969, Trudeau was booed and heckled in Regina while speaking to an outdoor crowd of about 700. A forty-man RCMP riot squad in steel helmets was secretly moved into the lobby of Trudeau's hotel while he was speaking from the back of a truck at the hotel entrance. There was no disturbance, and the riot squad quietly dispersed through a rear door out of sight of the crowd. The incident reminded me of the story told by leaders of the 1935 On-to-Ottawa Trek of unemployed, stopped bloodily by police at Regina, that when they met Prime Minister R.B. Bennett there were Yellowlegs (Mounties) hidden behind the drapes.

Trudeau was also apprehensive about the infiltration of French agents into Canada. France had been racked for years by terrorism, which included numerous attempts on the life of President de Gaulle. The RCMP guard on Trudeau was doubled and redoubled and a platoon of Mounties was assigned to his summer cottage on Harrington Lake. Undercover RCMP agents prowled around downtown near the Parliament Buildings.

15

Using a Sledgehammer to Crack a Peanut:
Trudeau Meets the FLQ

Trudeau was Pearson's minister of justice when de Gaulle made his notorious, and shortened, 1967 visit to Canada. It has since been shown that de Gaulle premeditated his "Vive le Québec libre" balcony speech. The evening before his arrival in Canada aboard the French cruiser *Colbert*, he had told officers at dinner that French Canada would have at least a degree of autonomy within a few years. Pearson was annoyed at the "Vive le Québec libre" call but what infuriated him was de Gaulle's comment that his drive from Quebec City to Montreal had exhilarated him like his liberation ride into Paris in 1944. Canadian soldiers died helping to liberate France, which had surrendered to Hitler in 1940 and whose resistance fighters during the next four years never numbered more than one per cent of the population. Don Peacock, a Trudeau aide, came up with the single word Pearson used to describe de Gaulle's words and actions: "unacceptable." I'm not sure but I think that Peacock was the first to apply this word to such circumstances; it has been widely copied ever since all over the world.

De Gaulle had been preceded to Canada by Philippe Pierre Rossillon, a member of the staff of the French prime minister's office whom Prime Minister Trudeau was to brand publicly in September, 1968, as a "secret agent of France" sent to Canada by the French government in an "underhanded and surreptitious way" to stir up separatist trouble. Rossillon had been coming to Canada since 1956 and had been in touch with Quebec separatists and persons subsequently convicted of terrorist activities. Trudeau took the unusual step of fingering Rossillon publicly as a warning to France that other French agents were known to Canadian authorities and were under surveillance. Another factor worrying Trudeau was that some two hundred French army conscripts were working in Canada, mainly as teachers, on behalf of the French foreign office. About one hundred and forty of them were in Quebec. The program was similar, the

French embassy said, to the Canadian University Service Overseas or the U.S. Peace Corps.

Still, Trudeau was justice minister for a year and prime minister for two without seeming to take over-seriously the terrorism by the Front de Libération du Québec. The FLQ was founded in 1963 and in seven years had carried out a hundred bombings resulting in six deaths, and maimings.

All of a sudden, at 8:15 a.m. on October 5, 1976, James Cross, forty-nine, British trade commissioner, was abducted from his Montreal home by the FLQ. Five days later, Quebec labor minister Pierre Laporte was also kidnapped.

This put terrorism on a different scale. It wasn't just armory caretakers and bomb disposal soldiers who were in danger. It was officialdom! Trudeau and his cabinet colleagues, especially those from Quebec, were frightened for themselves. Who else might not be carried off? "Perhaps me, or another minister," Trudeau was to say later in an interview on November 3. Jean Marchand, minister of regional economic expansion, told the Commons: "At the present time in the province of Quebec freedom is dead, people are afraid to go out, and this does apply to me, as I am no better than anyone else, nor do I have more courage.... The members from Quebec are afraid.... Some businessmen are in the same boat: I have met some here in Ottawa today who had run away from Montreal."

Marchand is not the type one would want near the nuclear button.

Physical fear fed wild exaggeration, even before Laporte's murder. Fewer than a dozen persons combined comprised the FLQ kidnapping cells, but Marchand maintained that the FLQ had a membership of 3,000 and was armed with "thousands of guns, machine guns, bombs and about 2,000 pounds of dynamite, more than enough to blow up the core of downtown Montreal."

On Sunday, October 11, the day after Laporte's abduction, the Quebec government asked Ottawa to invoke the War Measures Act, or to take similar action. Trudeau two days later called out the troops — but to guard himself, the rest of Ottawa officialdom and the diplomatic corps. No one in Ottawa was ever known to be in danger, but one soldier was killed accidentally, guarding Edgar Benson, the finance minister. Once the troops were on patrol in Ottawa, Trudeau said in his famous interview with Tim Ralfe of the CBC: "There are a lot of bleeding hearts around who just don't like to see people with helmets and guns. All I can say is, go on and bleed, but it is more important to keep law and order in the society than to be worried about the weak-kneed people who don't like the looks of an army." (This from a man who had shunned the helmet and gun in World War II.) "How far would you go?" Ralfe asked, and Trudeau said, "Just watch me."

His "just-watch-me" combination of bluster and sophistry turned into the proclamation, at 4 a.m. October 16, 1970, of the *War Measures Act*, and the kicking-in of doors in the pre-dawn darkness all over Quebec. The cabinet order, P.C. 1970-1807, said:

Therefore, His Excellency the Governor General in Council, on the recommendation of the Prime Minister, is pleased to direct that a proclamation to issue proclaiming that apprehended insurrection exists and has existed as and from the fifteenth day of October, one thousand nine hundred and seventy.

The proclamation did not explain how "apprehended insurrection" could actually exist, but that was only one anomaly in the wholesale invasion of civil liberties across Canada. (Why did the citizens of Saskatchewan have to lose their civil rights because of a situation confined to Quebec, asked Diefenbaker.) Three hundred and sixty-nine persons were arrested without charge; all were later released in dribs and drabs. Laporte was garroted with his own crucifix chain the day after the Act was proclaimed, though the government afterwards usually tried to insinuate that the murder had taken place beforehand and had led to promulgation. Tommy Douglas, the NDP leader, said, with his usual facility for the apt phrase, that the government "is using a sledgehammer to crack a peanut." But his voice, and that of Diefenbaker, were lost in general Canadian support for "putting Quebec in its place." From what I read and heard at the time, mostly from Conservative MPs, Trudeau was putting a stop to all that damned bilingual foolishness and dumb questions like,

"What does Quebec want?" Even Diefenbaker, though it was on another occasion, said of Trudeau, "He's my boy. He's for one Canada." The public thought so, too. Trudeau received 11,500 letters by October 29, 97 per cent backing him.

Though the "just-watch-me" policy produced the police rap on the door of innocent people, it didn't get tough with terrorism. On the contrary, the government was soft and compromising. Not only were the kidnappers safely conducted in a government plane to Cuba in exchange for Cross, but five FLQ members already in jail were offered parole. Trudeau and his cabinet continued their desperate fearmongering, no doubt based on their own nervous over-reaction. Portentously, the prime minister went on national television October 16 and began, "I am speaking to you at a moment of grave crisis, when violent and fanatical men are attempting to destroy the unity and the freedom of Canada."

He described the FLQ as an "armed, revolutionary movement." The criminal law was not adequate to deal with "systematic terrorism." The right to arrest and search without warrant, to detain people without charge, or bail, were necessary to deal with those promoting "violent overthrow" of the Canadian democracy.

Marchand was even more shrill. After describing his fear to go outside in Montreal, he told the Commons that the FLQ "had infiltrated every strategic place in the province of Quebec, every place where important decisions are taken." The FLQ was "made up of cells of two or three persons each, cells that do not know each other, that do not necessarily work hand in hand and that are now in touch simply through coded messages broadcast free of charge by our radio stations. What you might think are only speeches are in fact coded messages which are sent here and there."

Marchand went even further outside the Commons. The Front d'Action Politique, he said, was a front for the FLQ. This organization was then running candidates against Mayor Jean Drapeau, whose letter at 3 a.m., October 16 had warned Trudeau of "apprehended insurrection." (That phrase had been worked out in advance with Ottawa.) There was no evidence for Marchand's charge, and he had to withdraw it.

Justice Minister John Turner also took a hand in the scare

tactics. The government had secret information, he said, which would some day show why the War Measures Act had been invoked. (None has since been produced.) There was, Turner said, a "conspiracy" against "a legitimately constituted government" (Quebec's) and "hidden caches" of dynamite. The FLQ had infiltrated Quebec unions, universities and media. While its "prime target today may be the government of Quebec, there is every reason to assume — indeed I think there are many clear indications — that other governments and indeed the central government of this country fall within the purview of their endeavors." The FLQ's aim, added Turner, was a totalitarian state achieved by revolution.

Despite Turner's assertion that there was a conspiracy against the Quebec government, Marchand's claim that the FLQ had infiltrated every seat of decision in Quebec, and Trudeau's warning of an "armed, revolutionary movement," Trudeau several times accused the press of spreading rumors that there was a plot to depose the Bourassa government in Quebec. The government already knew — but left it to Conservative leader Robert Stanfield to say later — that the FLQ had no central structure or direction and was merely a group giving itself a name and purported credo to justify terrorism. But the myth of a conspiracy to overthrow the Quebec government — and perhaps even the federal government, in Turner's allegation — was needed to gloss over the invocation of the War Measures Act which in turn glossed over the panic in Ottawa. Trudeau even compared his manufactured crisis to the communist October revolution of 1917 which brought down the regime of Premier Alexander Kerensky in Russia.

What of civil liberties? On October 31, Trudeau said:

When, in a state of emergency such as this, the police are forced to take rapid action on a very broad scale, some obviously innocent persons may very well be detained temporarily for questioning. I am counting on the spirit of justice of every citizen to ensure that no such person suffers damage to his reputation or unfair treatment at work.

Cross was released December 3, the kidnappers were flown to Cuba, and the troops withdrawn from Quebec streets in early January, though not from bodyguarding in Quebec and Ottawa.

The courts pursued the government-led softness on terrorism. The five kidnappers of Cross remained in Cuba until 1974, when they were given political asylum in France. In 1978, they started returning to Quebec to plead guilty to kidnapping, forcible detention and extortion. Jacques and Louise Cossette-Trudel were sentenced to two years and paroled after six months. Jacques Lanctot was sentenced to three years, Marc Carbonneau to twenty months, and Yves Langlois to two years, serving only one-third of the sentence. A sixth kidnapper, Nigel Hamer, was arrested in 1980 and drew twelve months.

Four men were convicted in the murder of Laporte. Paul Rose and Francis Simard received life sentences and were paroled after eleven years. Jacques Rose drew eight years and Bernard Lortie twenty and both were released in 1978.

16

A Thoughtful Gift for a Millionaire

Every government and every politician in the long run disappoints the electorate. But in Trudeau's case, expectations of what he would achieve were higher than with most government leaders. The disappointments were correspondingly greater. But Trudeau was also a lot luckier than most politicians.

Trudeau and Marc Lalonde and five others in 1964 signed a "Canadian manifesto" which ended with the ringing sentence: "We will fight any action that tends to erode fundamental liberties and democratic institutions." Six years later Trudeau invoked the *War Measures Act* which not only eroded but temporarily cancelled fundamental liberties. The action was popular as a measure to fight separatism but in 1976 the Parti Québécois, dedicated to the partition of the country, was elected to power.

In December, 1970, Trudeau stated flatly: "Inflation no longer exists in Canada." Four years later, inflation was running at twelve per cent a year and the unemployed numbered more than one million. Conservative Leader Stanfield proposed wage and price controls. Trudeau ridiculed the suggestion, got re-elected on that basis and fifteen months later brought in wage and price controls.

Most of his able cabinet ministers quit: Eric Kierans, Ron Basford, Paul Hellyer, John Turner, Don MacDonald, leaving the likes of Bryce Mackasey. Other able ones were pensioned off to patronage posts: Paul Martin, Gérard Pelletier, Jeanne Sauvé, Don Jamieson, Jean Marchand. No potential rival for public attention was allowed to hang around. In 1964, Trudeau said social and economic problems were far more urgent and fundamental than obtaining a new constitution. He achieved a new constitution in 1982, but without Quebec. In the dying days of his regime in 1984, Trudeau set out on a so-called peace mission to mend East-West relations. The purpose was given away when the Norwegian embassy said officials in Trudeau's office had been making inquiries on how one went about being nominated for the Nobel peace prize. And finally, Trudeau bequeathed to his nation an enormous deficit which will take decades to pay off.

Just before he departed office in June, 1984, his Liberal caucus gave him a farewell present: $2,000 to buy furniture for his Montreal home; it was a thoughtful gift for a millionaire. At least it would provide the first occasion in nearly two decades when the taxpayer hadn't paid for Trudeau's furniture.

17
———

Some Tories Last Longer than Others

Whatever Mulroney has been up to since he took office in the fall of 1984, he understands his two basic problems: Canadian self-indulgence, and how to remain prime minister longer than those other Conservatives (reading backward) Joe Clark, John Diefenbaker, R.B. Bennett, Arthur Meighen, Charles Tupper, Mackenzie Bowell, John Thompson and John Abbott. Diefenbaker was the easy winner in this group with six years. Only two other Conservatives have been prime minister longer than Diefenbaker: Macdonald, nineteen years, and Robert Borden, nine. It is hard to tell which problem Mulroney ranks first but I suspect it is the latter. In any event, he grasps the first, which is of more immediate interest to all Canadians.

It is not all Trudeau's fault that when he took office Canada's net debt was $18 billion after one hundred years of Confederation and that, when he left it, was more than ten times that and climbing. Canadians wanted more and more of that easy living which most of them had come to expect since the 1950s. The interest to carry the debt now exceeds the cost of all social programs.

The general attitude of Canadians, Mulroney explained in an interview with two British journalists June 13, 1985, is:

You can do this or do that but by Jesus don't touch me. Whatever you do it's unconstitutional to touch me. This is what the last twenty years has done. No matter how much it costs, you want me to divert that river for you? I'll do that for you and what else do you want? Is there something else? We can do that for you, even though we're broke.

The Mulroney government's early attempts to handle tough problems showed only retreat. For instance, a special cabinet committee was struck in the summer of 1985 to deal with the problem of large importations of Japanese cars. The chairman of the committee, Sinclair Stevens, warned that 125,000 Canadian jobs were on the line and that the new Liberal government in Ontario could be expected to defend stoutly the province's car industry. Were the Ontario Liberals running the federal government? demanded Energy Minister Pat Carney. She drove a Japanese car and British Columbia liked doing business with Japan. Did the east intend to dictate policy to the west as it had under the Liberals? In any event, no action was taken and imports of Japanese cars actually increased.

The Case of the Tainted Tuna came to the attention of Charles Friend in the information branch of the fisheries department in December, 1984. The chief of the fisheries inspection branch showed him a can of Star-Kist tuna which had been rejected by the armed forces: it was a black liquid, with chunks floating in it. Friend is not a run-of-the-mill press officer. He has wide, and non-partisan, experience in government and has taken on a lot of nasty, difficult jobs, one being the government's attempts to stop the Greenpeace organization's illegal harassment of Canadian sealers. Friend told Fisheries Minister John Fraser that any attempt to keep bad tuna on the market would be political suicide, not to mention a health hazard. Fraser paid no attention. Friend warned Fraser at least four more times until Fraser, exasperated, went to Friend's superior, Arthur May, the deputy minister, and told him to keep Friend off his back. By this time it was May, 1985, and the bad tuna was still being sold. Fraser had not so much said "no" to Friend as he had just shrugged and walked away each time. Friend felt finally that he must inform the prime minister's office, and told two officials verbally. There is some question about what happened next because the two officials, Pat MacAdam and Ian Anderson, could not very well say sure, they'd told the prime minister and he didn't do anything about it either. Prime Minister Mulroney said he didn't know about the bad tuna until it came to public attention in September on the CBC program *The Fifth Estate*. But Fraser maintained he had told the prime minister. Fraser was promptly fired, not for allowing bad tuna to stay on store shelves for months, but for contradicting the prime minister publicly. The sequel was even more disturbing. The new fisheries minister, Tom Siddon, ordered Friend fired in February, 1986, on the grounds that he had been disloyal to Fraser. In the fall of 1986 Fraser was reincarnated as Commons speaker.

Erik Nielsen, on May 24, 1986, telegraphed his own political downfall when he arrived by military plane at Ottawa from Europe. The deputy prime minister and minister of national defence tried to bring twelve meat pies into the country. Such produce isn't allowed under agriculture department regulations. The agriculture inspector seized the pies. Nielsen said he would have them, or else. The agriculture inspector chucked them into the incinerator. Two weeks later, Nielsen was dropped from the cabinet. A politician who can't hang onto a dozen meat pies isn't likely to hang onto power.

PART TWO

THE PARLIAMENT HILL PLAYERS

A bull, Mr. Speaker, has no gender in this House.

Sheila Copps, MP, Hamilton East, February 6, 1986

Prologue

Pierre Elliott Trudeau was cruelly accurate when he said in 1969 that fifty yards away from Parliament Hill opposition members were "just nobodies — they are just nil."

Even apart from his everyday arrogance — "There but for the grace of Pierre Elliott Trudeau sits God," said the New Democratic Party's then deputy leader, David Lewis — the derision was well aimed. Today, one would have to include as nobodies the MPs of all parties, and most of the cabinet.

Parliament has lost its stature for basically four reasons: television; replacement of the principle "What can I do for the public?" with "What can the public do for me?" (this is even more pronounced in the civil service than among politicians); Parliament's loss of control over expenditures to the executive and the civil service; and Parliament's relinquishing of responsibility for human and individual rights to the courts. To take them in turn:

1

Best on the Box

Before television, the local Member of Parliament was a power to reckon with back in the constituency. The MP knew what was going on in Parliament and, if on the government side, knew what was going on in government because the government, and not the civil service, still ran the government and usually consulted its caucus of MPs. When the MP went home (and it wasn't often except for Quebec and Ontario MPs because Parliament used to work hard) constituents expected to learn how things were going and to get answers to questions while the MP sounded out as many people as possible on what they thought about all the major issues. Even the MP's role as a sounding board has been eliminated. Now the civil service or professional polling is used for such purposes. Here is an extract from a cabinet document dated July 31, 1981, and entitled "Government Communications: A Priority Initiative" which makes this very point:

> Government has a corresponding responsibility to make every reasonable effort to learn of the concerns and views of Canadians, with particular attention to differences of views in different regions of the country, so as better to inform itself in establishing priorities, in developing policies, and in implementing programs which serve the interests of Canada; ... Line departments and agencies have the primary and paramount role in obtaining, using and providing the information needed by the government, by Canadians and by the officials of the department and the central agencies with whom they work....
>
> It [this role] is carried out by departmental officials providing their senior management and Minister with regular information on what clients think of government policies, programs and services administered by the department. This information is obtained partly through ongoing media monitoring responsive to the Ministers' public communications priorities and objectives.

That's how cabinet documents read. "Clients" is the official word for public. Nowhere in this twenty-seven-page cabinet directive is there a single mention of Members of Parliament. Literally hundreds of civil servants have no other job than to scan newspapers and radio and television tapes for items of interest about government departments and crown corporations. Articles and editorials about ministers receive top priority, and some ministers demand to see such clippings first thing every day. Publicly, Liberal Finance Minister Marc Lalonde used to wave aside any suggestion that he might pay the slightest attention to what the press was saying about him. But his press clippings were chauffeured to him at home first thing every morning, and his staff caught hell if Lalonde later spotted an item which had not been included.

Radio and television have been allowed on Parliament Hill for fewer than thirty years, but in that time they (especially television) have emasculated Parliament. The smart cabinet ministers saw and seized the opportunity afforded by the new broadcast outlets to grab and hold public attention with the quotable quote that would fit the standard fifteen seconds, the attention span of a TV reporter. This obviated the need for a cabinet minister to learn policy or other subject thoroughly in case called upon to explain it. Radio and television could use only a few brief sentences, and if the minister had to make a speech in the Commons or elsewhere, he had a political and a civil service staff to write one for him.

For the backbencher and local MP, television was a disaster. If the public can see and hear the prime minister and senior cabinet ministers on the home screen every night, and sometimes the leaders of the opposition parties, who wants to hear secondhand stuff from the lowly MP? If an MP manages to get on a local station, what is there to say? The bigshots were there ahead of time, nationally, giving their perfunctory fifteen-second assessments of complicated policies. In short, who needs the MP except as a voting machine in the Commons and party candidate at election time? Nobody — and the MP knows it.

This accounts for Parliament's ceaseless quest for so-called reform. Reform is not aimed at streamlining or speeding up Parliament's work because Parliament can't fill advantageously the time it has now (thus the three-month summer vacations and three or four weeks off at Christmas and Easter.) Reform is aimed at making the backbencher feel important, whether he is or not. The purpose of the 1985 plan to set up comparatively small (seven members) parliamentary committees to examine government operations and legislation is to give each MP on a small committee a better chance at recognition through more opportunities to speak and question. This assumes that the press is going to cover every committee and find time to fit in, between prime ministerial and ministerial fifteen-second clips for television, the views, reasoned or otherwise, of some MP too low on the scale to be considered for an assistant parliamentary secretaryship to a cabinet minister. Many cabinet ministers themselves have a hard time getting any recognition. There are so many of them, the names of most are unknown to the public.

Nobody ever devised a better system for gaining recognition as a backbench MP than did John Dienfenbaker. He used to wangle his way onto several Commons committees. He knew which ones were covered by the press, and he would go from committee room to committee room, sit down long enough to catch the gist of the subject under discussion, throw out a quotable quote, and move on to the next committee and deliver another telling phrase which the press as a rule gobbled up happily because most committees by their nature were deadly dull. Diefenbaker never was. It was not unusual for Canadian Press reporters (CP was the only service which covered all committees, or nearly all) to find after the Tuesday and Thursday committee meetings that all their stories started the same way: "John Diefenbaker (PC — Lake Centre) said today . . . ."

One of the prime duties, if not the very first, of a cabinet minister is to explain government policy, and particularly his department's policy, to the public through the press. This is seldom done today. Few reporters are able to swim the moat and climb the battlements of ministerial executive and special assistants and purported spokesmen who never know the answer to the question asked, only to the question never posed. Ministers routinely used to invite into their offices, on a regular basis, reporters they trusted — and often some they didn't — to tell them, simply, what the hell was going on. Today the minister himself may not know what is going on until he is briefed by civil servants.

Even if a minister wanted to go through the press to give the public an accurate outline of all the ramifications of a firm, decided policy, why risk an unguarded remark when all that's necessary is to issue a press statement and rehearse a few sentences for easily satisfied radio and television? Why take a chance on being daringly human when you can be a robot?

The thing is, MPs are human. They want to do the right thing in the right way. They have ideas, most reasonable, some outlandish, for benefitting the common weal. They want to speak out independently on a lot of issues. They don't like being ignored or used as voting machines. They sometimes get angry at their leaders. They seldom stay angry at each other for very long. The spirit of the Commons is not that of an evangelical football locker room, but neither is it of feuding partisanship. MPs are educated and civilized and good-humored, even with so many lawyers among them.

But the system is degrading them. For television, whose coverage of Parliament is based solely on confrontation and not the public interest, MPs are expected to applaud wildly the most innocuous ministerial statement or sally while barracking even the mildest rebuke from the opposition. Most debates in the Commons are so dull they can't hold the attention of even their central figures, but television requires that all the seats around the leaders be kept filled so that no impression is allowed to seep out that anything being said is other than crucial to every Canadian. Confrontation has been raised to such a high (and false) level by television that every minor error or contradiction automatically is described as a scandal or a crisis or both. Television is the boy who cried wolf.

2

What's In It for Me?

Stripped of any adequate means to give their views weight in Parliament, and denied any recognition even at home, most MPs have settled into the routine of playing automaton for radio and television, taking the pay, the airline pass, the pension, and other perks, and doing their best to catch the eye of the prime minister so that they can one day join the cabinet, where the real perks are: personal staffs, individual jetline service, limousines, $113,000 a year, and maybe, just maybe, a summons to escort the Queen on a visit to the home riding.

Bills that receive the quickest passage, usually without any debate at all, concern increases (never decreases) in MPs' pay and pensions. The backbench MP in 1987 was paid a basic $75,000 for part-time work (even more than some civil servants), and a pension for life starts after six years in the House of Commons. The pension plan for members of the Commons and Senate ran a deficit in 1981-82 of $90 million. By the end of 1985, there was no suggestion that the benefits be cut or that contributions — except by the taxpayer — be increased. In the 1930s depression, MPs used to take annual pay cuts of ten or five per cent to set an example for the rest of the country. The 1986 cut was 1.3 per cent — after an increase of five per cent. Not only does the retired (that usually means defeated) MP receive a fat lifetime pension of as much as $60,000 a year the moment he leaves Parliament, no matter how young, he more often than not gets a fat government job, like a judgeship, besides.

When I came to Ottawa in 1953, MPs' lives were pretty frugal. They shared offices and if one of them wanted to dictate a letter (to a secretary from the pool) of a private or confidential nature, the colleague had to be invited to leave the room. I recall Defence Minister Pearkes telling me that when he was a backbencher he and his roommate, John Hackett, MP for Stanstead, were always fighting about Hackett's smoking; Pearkes was continually throwing open the window, even in wintertime. In those days, all MPs, including the cabinet, were crammed into the Centre Block of the Parliament Buildings. Today each MP has a private office, anterooms, other rooms for staff, private secretary, and a constituency office back home. To provide all this space the parliamentary precinct has been extended to the West Block, the Langevin (or South) Block, the Confederation Building, and, most recently, the former palace of a life insurance company. That's four additional buildings to accommodate an increase (to 282) of only seventeen MPs during all that time. Three persons are employed full time making up security passes for an incredible 6,000 people who need them for entry to the Parliament buildings. Parliamentary staff has grown almost as fast as the civil service. It costs about $160 million a year to run Parliament and that figure is, of course, growing.

It used to be said that Parliament would improve if MPs' pay could be increased as an attraction for "better quality" members. What higher and higher pay has attracted is the money-grubber, not the person committed to public service who was never chiefly interested in the money anyway. There were always a few MPs who made a public refusal of general pay increases (there are no increases given for merit). Being only human, they didn't cash the cheques until the public outcry against this latest fleecing of the taxpayer had died away. So prevalent was MPs' acceptance of freebies that in 1985 the government asked members to record publicly their trips paid for by lobbyists, whether business interests or foreign governments.

Devotion to money-grubbing instead of the public interest has resulted in a severe loss in stature for Parliament, much to the professed amazement and indignation of its members. Nobody listens to the debates any more, even the press or MPs themselves. The only time the galleries are full is for such events as budget night, which is now more a social occasion than anything else. People like to be seen near the economic mighty and near-mighty. Besides, they often get a chance to cadge a free drink at the self-laudatory parties afterwards or to get into a corridor camera shot of one of the television networks. And, of course, it is one of the few times in the life of a Parliament that all the members show up, offering a chance to spot your member, if you can remember the name or that of the constituency.

3

Is There a Deadly Serious Comic in the House?

There are few outstanding people in Parliament now compared with those of only a few years ago: Pierre Trudeau, the complete master of the Commons either by contempt, ridicule or persuasion; cadaverous Stan Knowles, fighter for the poor, the old, and the handicapped; Mike Pearson, shy and flustered but ramming through his policies with energy and humor; Judy LaMarsh, big bundle of verve and commitment; John Diefenbaker of the thrashing finger; Louis St. Laurent and M.J. Coldwell, always courteous opponents; C.D. Howe, leaning out into the Commons' centre aisle to explain the policies of his far-flung empire (one day, he pulled a policy statement from a pocket and began reading it, stopped suddenly, thrust the statement back into the pocket, dived into another pocket for another statement and said, "ah, here's today's announcement"); gentleman Davie Fulton, whose cares and defeats carried him into alcoholism, from which he bravely recovered; coal miner Clarie Gillis from Glace Bay; little Tommy Douglas, the deadly serious comic; and Jimmy Gardiner of Saskatchewan, the minister of agriculture, snapping his galluses over a capacious stomach as he took the Commons into his confidence.

Gardiner was a masterful user of statistics, though not in the usual sense. One occasion which comes to mind was a meeting of the Canadian Federation of Agriculture in Regina. Gardiner knew the federation was itching to get at him. He tossed out statistics purporting to show that farmers were never better off. He got the meeting so mad arguing over his statistics that the delegates forgot to nail him on all the important matters they wanted to broach. Gardiner slipped away and back to Ottawa and an experienced delegate, wagging his head in wonder, told me that "The son of a bitch did it to us again. That's three years in a row he's got off scot free." About the only man of stature in the Commons now, who puts the public interest ahead of his own, is Don Mazankowski, deputy prime minister.

MPs often become great by rising to great issues. But there have been precious few great issues which have exercised the public since the invoking of the War Measures Act in 1970, and even this was not a great parliamentary issue because nearly everyone was on the same side of the argument. Big issues today have mainly to do with money in sums so huge as to be incomprehensible to the public. Time allocation in debate and the now untainted use of closure of debate have also tended to keep issues from becoming public property. Before a debate can come to full public attention it must endure for nearly a month, and it must be over an issue involving principle, not principal.

The last great debate, in 1956, was about a government loan of $80 million (was the amount really that small?) to Americans to build a section of the trans-Canada oil pipeline. The debate was not about oil or pipe or money but about the will of the government to impose closure to meet its own legislative deadline and the equal determination of the opposition to thwart the government. Davie Fulton did most of the work for the Conservatives, and Diefenbaker reaped the political profits by riding the issue into the prime ministership in 1957. Stan Knowles of the old CCF (Co-operative Commonwealth Federation, now the New Democratic Party) was Fulton's main colleague in the fight and, as the expert on parliamentary rules, devised most of the opposition's tactics, with brilliant red-herring additions by Colin Cameron of the CCF. Diefenbaker was so grateful he later offered Knowles the speakership of the Commons, which Knowles declined on the grounds that he could never desert his party.

All during the pipeline debate, Knowles used to come to the parliamentary press gallery late in the evening, when an exhausted Commons had adjourned, to explain to baffled reporters, including me, the intricacies of his and Fulton's strategy against the government. It was only because of Knowles that the press was able to present a coherent daily story of what was going on and, for a change, its significance. Throughout, Knowles was straightforward with the press as he plotted opposition moves and government counter-measures for us. His honest, non-partisan nightly briefings carried us through the debate as astute and well-informed chroniclers. I remember that we all thanked Knowles every night, but I don't think any of us ever thanked him in print. Well, it wouldn't look good, you see: the leader in the affray, and a CCFer to boot, supplying all the information and direction, how could he be regarded as a dependable source?

In the end, Knowles and Fulton lost, as they knew, inevitably, they would, but their fight had given Parliament one of its great occasions — and the Conservatives power, only a few months later, after twenty-two years. Howe, the minister of trade and commerce and defence production, and the great Liberal "doer," pushed through the Liberal legislation; national development could not wait for a single day. St. Laurent sat hunched down in his Commons seat, fingering his moustache, unable to halt the rush to a Liberal debacle. Howe, beaten at the polls by rookie Doug Fisher, said with a wide and good-natured grin that he had been "dismissed" by his Lakehead constituents. A large crowd of senior civil servants was at the airport to meet Howe when he came back to Ottawa for the last time to surrender his cabinet portfolios. "I didn't care whether the Conservatives fired me on the spot," said Dave Golden, a deputy minister. "He was a great man and we wanted to make it plain that we knew he was."

Today, Howe wouldn't have been met by a porter. There is no regard in Ottawa any more for a loser, even a big one. Ask Bob Stanfield.

We do not see great national issues any more because the most difficult choice of all — can we afford it? — has been ducked by simply borrowing public money for every major undertaking, usually regional and seldom national. Our high purpose and national effort of the Second World War are not fancy or nostalgia. They are historical fact, like our achievement of nationhood in the First War when the hundreds of thousands of men in Flanders' trenches became Canadians instead of representatives of regions in Canada. (The men of the trenches could never be "provincial" again, said their commander, Gen. Sir Arthur Currie.) Almost forty years of self-indulgence have replaced national will. Nowhere is national will less evident than in the cabinet room where ministers fight savagely as despots of regional fiefdoms. Energy Minister Pat Carney's shouted insistence in 1985 that now was the time for the west to get the spoils instead of central Canada brought remonstrances from even some Quebec ministers that the government, after all, was supposed to represent Canada, not regions of it. Indeed the abilities of most cabinet ministers prompt the argument that cabinet appointments should pay no attention whatever to regions — just pick the best forty, or fifty, or sixty, or whatever the number will be before long, and get on with it.

Our effort in the Second World War is astonishing because it was carried out despite the politicians. Under Prime Minister Mackenzie King, we weren't allowed to command any of our own higher formations — the fourth most powerful air force in the world, for instance. This was driven home to me not long ago when I was reading in the Public Archives of Canada the war diary of my RCAF squadron, 418 City of Edmonton. There was only one letter in it. Dated December 20, 1944, it was from the air marshal commanding the RCAF overseas, Lloyd Breadner. It questioned our spelling of one of our targets in Germany, Dedelsdorf. He did not have operational command over a single Canadian airman and writing such letters was his only headquarters occupation. Despite King, we believed in our cause, even to the extent of providing colonial cannon fodder for Britain, e.g., at Hong Kong, Dieppe, RAF Bomber Command, and the Murmansk run.

4

Gas Tanks and Leaky Revenues

If Parliament had managed to retain some control over government expenditures, it might have been able to help channel public money into undertakings that would have benefitted the whole country (why was the natural gas pipeline not extended years ago into the Maritimes?) instead of watching helplessly as funds were frittered away in piecemeal regional projects which had to be continually propped up with more public money, and then often disposed of at firesale prices.

Certainly the rules of Parliament needed overhauling. One or two MPs could play dog in the manger, sometimes in a good cause like ridding the House of Commons of divorce cases, more often simply grinding local axes. But Parliament kept unnecessary procedures, such as Rule 21 which allows MPs to spout trivia at the start of each sitting, while giving away its crucial weapon: the right to hold up approval of government expenditures until satisfactorily explained. It cracked under heavy Liberal government pressure in 1968 and put time limits on consideration of estimated expenditures running into billions of dollars. When the restricted time is up, all estimates, approved or not, even debated or not, are automatically passed. If Parliament had given up everything else, even the daily question period, but kept control of the public purse, it would still be the country's supreme lawmaker. Now it is simply another stage, albeit sometimes a troublesome one, in the bureaucratic process of spending your money — lavishly.

So devastating was this sell-out (there were others, as we shall see in a moment) that the government now does not even take the trouble to inform Parliament of huge expenditures, let alone seek its approval for them. The Lambert Royal Commission on

Financial Management and Accountability complained about this in 1979, as had the Independent Review Committee in 1975. Since their reports came out, the situation has worsened, as Auditor-General Kenneth Dye illustrated in his 1984-85 report to Parliament. Billion-dollar tax remissions, Dye said, represent "a huge hidden budget in the financial affairs of Canada." He cited a previously unannounced gift of up to $1 billion to Dome Petroleum under a tax-remission order approved before Parliament was even asked to amend the law to accommodate such generosity. Dye added:

> There is something very wrong with a system that allows a one-billion-dollar policy decision to be made by way of a tax expenditure with Parliament having so little information on the transaction. We are, after all, talking about public money, provided by Canadian taxpayers who elect MPs to look after their interests.

In 1985, Dye appeared to be the only one in Ottawa looking out for taxpayers' interests. Certainly the cabinet wasn't as it collectively bailed out the uninsured depositors of failed banks and individually billed the treasury for holidays abroad. MPs of all parties junketed here and there, and their Speaker sought hundreds of thousands of dollars for refurbishing a home already supplied to him free. Dye seemed almost a voice in the wilderness as he kept pleading for information from the government on still undisclosed aspects of Petro-Canada's 1981 acquisition of Petrofina. He said: ".... in 1984, Parliament enacted amendments to the Income Tax Act that may well allow Petro-Canada to reap benefits of hundreds of millions of dollars in reduced taxes. But MPs were not informed — and had no way of knowing — that these huge tax benefits might accrue to Petro-Canada when they enacted that legislation." Dye provided this colorful simile:

> A cost-conscious Parliament is in the position of a team of engineers trying to design a more fuel-efficient automobile. They think they have succeeded, but the engine seems to go on consuming as much gas as it did before. They cannot understand the problem until they notice that, hidden from

view, myriad small holes have been punched through the bottom of the gas tank. This is too often the way of tax expenditures. Revenue leaks away, and MPs do not know about it until it is too late.

Tax remissions represent a much bigger hogshead of patronage than the thousands of appointments in the power of the prime minister — and with practically no publicity. The minister of national revenue spends a good part of each working day signing remission orders granting relief, deserved or otherwise, from all kinds of taxes, from personal income tax to Customs duties. By law, these orders appear in the *Canada Gazette*, but the press never looks at them.

While Dome and Petro-Canada and several banks were receiving tax remissions or otherwise being favored by public money, the revenue department was going after back taxes from Newfoundland fishermen who had just had their worst catches in years. We deal with this in the chapter on government.

Dye returned to the theme of remissions in his 1986 annual report, saying that government forgiveness of taxes for certain groups is undermining our self-assessment tax system so that legal tax avoidance before long slips into illegal tax evasion and the public no longer sees the Income Tax Act as fair or credible. Parliament, he wrote, is being "foiled and frustrated in its twin tasks of approving proposed expenditures and holding the government accountable." Lack of control in the use of tax remissions "may well represent one of the most serious voids in parliamentary control over the public purse in Canadian history."

The special committee on reform of the House of Commons sounded plaintive in its June, 1985, report:

Years ago, Parliament was the primary source of legislative issues. Today, the legislative role of Parliament and its members is not to formulate but, at best, to refine policy. . . . . It is time to change this situation. Private members must once again become instruments through which citizens can contribute to shaping the laws under which they live. The formulation of legislation used to be a central task for Members of Parliament, and it must become so once again.

Fat chance. Not only did Parliament effectively give up its right to deny the government money, it had another part of its rights stripped away when the charter of human rights and freedoms was inserted in the Constitution where it cannot be amended by a simple enactment of Parliament.

5

Take It to the Courts

Before the Charter, nowhere was Parliament's supremacy more evident to the public than in its ability to deal quickly with cases of individual and human rights. A case could be brought to the floor of Parliament almost immediately and thoroughly aired. Parliament not only did good work protecting a citizen's rights, it looked good doing it. Now it has no power in that most important of all aspects of a democracy. Non-elected judges instead of elected Members of Parliament sit in judgment in all cases of individual liberties and human rights.

Parliament was always extremely sensitive to cases of individuals harassed by government officialdom. Such cases popped up almost overnight in the Commons, were debated until action was promised (usually quickly to reduce already bad publicity) and then dropped, the names never to be heard in public again. For instance, Clifford Williams of Montreal was sentenced to twenty-eight years in prison for a first offence, armed robbery with a toy pistol. The opposition pressed the case until the sentence was reduced. Today the government can say, "Take it to the courts."

Constant questioning by the opposition finally resulted in the deportation of French war criminal Jacques de Bernonville. Harry Allen Read, an air force veteran, got proper medical treatment for his back, broken in a wartime bail-out over Germany, after an opposition member put more than twenty questions to the government on the case. The government's doctors had told Read it was all in his mind. Flight Lieutenant Jean-Jacques Desrochers received rapid attention in Parliament when he said he had not been promoted in the RCAF for eight years and had finally been discharged because he insisted on speaking French.

These are examples of human problems which don't come before Parliament any more. But animal problems do. Here's a House of Commons exchange of June 28, 1972:

P.C. Noble (Conservative — Grey-Simcoe): In the interest of reducing the heavy losses of cattle in transit from west to eastern feed lots, is it the intention of the minister to give favorable consideration to the request of the Canadian Cattlemen's Association for an extension of the 36-hour limit in the Criminal Code to 42 hours for rest periods during the movement of cattle by the railways? This would shorten the trip between Winnipeg and Toronto by approximately 18 to 20 hours.

Hon. Otto E. Lang (Minister of Justice): Following the representations from the association I asked for some special studies to be undertaken to see whether it would be within the tolerances of humane treatment if there were such an extension. I propose to institute some special studies in this regard forthwith in order to see if any accommodation can be arrived at.

Did you ever hear of an MP proposing special studies to cut the length of trips for VIA Rail passengers?

The courts have been only too happy to take over a field removed from its proper parent, Parliament. And like all bodies with power, it wants more. Chief Justice Brian Dickson of the Supreme Court of Canada proposed in the summer of 1985 that the Constitution should be amended to recognize the judiciary as an independent body separate from the government. He was increasingly concerned, he said, about extra-judicial activities which could politicize the role of judges and damage their status of impartiality: "I think there's always a great danger of a judge engaging in a royal commission most of which are highly political and highly contentious, that his objectivity and impartiality, his independence may be prejudiced."

But Dickson did not make a murmur when one of his own court, Willard Estey, was appointed only two months later by the government to the highly political job of looking into the collapse of two Alberta banks. In any case, the courts were already embroiled in political questions such as abortion and testing of the cruise missile in Canada, matters obviously for Parliament but which the courts have usurped.

The government, civil service, and judiciary have all gained at Parliament's expense. The public has lost. We now have such spectacles as the ludicrous judgment of the Supreme Court that penis-shaped vibrators and inflatable dolls are "publications" under the Criminal Code. Dickson himself explains: "What matters is not what Canadians think is right for themselves to see. What matters is what Canadians would not abide other Canadians seeing because it would be beyond the contemporary Canadian standard of tolerance to allow them to see it."

So much for individual freedoms. The Supreme Court's message can be summed up in one word: conform.

Twenty years ago, a justice of the Supreme Court, Wishart F. Spence, went so far as to hold that he could sit in judgment on political decisions. A Liberal appointee, he quickly agreed in 1966 to take on the Munsinger case as a royal commissioner when all other justices on the court refused. Spence did so at the urging of his old school pal, Paul Martin, then minister of external affairs.

The essence of the case — a court, after the event, pronouncing judgment on a prime minister's decision — was lost in its sensational aspects, mainly the "physical relationship" between Associate Defence Minister Pierre Sévigny and a German tart, Gerda Munsinger, who was said to have also taken Soviet agents into her bed. Gerda wasn't a spy, and when the matter was presented to Prime Minister Diefenbaker in 1961 as a possible security risk, he told Sévigny to stay away from her and that was that. But the Liberals were smarting over the 1964 Rivard case — an official named Raymond Denis in Immigration Minister Guy Favreau's office got two years in jail for trying to spring drug runner Lucien Rivard from prison — and when they asked the Mounties what they had on the Tories, the RCMP could hardly wait to tell Prime Minister Pearson about Gerda. (The Rivard case provided one of the great political lines of this century. Rivard had escaped jail in Montreal by scaling the prison wall on a garden hose in 45° F weather after telling his guards he was going out to water the rink. During the 1965 election campaign, when crammed meeting halls became hot and sweaty, Diefenbaker would say, "It was on a night like this that Lucien Rivard went out to water the rink." Diefenbaker brought the house down every time with this, no matter how often he used it. Sometimes, when he didn't use the line, people in the crowd would shout, "Tell us about the rink, Dief." It was generally believed that Tom Van Dusen, Diefenbaker's press-and-every-other-kind-of aide, gave The Chief the line, but Van Dusen insists to this day that Diefenbaker himself was the originator.)

Spence permitted the lawyers for the royal commission and for Justice Minister Lucien Cardin, who had deliberately blurted out the name Munsinger in the Commons (he pronounced it monsignor, alarming state and church alike), to give opinions which he, as chairman, then characterized as allegations of misconduct against Diefenbaker and Davie Fulton, justice minister at the time. Spence also held a secret meeting of the commission to take evidence without Diefenbaker or Fulton being allowed to see the transcript, and issued a summary of the secret meeting — he referred to it as a "handy document" — which removed the names of known criminals but left in the names of Conservative cabinet ministers implicated by commission innuendo. The "handy document" alleged political pressure by the Conservatives on the RCMP to drop charges against Gerda even after RCMP Commissioner Cliff Harvison had already testified that the Mounties on their own had requested, without consultation with any member of the Conservative government, that charges be dropped. (Eddie Goodman, counsel for George Hees, couldn't resist a joke in even the direst circumstances. He was questioning a witness about seeing Hees and Gerda together in a Montreal bar. The witness allowed that it was pretty dark but that he could make out the pair all right. "It wasn't nearly dark enough," Goodman said.) Spence carried out his duty to the Liberals and found, as everyone expected he would, that Diefenbaker should have dismissed Sévigny from his portfolio.

In 1981, the Liberals hauled Spence out of retirement to provide them with another self-serving report, this time on the findings of the McDonald royal commission that there was "institutional acceptance" in the RCMP of disregard for the law. Liberal Solicitor-General Robert Kaplan maintained that it wasn't a crime for police to break the law in line of duty and, to support his argument, made public a specially commissioned report by Spence and Robert J. Wright, a Toronto Liberal lawyer. Spence said that such a thing as barring the RCMP from carrying out electronic surveillance "would be an unwarranted interference with the efficiency of the operation."

Is this the kind of person we want on the Supreme Court, making judgment on human rights and individual freedoms? Can we entrust our freedoms to an appointed, non-accountable court which harbors such members?

6

Don't Anybody Point a Finger at Me!

In Ottawa, nobody is accountable for his actions, except when the odd project works out and everybody seeks acclaim. This is mainly due to the Trudeau system of committees reviewing committees reviewing committees so that what responsibility might be detected in this maze is shared collectively and no one can be singled out as the accountable party. The higher the position, the less the accountability.

In my thirty-odd years in Ottawa, I can recall only one case of admitted mistake. The Second World War history of the army had just been published in which it was said that the war was prolonged into 1945 partly because 1st Canadian Army didn't close the Falaise Gap swiftly enough to trap the entire German 7th Army. I was sent down to army headquarters to see Maj.-Gen. George Kitching who had commanded the 4th Canadian Division at Falaise — and been sacked after the battle. The conversation went something like this:

Me (referring to the appropriate section of the history): Is this true?
Gen. Kitching: Yes.
Me: What happened?
Gen. Kitching: I goofed it.

He offered no qualifications and made no attempt to attach blame to anyone else, superior or subordinate. He went on to explain that the Polish division beside the Canadians couldn't communicate because they had not been supplied with enough interpreters. That, Kitching said, was his fault. (My other favorite general was Maj.-Gen. Harry Wickwire Foster of Halifax who, after retirement, confided to a friend that he had discovered how to save $365 a year: "There's a new brand of scotch in the liquor store which is $1 cheaper a bottle than what I'm drinking.")

Parliament has long grappled vainly with the problem of accountability by ministers and civil servants. The special committee on reform of the Commons said in 1985:

> The idea of a minister responsible for everything that goes on in a department may once have been realistic, but it has long since ceased to be so. A minister cannot possibly know everything that is going on in a department. The doctrine of ministerial responsibility undermines the potential for genuine accountability on the part of the person that ought to be accountable — the senior officer of the department. We have heard many arguments that a new doctrine of deputy ministerial responsbility relating exclusively to matters of administration should be established. In this context administration includes policy implementation. Such a doctrine would set out the obligations of senior public servants and include the obligation to testify before parliamentary committees on matters of administration. Under this system, the testimony of deputy ministers before committees would be an everyday occurrence. Furthermore, regular open contact between the senior public service and Members of Parliament should lead to a more realistic understanding of administrative practices and more precise pinpointing of accountability.

Don't hold your breath. In November, 1985, Gerald Bouey, governor of the Bank of Canada, was testifying about the collapse, two months earlier, of the Canadian Commercial Bank, and his statement, in May that same year, that the bank was solvent. Bouey told the Commons finance committee that he had based that statement on information given him by William Kennett, the inspector-general of banks. It was up to the inspector-general to decide whether a bank was solvent, Bouey said. The Bank of Canada relied on the inspector-general's opinion.

Over to Kennett as witness before the same Commons committee a few days later. It wasn't his fault, Kennett said, that the extent of the bank's problems went undetected. Whose fault, then? he was asked. Kennett had ready a field of scapegoats: the recession in western Canada, declining oil prices, the bank's auditors, and the whole system of inspection of financial institutions. Kennett even went one step further and blamed Parliament itself for not updating the inspection system since 1923. It was very unfair, he protested, that anybody point the finger at him. What about the bank's management, its board of directors, internal and external auditors?

Earlier in 1985, the Commons public accounts committee dealt with another text-book case of blame-shifting in a $42-million loss to the taxpayer from renegotiation of leases of several government-occupied office towers in Ottawa. The public works department blamed the loss on ministerial decisions, but it turned out that the ministers involved were not informed by their civil servants of all the key factors. Auditor-General Dye commented on the case:

> This issue is therefore two-edged; the sword of accountability cuts both ways. MPs may think that officials in a department have initiated and carried through a major decision when, in reality, the decision resulted from ministerial intervention. In another instance, MPs may believe that ministers are the architects of actions. But, in fact, departmental officials have not only taken the decision but have kept ministers at least partially in the dark as to the action they have assented to. All of this makes pinning down where accountability lies very difficult.

Parliament itself ducks responsibility. The special joint committee of the Commons and Senate on Canada's international relations spent two months in the summer of 1985 receiving 700 briefs and hearing 300 witnesses on the issues of free trade with the United States and the U.S. Strategic Defence Initiative (Star Wars). It declined to recommend anything on either issue. On trade, it said there should be talks with the U.S. On Star Wars, it said, let the government decide. Parliament thus took itself out of debates which it continuously clamors to enter.

I guess I haven't given a very nice picture of Parliament, but I love the place and hate to see its powers eroded. It hasn't any illness which can't be cured. But it will take years of skill and determination to wrest back from government, the courts, and the civil service the powers properly vested in Parliament and which have been allowed to slip away by weakness and oversight. A return to its former greatness will also require the co-operation and forthrightness of government willing to give back some of its enormous powers, especially over expenditures.

When I used to leave the press gallery late at night, whether after an evening of dull or raucous debate, I used to pat the sandstone walls of Parliament's columns and corridors and say to myself, "Boy, are you ever lucky being able to work at the very heart of freedom." Really, that's what I said to myself, though sometimes in less maudlin phrases. I meant it too. And I still mean it. All Parliament needs is a stiffer spine.

PART THREE

CANADIAN DEFENCE: The Secrets Are All American

Military intelligence is a contradiction in terms.

Groucho Marx

1

Horses on the Payroll

Canadian ministers of national defence have gone as unthanked as their colleagues in the finance portfolio, and the more honorable they have been, the harsher their undoing. One defence minister, Sir Mackenzie Bowell, and one finance minister, Sir Charles Tupper, made it to the prime ministership, but only as short-lived stopgaps in the grab-bag of four Conservative administrations which followed, within five years, the death of Sir John A. Macdonald in 1891. The first Liberal defence minister, William Ross, lasted only eleven months before he was shunted off to Halifax in 1874 by Prime Minister Alexander Mackenzie as collector of Customs. The department of Customs was then as big a political dumping ground as external affairs is today — and would still be if the salaries came up to the standards set by dumpees.

The most honorable defence ministers fared worst: Sir Sam Hughes in the First World War because he was a bit of a kook; J.L. Ralston in the Second World War because his head was required by his leader for the anti-conscription pike; Gen. Andrew McNaughton because he was a political innocent; Brooke Claxton because he was trapped in his own quicksand of detail; George Pearkes because the cabinet went on a disarmament bender; and Douglas Harkness because his head was required by *his* leader for the anti-nuclear pike.

Claxton, the defence minister from 1946 to 1954, had been a sergeant-major during the First War and he loved to discuss world military strategy with his executive assistant, Paul Marshall, before a huge wall map, both men waving enormous drinks as pointers to soft underbellies and critical fluid fronts. On Claxton's military transport plane, the bar opened before the wheels came up, the steward rushing headlong down the canted aisle with the first for the minister. Claxton loved a party, and was always the last songster still upright at the piano, still fending off his wife Helen, who kept trying (vainly) to steer him home or, if they were out of town, to their barracks or hotel room

Claxton insisted on seeing nearly all files. He could not delegate work, important or trivial. The files grew floor-to-ceiling in his office in the ramshackle old wooden defence headquarters on Elgin Street (in the days before the pay and accommodation of civil servants became more important than policies). The files and the detail finally did him in because he couldn't keep up, with or without booze. A minor scandal of detail which he hadn't had time to deal with (it was too far down in the pile) became public and set the country giggling: horses on the payroll of the Army works service at Camp Petawawa, Ontario. Claxton furiously maintained that there were no horses on the payroll. But they were there all right, as entries of teams which turned out to be non-existent but whose teamsters, pocketing the money, were real enough. And there was the matter of the missing railway spur line at the camp, pulled up surreptitiously and sold for scrap. Prime Minister St. Laurent handled the affair easily and lightly in the 1953 election campaign: "Boys will be boys," he said, and everybody smiled and the Liberals breezed to another re-election.

I think the maddest Claxton ever got was on receipt of a letter dated April 24, 1953, from Field Marshal Montgomery, then deputy Supreme Allied Commander, Europe. Monty had just toured Canada, to considerable public and private acclaim, and he proceeded, on the very date of his return, to give Claxton "some of the more important impressions I have gained." The first one was: "Today, the Canadian Army is not organized on sound basis." Many of the senior officers were incapable of command and should be retired. Canada should have national compulsory service. The militia was wasteful of money. And so on.

"I am sure you will understand that this letter is intended to help you in your great task," Monty said. "If there is ever anything I can do to lend a hand, you have only to ask."

There was one more shot to come. Montgomery said he had

sent a copy of his letter to Lt.-Gen. Guy Simonds, chief of staff, Canadian Army, "a really high-class officer" and "well qualified to advise you." Gen. Charles Foulkes, chief of defence staff and Simonds' superior, did not receive a copy of the letter, was not mentioned by Montgomery, and was even madder than Claxton.

Claxton wrote back coldly to Monty May 12, 1953, that his "personal views .... raised major questions which are, of course, matters of policy to be decided by the government of this country." With some trepidation, Claxton sent Montgomery's letter to Prime Minister St. Laurent and noted that Monty was coming back to Canada in August to open the Canadian National Exhibition, adding: "On this occasion he will make a speech and it is entirely likely that .... he may be indiscreet." But Monty held his tongue, in public at least.

Claxton became president of the Canada Council and sponsored a competition to name the most popular ten songs of the First and Second World Wars, which he had printed as songsheets. On his cancerous death bed in 1960, Claxton ordered the hospital gadgetry removed, and went home to die, alone with his wife.

Ralph Campney succeeded Claxton in defence for the last three years of the twenty-two-year Liberal rule before John Diefenbaker surprised everybody except himself by winning the prime ministership in 1957. Campney had been a flier in the First War when castor oil was used as a lubricant in aircraft engines, frequently spraying the planes' occupants, and he was fond of saying that he had never afterwards needed that type of medication.

The self-effacing Campney once told me how he got his start in law and politics in Vancouver. A rookie member of his club, he one day encountered a drunken businessman who asked him to fix a brief for him. Campney worked day and night for a week to get it ready. He was about to deliver it when he ran into the businessman, this time sober, in the club. The businessman again asked Campney to prepare a brief, forgetting that he had done so a week earlier. "I can have it for you tomorrow," Campney said. "Impossible," the businessman said, "that job will take at least a week." Campney handed over the brief the next day and the businessman for months could be heard telling everybody at the club, colleague, acquaintance or stranger: "If you want a good job done fast, get that new guy, Campney."

Campney was the smoothest minister with his departmental

estimates I ever saw. In those days, ministers had to put through the Commons, on their own, their departments' planned expenditures for the fiscal year. This always occurred in the dog days of August, the last item on the Commons order paper, everybody dying to get away from the un-air-conditioned chamber. (Now the Commons has lost practically all control over government expenditures and, anyway, it wouldn't dream of sitting through July and August, though the chamber has factory air.) It took only a few determined opposition members to drive nearly everybody insane, not letting the estimates pass until they got the answers they wanted, keeping the House in session one more day, vacation time slipping away. Claxton bristled at almost every question, taking each as a personal test of his knowledge of his department. It only prolonged the grilling. Campney, on the other hand, jumped to his feet at every opposition suggestion: "What a marvellous idea," he would exclaim, "we'll have a look at that right away and see how fast we can implement it." The opposition member beamed; he had influenced government policy. The estimates passed quickly, no more was ever heard of the suggestion, and Campney was enjoying the balm of Vancouver.

Campney failed in one endeavor: trying to persuade Air Commodore Len Birchall of the Royal Canadian Air Force to write a memoir of the three and a half terrible years in Japanese prisoner-of-war camps. Birchall was the "savior of Ceylon" for warning of the approach of a Japanese fleet before being shot down in his flying boat in 1942. His prison experience included being marched to a chopping block for beheading by sword and then told: not today, maybe tomorrow. Birchall was appointed an aide to Campney for a ministerial tour of Canadian bases in Europe and Campney spent a good deal of time cornering Birchall in hotel rooms to impress upon him the enormous dearth in Canada of war diaries and memoirs and how he could help fill the gap. Years later, Birchall wrote an account but felt that the worst details of prison life should not be revived. On that same trip to Europe, Campney discovered that the RCAF had lied to him about a crash which had wiped out its aerobatic team. The air force had said an explosion in one of the four close-flying planes during practice near the French-German border had caused all four to crash, with loss of the four pilots. What had actually happened was that the Sabre jets had come out of a loop and that three had followed their leader into a hillside. Campney immediately banned all such flying and aerobatic teams were not revived until long after he had left the ministry.

George Pearkes and Douglas Harkness, like most defence ministers, were war veterans, and their greatest political danger often lay in their friendship, or at least acquaintanceship, with most of the senior officers and civilians running the department. They had fought beside them in the war. (We leave aside here the question of whether, after nearly half a century, the government should hold another war to replenish the supply of veterans for the Canadian Legion and for the veterans affairs portfolio.) Harkness ran into an early embarrassment as defence minister: as one measure to cut costs, he ordered the navy not to show the flag at exhibitions and fairs in Canadian and foreign ports. The navy promptly dispatched a flotilla to the annual fisheries exhibition at Lunenburg, N.S. Harkness was outraged at this defiance of a direct order. "Why didn't you fire an admiral or two?" I asked him. "How can I?" he said, "they're all my friends." But the navy didn't do it again.

Pearkes was quickly dragooned in 1957 by Gen. Charles Foulkes, the chief of defence staff, into signing the North American Air Defence agreement with the United States before the new Conservative government had a chance to grasp all its details and implications. There wasn't anything wrong with the agreement, which has endured until now, but the government didn't anticipate all the questions which were going to be raised, especially by the Liberals, who pretended it was all news to them but who, as Foulkes said publicly later, had not only known about it all along but had been on the verge of signing when rudely thrust from office by Diefenbaker. Foulkes simply placed the same piece of paper in front of the Conservatives. I once interviewed Foulkes in his defence headquarters office in winter. The heat was turned off, the window was open, and the curtains were drawn, soaring into the room occasionally on a frigid draught. Foulkes was working by a tiny gooseneck lamp which threw a small blob of light on his paper in the darkened room. The interview went on for some time and I left frozen. I waited for summer before I interviewed him again, at least in his office.

2

The Secrets Are All American

I used to see all the generals and admirals and air marshals in those days. They were almost as accessible as the politicians, though not always as knowledgeable on defence matters. The service public relations officers kept encouraging me to make appointments to see the brass because they seized the opportunity to sit in to find out what was going on. Like all public relations officers in the government, they were the last to be told anything, if they were told anything at all; usually they were kept in the dark as a routine procedure. Generally, ministers and deputy ministers do not trust departmental public relations officers, not because they are disloyal but because they never have a grasp of what is going on in a department and therefore cannot judge the import of a question; this, in turn, is because ministers and deputy ministers never take these officers into their confidence. Instead, they have a press officer of their own, usually under the name of a special assistant, who, of course, needs a staff. There are thus two public relations organizations in each department, one handling information and the other the typing for the standard press release.

As a rule, appointments had to be made to see senior officers. But for lesser ranks I could walk into defence headquarters off the street and make my way up and down peeling, linoleum corridors in the departmental labyrinth of "A", "B" and "C" buildings searching for a particular officer without ever being challenged at the main door or elsewhere. Today you need a military escort, if you can get in at all, lest you stumble onto some secret. The secrets are all American and the Canadian military, having none of their own, can enjoy only a vicarious thrill out of protecting them.

In the two decades after the Second War, there were a lot of important defence decisions taken: to enlist in NATO, NORAD and the Korean war, to pour treasure into a new defence build-up only five years after finishing a war, to refuse nuclear weapons, to accept nuclear weapons.

The decision that brought down the greatest abuse on the

government was the 1959 cancellation of the Avro Arrow jet interceptor. Avro had made one lousy interceptor, the CF-100 (the RCAF crews called it — and not affectionately either — the "clunk"), a transport jetliner which needed sand in the tail to fly (in C.D. Howe's famous description) and here it was milking taxpayers of millions of dollars for a plane advertised as the greatest of its type in the world but which had never flown with its own engine in it. Avro had a cost-plus contract, which meant it was guaranteed all costs plus a percentage for profit. The higher the cost, the higher the profit, so Avro threw into the cost account such items as company cocktail parties. The contract had driven defence spending to its highest figure since 1945, and the course was still up, up.

It is often said by those who still vilify Diefenbaker for cancellation of the project that he acted on a whim. Far from it. The cabinet debated the issue for months and it well knew what the economic and political repercussions were going to be. Avro just didn't believe cancellation was possible, though repeatedly warned that the government had just that in mind because of costs. Crawford Gordon, the president, went in to see Diefenbaker with jaunty air and came out spluttering and purple-faced. He had thought, until suddenly and harshly disabused of the idea, that the defence industry ran the government, as in the United States.

Cabinet papers which I was not allowed to see until 1985 show that it was the chiefs of staff committee in the first instance who recommended killing the Arrow because its cost far outweighed its advantages and the main threat to North America was shifting from the bomber to the missile. Here is the actual wording of the recommendation to cabinet August 22, 1958:

The Canadian Chiefs of Staff have grave doubts as to whether a limited number of aircraft [100 Arrows] at this extremely high cost [$2 billion] would provide defence returns commensurate with the expenditures in view of the changing threat and the possibility that an aircraft of comparable performance can be obtained from U.S. production at a much less cost and in the same time period, 1961-62.... Therefore the Chiefs of Staff consider that to meet this modest requirement for interceptor aircraft it would be more economical to procure a fully developed interceptor of comparable performance from U.S. sources.

In other words, the U.S. already had in squadrons an interceptor comparable to the Arrow, which was still in the development stage. The cabinet eventually took the chiefs' advice and bought sixty-six American F-101B Voodoo interceptors which lasted more than two decades. Figures accompanying the presentation to cabinet showed that Arrow development would cost a total of $862 million, of which $476 million had already been committed, and that production of one hundred planes would cost an additional $1 billion.

The cabinet did not accept immediately the chiefs' advice but decided to continue development of the Arrow for the rest of the 1958-59 fiscal year and then get an updated opinion from the chiefs of staff committee. The chiefs' opinion didn't change. Here is the decision of the cabinet defence committee in the form of a memorandum to cabinet (cabinet document 46/49, top secret) February 6, 1959:

1. At a meeting on February 5th, the Cabinet Defence Committee had before it recommendations of the Minister of National Defence that further development of the CF-105 aircraft [Arrow] be discontinued now and that the Chiefs of Staff be asked to present at an early date their recommendations on what requirements, if any there were, for additional air defence missile installations in Canada and for interceptor aircraft of the nature of the CF-105 or alternate types.
2. During the consideration of these matters, the Chairman of the Chiefs of Staff Committee [Foulkes] reported that the Chiefs of Staff had reviewed the position concerning the production of the CF-105 and that "they are still of the opinion that the changing threat and the rapid advances in technology, particularly in the missile field, along with the diminishing requirements for manned interceptors in Canada, create grave doubts as to whether a limited number of aircraft of such extremely high cost would provide defence returns commensurate with the expenditures."

3. The Committee concurred in the recommendations of the Minister of National Defence and agreed that they be submitted to the Cabinet for consideration at an early meeting. W.R. Martin, Secretary, Cabinet Defence Committee, Privy Council Office, February 6th, 1959.

On February 20, 1959, the government killed the Arrow, and on March 26, Air Marshal Hugh Campbell, chief of air staff, recommended that the airframes already built be reduced to scrap. The government on September 21, 1960, decided on the Arrow's replacement with the American Voodoo. On December 23, 1960, Harkness sent to Diefenbaker a paper on North American air defence by Air Marshal Frank Miller, new chief of the defence staff, estimating Soviet bomber strength at 160 heavy bombers and 1,000 medium Badger bombers of which 400 could "arrive over continental North America." However (and Diefenbaker underlined this in his copy of the memorandum), Miller added that the intercontinental ballistic missile would be the principal intercontinental weapon by 1963. This confirmed Diefenbaker's premise for cancellation of the Arrow and acquisition of the Bomarc-B anti-aircraft missile: the threat of the manned bomber was shifting to the long-range missile. (In saying this on February 20, 1959, Diefenbaker was echoing, almost word for word, the secret advice of the military.)

Though the Arrow flew at mach 1.9 (that is, at 1.9 times the speed of sound) at 50,000 feet and reached 59,000 feet without trouble, there can be no doubt that the decision to scrap it was the right one. It is argued that the cancellation broke up a magnificent engineering team at Avro, though the Canadian Iroquois engine which was supposed to go into the Arrow never ran properly and the Canadian Astra-Sparrow armament control system and missile had to be ditched in favor of the American Falcon. What would have this team done? Build a missile inferior to the American product? Build a transport plane (the Avro jetliner had already been dropped)? De Havilland and Canadair made such planes, and they didn't sell. After the government took over de Havilland and Canadair as crown agencies, their records rapidly worsened as the bureaucratic cloud settled down over an industry already beset with enough problems. Continuation of the Arrow would not only have meant a halt to all other capital defence projects but a serious drain on the over-all federal budget. The government would have been able to do little spending except ladle out funds to Avro, including the price of its booze.

3

The Nuclear Bells of Howard Green

In its 1957-58 agony over reaching the "inescapable conclusion" (Harkness' words) that the cost of the Arrow was out of proportion to its military value, the cabinet ignored the significance of acquiring the Bomarc, including its nuclear warhead. Almost routinely, on October 15, 1958, the cabinet approved initiation of negotiations with the United States for the acquisition and storage of defensive nuclear weapons for the use of Canadian forces. This was accepted as a necessary step for Canada to meet its air defence responsibilities under the NORAD agreement signed the previous year. In November, 1958, the nuclear negotiations began between the Canadian chairman of the chiefs of staff and the American chairman of the joint chiefs of staff. The following February, Diefenbaker announced the pro-nuclear decision and that seemed to be that. A document called "general principles governing the acquisition by Canada of nuclear warheads for Canadian forces in Canada and Europe" was drawn up. Section B2 of this document said:

The procedures under which the nuclear warheads will be released and employed will vary depending on the types of weapons and the operational theatres in which they are to be employed. These procedures will be the subject of separate governmental agreements and will be based on the principles of joint responsibility.

In July, 1960, the United States seemed to entertain no doubts that Canada would not only accept nuclear weapons for its own forces but would not object to the storage of nuclear warheads for American forces stationed in Canada. It was not public knowledge at the time, but the U.S. sought permission from Canada to store air-to-air nuclear missiles at its Newfoundland bases at Goose Bay and Stephenville; to store anti-submarine nuclear warheads at its naval base at Argentia, Newfoundland; and to store nuclear strike weapons for U.S. Strategic Air Command at Goose Bay. Canada agreed with the first but demurred at the last two. With its request to put offensive nuclear bombs at Goose Bay, the U.S. pushed too hard and too far and set off alarm bells in the external affairs department.

Those bells were already being tinkled by Howard Green, who became external affairs minister in 1959 after the sudden death of Sidney Smith who had tried, heroically but vainly, to keep up with the stacks of paper his officials kept piling in front of him (he died in his office reading one of these unnecessary, and probably irrelevant, papers). Pearkes was a brave and very gallant gentleman — the citation for his Victoria Cross in the First War is a hair-raiser — but he was no match for Green, another British Columbia war veteran. Green embarked on a laudable disarmament policy, one copied, without credit, by Prime Minister Trudeau a quarter-century later. Green appointed a disarmament negotiator, subtly attacked the government's nuclear warheads acquisition policy, and went so far as to insist on a defence department blackout on any announcements about military formations, equipment or even exercises. I happened to be talking with Pearkes in his defence department office the day the military had announced a routine NORAD exercise. Green came on the telephone. I of course got up to leave until the conversation was over but Pearkes, always polite and considerate, waved me back into my chair in front of his desk. Pearkes' side of the conversation consisted mainly of "yes, Howard" to Green's obvious complaint about how in hell could he establish credence for a government policy on disarmament while the defence department kept harping on war games and weapons and all that military stuff. Pearkes put back the phone and said mildly, "My, but Howard does get worked up." But from then on, during Pearkes' remaining time at defence, the military stayed well in the background and their announcements dealt with little more than routine promotions and transfers of senior officers and snappy features on a warship's daily menu or cold-weather tenting at Fort Churchill, Manitoba.

But some of Green's own officers tried to subvert their minister's anti-nuclear policy. In late 1960, Escott Reid, Canadian ambassador to West Germany, proposed a special military mission to Europe to sell Canadian-produced CF-104 nuclear strike planes to NATO members. Reid returned to Canada to promote his idea and saw Diefenbaker, Robert Bryce, secretary to the cabinet, and Norman Robertson, deputy minister of external affairs. But he stayed away from Green. In a confidential memo December 16, 1960, after his return to Bonn, Reid said Lockheed of California was claiming that Canada had no right to sell the company-designed plane to the Netherlands, Belgium, Italy and West Germany. Canada should, Reid said, offer to train European CF-104 crews, buy armaments from Europe and send to Europe a mission headed by Harkness who would first exert pressure on NATO's military commander, Gen. Lauris Norstad of the U.S. Harkness declined to be a salesman and no more was heard of the proposal.

4
___

What's a Rocket without a Warhead?

Pearkes left in 1960 to become lieutenant-governor of British Columbia and Harkness, who could not be cowed by Green — or Diefenbaker — succeeded him for three highly entertaining years, entertaining years for the public, at least, because the Tories, to paraphrase Sir William Connor, are always hacking themselves in two and leaving both parts to writhe in public. Harkness maintained from the start (and at the start he was accurately enunciating government policy) that because Canada had acquired from the Americans the carriers for nuclear weapons (the Bomarc, the Voodoo and Starfighter planes, and the Honest John artillery rocket) it should also acquire the nuclear warheads to go with them. The Bomarc-B, the type positioned in Canada (at North Bay, Ontario, and La Macaza, Quebec), was not even designed to carry a conventional warhead. Pro-nuclear policy was still official. The cabinet decided December 6, 1960:

That discussions (or negotiations) with the U.S. Government concerning arrangements for the essential acquisition of nuclear weapons or warheads for use by the Canadian forces, in the manners already decided, may proceed as soon as they can usefully be undertaken but the acceptance of joint controls to be a basic principle.

Draft agreements were prepared by external affairs but the department's own minister managed to avoid any actual negotiations with the United States. Green and Harkness wrote back and forth on the subject, always polite and proper. But privately Harkness said that Green was obsessed with disarmament and Green said Harkness was obsessed with weaponry. Diefenbaker was apparently on the fence, because R.B. Bryce, secretary to the cabinet, reported to Harkness March 2, 1961:

When the Prime Minister returned from Washington last week he outlined in Cabinet the following day, Tuesday, February 21st, the substance of his talks with President Kennedy. Part of these dealt with the Canadian position on storage of nuclear weapons, and I thought you should have a note on what I propose to record on this matter.

Mr. Diefenbaker said he had stated that negotiations should continue regarding such storage at Harmon Field [Stephenville] and Goose Bay, but that Canada would insist upon joint custody and control, and joint authority over use. The President had seemed to raise no objection. Regarding the submarine base at Argentia, Mr. Diefenbaker said he had stated that Canada would require joint custody, but that use should be determined by NATO. He had further stated that, so long as serious disarmament negotiations continued, Canada did not propose to determine whether or not to accept nuclear weapons for the Bomarc bases or for the Canadian interceptors; but that, if such weapons were accepted by Canada, this country would require joint custody and joint control, and use would be determined in the same manner as on U.S. bases. Negotiations for the necessary agreements should now continue on the basis of a "package deal," no one agreement being signed before the others had been worked out. There would be no hold-up if war should occur. The President had asked whether the same sort of "two-key" arrangement as the United Kingdom had would be satisfactory and Mr. Diefenbaker had said it would.

You will remember that Mr. Green pointed out that President Kennedy had indicated that the new U.S. government hoped to determine its basic policy on disarmament before participating in international discussions on the subject. The Cabinet noted with approval the statement of the Prime Minister on his discussions with President Kennedy in Washington on the previous day on the storage of nuclear weapons in Canada.

It is my understanding that negotiations on the basis outlined above were to proceed forthwith.

I have written a similar letter to Mr. Green.

That might have been Bryce's understanding, but it didn't happen. Harkness kept putting on the cabinet agenda the subject of nuclear negotiations with the U.S., only to have Diefenbaker pass over it entirely, or call it in the dying minutes of a meeting. Diefenbaker's last word would be that he would call the item at the next cabinet meeting, but he never did. Asked in the Commons external affairs committee whether it was still government policy to obtain nuclear weapons, Green said the question should be addressed to the defence department; his own department was "sticking to its own knitting." Over to Harkness: all he had to do was point to Diefenbaker's announcement of February 20, 1959, that nuclear weapons would be acquired from the United States on the grounds that defensive weapons could achieve their full potential "only when they are armed with nuclear warheads." Thus the government went through the tortures of the damned backing and forthing on the nuclear issue, arguing incessantly internally, contradicting each other in public, amending statements already amended, blaming the press for awkward disclosures. Even when it was more or less decided (there was never a clear statement from Diefenbaker) to reject a nuclear role in defence, the government so deliberately fudged its hesitant policy that the public decided that Diefenbaker couldn't make up his mind about anything and threw him out of office in 1963.

5
———

Not an Acceptable Military Solution

One of the problems in deciding the nuclear issue — to have or not to have — was Diefenbaker's distrust of the external affairs department. He was given a very good reason in 1957 on his first day in office; when he asked to see some foreign policy documents he was told they were secret and that he couldn't have them. Diefenbaker's aides had to go to the just-ousted prime minister, St. Laurent, to get approval for the new prime minister to see government papers.

Just a few day later, Diefenbaker went down the corridor from his East Block office and when he came back a few moments later his desk had been swept clean and he couldn't find the papers he had been working on. In both cases, the official involved in keeping Diefenbaker in the dark was John Starnes who, incredibly, remained director of communications security in the East Block until 1959, later was ambassador to West Germany and, still later, the first civilian head of Canada's security service. (Starnes turned inside out one day at Bonn when the visiting Canadian Commons defence committtee got off the bus in front of the hotel and a Liberal MP shouted, "So this is the place where they make the lampshades." Starnes was always preaching that it was time that we stopped being beastly to the Germans.)

Partly as a result of the two Starnes East Block incidents, Diefenbaker had seconded to his office two experienced officials from external affairs: Ross Campbell and Basil Robinson. They became the channel for foreign policy and, when Green took over that portfolio, his close advisers. Unlike many civil servants, mostly in external affairs, who sabotaged Diefenbaker at every opportunity, Campbell and Robinson, in the very best (and by that time past) tradition of the civil service, remained loyal to government and government policy throughout, though this sometimes meant devising, and defending, some tortured tactics to support some questionable policies.

The prime example was the attempt to work out a scheme whereby nuclear warheads for Canadian forces would be held in the United States and flown to Canada in a war emergency. This would permit the government to say there were no nuclear weapons on Canadian soil. But militarily it made no sense. The military said there was unlikely to be much more than two hours' warning of an attack on North America and that, under ideal weather and other conditions, it would take fifteen hours to transport the nuclear warheads to Canadian bases. The Americans expressed this view in May, 1962, at a meeting of the Canada-U.S. Permanent Joint Board on Defence and Harkness sent the appropriate minutes of the meeting to Diefenbaker. On August 17, 1962, Air Marshal Miller, chief of defence staff, told Harkness that fifteen hours to move nuclear warheads to Canada was not an "acceptable military solution" for the problem.

Thankfully, the fifteen-hour scheme never had to be put to the test. It could have been, in the Cuban missile crisis in October, 1962, but Diefenbaker refused to recognize it as an emergency (though Harkness did and put Canadian forces on the alert and sent the navy to sea, without cabinet approval). It was three days before Diefenbaker agreed to an official increased state of readiness. (The U.S. had the bad taste to send Livingston Merchant to Ottawa to brief Diefenbaker, Green and Harkness — Bryce, Miller and Norman Robertson, undersecretary of state for external affairs, were excluded by Diefenbaker at the last moment — on what the U.S. proposed to do about the Russian arms build-up in Cuba. Merchant had just completed his term as ambassador to Canada, during which he had spent a good deal of his time trying to undermine Diefenbaker.)

Green had expressed interest in the Cuban problem from the beginning because it looked like an opportunity to practice disarmament, or, at least, avoid armament. In May, 1961, Art Gavshon of the Associated Press and I hitched a ride with Green from a NATO meeting in Oslo to Geneva. (Green took great delight in flying in an ancient Dakota while other foreign ministers were arriving at Geneva by shiny jet — I think the Dakota was supposed to symbolize disarmament.) In his talk with us during the leisurely flight, Green remarked that Canada might be willing to act as an intermediary between the feuding United States and Cuba. Diefenbaker didn't like the idea at all and, in a typical method of handling such situations, simply said Green had said no such thing.

My boss, Gillis Purcell, general manager of Canadian Press, didn't like the idea of Diefenbaker saying Green hadn't said something which he had said to a CP reporter. Purcell issued a statement saying CP had full confidence in the accuracy of my report which, on the strength of some pieces I had written, was more confidence than I might well have expected, or deserved. When I next saw Green, he grabbed me by the elbow, laughed, and said, "Boy, you've got some boss. He really backs you up." There was not the slightest suggestion in Green's remark that he was drawing a comparison between my relations with my boss and Green's with his.

The Diefenbaker government's decisions taken between September, 1958, and June, 1961, to acquire the four American nuclear carriers, Bomarc-B, CF-104 Starfighter jet bomber (the widow-maker), Honest John artillery rocket, and CF-101B Voodoo jet interceptor, represented a very large outlay of defence funds: at least $700 million. Even at that, Canada was getting them cheap, because the U.S. had a vested interest in seeing that the Bomarc and Voodoo were placed in this country; every Soviet bomber shot down over Canada would crash in Canada, not the U.S. (The best defence strategy for Canada I ever heard was devised by Rawhide — Max Ferguson — on his early-morning CBC radio show: Canadians should tramp out in the snow, or in wheat-fields in summer, huge arrows pointing to Chicago.) The U.S. tried unsuccessfully to write into its agreement for Canadian purchase of the Voodoo a clause that these interceptors would be armed in the same way as in the U.S., that is, with the Genie nuclear air-to-air rocket or Falcon nuclear air-to-air missile. Where did they think Diefenbaker came from — the sticks? The Americans would have to devise a much more elaborate trap than that to catch Diefenbaker. They did, eventually, but the trap was about as elaborate as a street-corner mugging.

6

Suddenly, Whammo!

Meanwhile, Harkness was beavering away in support of nuclear weapons, the original and still official government policy. He approved in advance a speech by Gen. Laurence Kuter, former American commander of North American Air Defence Command, in Toronto September 1, 1961, outlining how, theoretically at least, nuclear warheads would not only destroy the Russian bomber but "cook" its nuclear bomb, rendering it unexplodable. Harkness later used this dubious argument himself in speeches and statements.

By this time, the armed forces had taken delivery of all their American nuclear carriers and Harkness began to insist that it was time to conclude negotiations with the U.S. for the warheads. Finally, in November, 1962, a month after the Cuban crisis, Diefenbaker agreed to preliminary negotiations and named Harkness, Green, and Gordon Churchill as the negotiating team. Some negotiations actually took place. Then Harkness went to the annual NATO meeting in Paris in December and from there to Egypt to visit Canadian troops on United Nations peacekeeping duties in the Sinai desert. He returned January 4, 1963, expecting to find the nuclear negotiations advanced. Instead, all hell had broken loose the previous day.

Gen. Lauris Norstad, the American military commander of NATO, had just retired and was paying the customary farewell visits to NATO countries to thank them for their contributions to the alliance. His thank-you suddenly turned into a slap in the face for the Canadian government.

Norstad claimed afterwards that he was badgered by reporters into saying what he did and that he was unconversant with the Canadian political situation. It is hard to believe that a general as astute as Norstad, and knowledgeable about the political vagaries of all alliance members, would not have known what he was getting into. On the other hand, the Canadian military, without Harkness' approval and in his absence, made delighted use of Norstad's remarks.

The transcript of Norstad's press conference at Uplands, the military airfield at Ottawa, now called Ottawa Base South, shows this exchange:

Q: Have you always been satisfied with Canada's contribution to NATO even though it was non-nuclear all along?

A: It's a mistake for anyone ever to say he is satisfied with anything. And if you find a commander that would say that he was satisfied he should be relieved, or should have been relieved. Canada has made certain commitments to the alliance which bear every reasonable relationship, I believe, to Canada's ability to commit forces to the alliance. Canada has met those commitments in numbers and, in general, in quality during the entire life of the alliance. So Canada has been quite outstanding in meeting its NATO commitments.

Q: General, do you consider that Canada has committed itself to provide its Starfighter squadrons in Europe with tactical nuclear weapons?

A: That is perhaps a question you should direct to the Minister rather than to me, but my answer to that is 'Yes.' This had been a commitment that was made, the continuation of the commitment that existed before, and as the air division is re-equipped that air division will continue to be committed to NATO and will continue to play an extremely, an increasingly important role.

Q: In the field of tactical nuclear ... ?

A: That's right.

Q: I'm sorry, sir — will play an extremely important role with or without tactical nuclear weapon?

A: I would hope with both. Is Air Marshal [Frank] Miller [chairman, Canadian chiefs of staff committee] here? I don't want to release anything you people haven't released here on this.

Air Marshal Miller: I think you're right on that, quite right on that ...

Norstad: We established a NATO requirement for a certain number of strike squadrons. This includes tactical atomic strike squadrons and Canada committed some of its force to meet this NATO-established requirement. And this we depend upon. Again, we depend upon it particularly because of the quality of the air division.

Q: Does it mean, sir, that if Canada does not accept nuclear weapons for these airplanes that she is not actually fulfilling her NATO commitments?

A: I believe that's right. She would be meeting it in force but not under the terms of the requirements that have been established by NATO. . . .

Whammo! The military could hardly wait to rush out a transcript. Diefenbaker hit the roof. To him, this was just another example of the Canadian civil service trying to undermine him, a belief for which there was considerable justification (see chapter on government and civil service).

Harkness maintained that Norstad hadn't said anything that the prime minister himself hadn't said. True enough, but it was what Diefenbaker had said five years previously, not the day before yesterday. In the intervening years, vacillation had had plenty of time to set in. And so it had with the Liberals. On January 13, 1963, Liberal Leader Mike Pearson did a perfect backward flip and came out for acquisition of nuclear weapons, which brought on his denunciation as the defrocked prince of peace by Pierre Trudeau, who was to succeed him five years later as prime minister. The Liberals had reversed policy the moment a Gallup poll showed a large majority of Canadians in favor of obtaining nuclear warheads.

Harkness breathed a sigh of relief. He thought this would settle the issue, leaving the New Democratic Party as the only party opposed to nuclear weapons. But Diefenbaker wasn't going to agree with anything Liberal; Pearson's position must be opposed and any acquisition of nuclear weapons delayed. On January 18 and 19, the Conservative party's annual meeting passed a watery resolution on nuclear arms, leaving the issue to the government to decide. Diefenbaker's interpretation of the resolution was a vote against nuclear weapons. Senator Solly Thorvaldson, the retiring president of the Progressive Conservative Association, had chaired the association meeting and he complained afterwards to Harkness that there was no doubt but that the party had to get rid of Diefenbaker. Harkness recounted in his reconstruction of the nuclear question: "I said to him [Thorvaldson], 'why didn't you do something on it while president instead of having just finished saying, at the meeting, what a great leader Diefenbaker was.' His reply was that he couldn't do anything else as long as Diefenbaker was still leader. This was typical, I thought, of the situation of a lot of Conservatives, then and later, who wanted to get rid of Diefenbaker, but wanted someone else to bell the cat."

Harkness had told his wife, Fran, in early January that he was considering resigning, but he did not inform anybody else until January 16 when he told Green, Churchill, Richard Bell and Paul Martineau, all cabinet colleagues, that he would resign if the government did not agree with a position on nuclear weapons which he could accept. On January 19, he told his son, Ken, and Dr. John Porter, the president of his constituency association. Davie Fulton tried vainly to rally cabinet ministers to remove Diefenbaker on the grounds that he was unreliable, as in the Cuban crisis. Discouraged, Fulton retreated to the Conservative leadership in British Columbia.

During the week of January 20, 1963, the cabinet thrashed away at the issue with Harkness poised to resign and, in one fanciful moment, Diefenbaker saying he would rather resign himself than see Harkness go. Most ministers, including Trade Minister George Hees, and Associate Defence Minister Pierre Sévigny, said they backed Harkness.

On Friday, January 25, the Commons met at 11 a.m. and after routine business was cleared away (introduction by the speaker of visiting provincial speakers, and the like) Pearson led off a debate on defence and foreign policy and gleefully quoted at length from the transcript of Norstad's press conference. When Diefenbaker got the floor, he rambled on and on, leaving a trail of red herrings which would have confused a shark. Here are two direct quotations from his speech that day:

1. "We will do nothing to extend the nuclear family."
2. "We will negotiate with the United States so that, as I said earlier, in case of need nuclear weapons will be made readily available."

Harkness seized on No. 2 while nearly everybody else thought Diefenbaker had come down more heavily on the side of No. 1. The press, as usual, went with the majority and wrote (at least, I wrote) that it looked like $700 million worth of nuclear carriers was going to be scrapped. Harkness was (he told me) taken aback at my story and pointed out to me the parts of Diefenbaker's speech which represented a pro-nuclear stand (No. 2, above). Harkness decided to clear up the matter — and he did, in a way — by issuing a press release explaining how Diefenbaker had outlined a policy for acquiring nuclear weapons. It wasn't long before Harkness was hauled onto the prime ministerial carpet. A five-minute shouting match took place, with Harkness apparently getting the last word, which was that he had every right as defence minister to clarify the government's — and his own — defence policy, which, he contended, were one and the same.

The next day, Tuesday, January 29, another furious round of meetings began between and among ministers. At a Wednesday cabinet meeting, Diefenbaker and Harkness restated their positions. Harkness left and dictated his resignation to his secretary, Mrs. Phyllis Jones, who began to type it out. Half a dozen ministers descended on him and persuaded him to hold off a while longer. That evening, the United States, uninvited and unwelcomed, jumped into the debate with both cloddish feet and the question of Harkness' resignation retreated temporarily into the background. The U.S. State department, out of the blue, issued a statement which said:

In 1958 the Canadian Government decided to adopt the Bomarc-B weapons system. Accordingly two Bomarc-B squadrons were deployed to Canada where they would serve the double purpose of protecting Montreal and Toronto as well as the U.S. deterrent force. The Bomarc-B was not designed to carry any conventional warhead. The matter of making available a nuclear warhead for it and for other nuclear-capable weapons systems acquired by Canada has been the subject of inconclusive discussions between the two governments. The installation of the two Bomarc-B batteries in Canada without nuclear warheads was completed in 1962....

In addition to the Bomarc-B, a similar problem exists with respect to the modern supersonic jet interceptor with which the RCAF has been provided. Without nuclear air-defence warheads, they operate at far less than their full potential effectiveness. Shortly after the Cuban crisis in October, 1962, the Canadian Government proposed confidential discussions concerning circumstances under which there might be provision of nuclear weapons for Canadian armed forces in Canada and Europe. These discussions have been exploratory in nature; the Canadian Government has not as yet proposed any arrangement sufficiently practical to contribute effectively to North American defence....

Reference was ... made in the [Jan. 25 Commons] debate to the need of NATO for increased conventional force. A flexible and balanced defence requires increased conventional forces, but conventional forces are not an alternative to effective NATO or NORAD defence arrangements using nuclear-capable weapons systems. NORAD is designed to defend the North American continent against air attack. The Soviet bomber fleet will remain at least throughout this decade a significant element in the Soviet strike force. An effective continental defence against this common threat is necessary.

The provision of nuclear weapons to Canadian forces would not involve an expansion of independent nuclear capability, or an increase in the "nuclear club." As in the case of other allies custody of U.S. nuclear weapons would remain with the U.S. Joint control fully consistent with national sovereignty can be worked out to cover the use of such weapons by Canadian forces.

The statement was aimed at Diefenbaker's throat: he had suggested that more conventional forces were needed in light of a preponderance of American nuclear strike weapons; that the threat to North America had changed from the Russian bomber to the intercontinental missile; and that Canada would have to give up some of its sovereignty if it signed a nuclear control agreement with the U.S. The opposition parties the next day, January 31, perfunctorily accused the U.S. of unprecedented and unwarranted interference in Canadian affairs, then happily quoted at length from the State department statement and overturned the speaker's ruling by a recorded vote so that the Commons could hold a special debate on the issue.

Harkness was left in the awkward position of replying for the government. He never pretended to be an orator and he had a dreadful time finishing sentences, so that he usually concluded them by saying "and so on" or "and so forth" or combined the two: "and so on and so forth." Despite his extreme nervousness, Harkness made a rather neat job of it, quoting from Diefenbaker's speech of six days earlier the scattered and rather tenuous references which supported Harkness' own position. He was applauded by all sides of the Commons (this also flummoxed him), not because he had made a particularly telling speech, but because he was an honorable man.

7

The Honorable Thing to Do

There was little doubt at the time, and there is even less now, that President Kennedy was trying to bring down Diefenbaker by whatever means at his disposal, and he considered helping Pearson as one means. Diefenbaker taunted Pearson: had the leader of the opposition received his daily briefing from the Americans yet? In the Cuban crisis, Canada had received only ninety minutes' warning of the U.S. blockade. What a way to treat an ally in NATO and NORAD, Diefenbaker said. The January 30 statement by the State department was handed to the external affairs department only an hour before it was made public. Moreover, for weeks before the statement, officials of the U.S. embassy in Ottawa kept feeding material to Canadian reporters designed to embarrass Diefenbaker and his government. Merchant himself had gone so far as to hold briefings in the basement of his house. I recall that one U.S. embassy officer invited me to lunch and filled me with a lot of cock-and-bull about how Diefenbaker was destroying the NATO alliance by his intransigence on nuclear weapons. Other reporters were stuffed with the same thing, but little if any of it got into print. Diefenbaker had made such a mess of things all by himself he didn't need any assistance from his enemies.

The extent to which Kennedy interfered in Canadian affairs was revealed more than two decades later when A. Edgar Ritchie, former undersecretary of state for external affairs, disclosed that Kennedy had asked Pearson at Hyannisport, Mass., some months after Pearson had become prime minister, whether the State department press release and similar U.S. actions had been helpful to Pearson, and by how much. Pearson replied that the U.S. intervention had probably cost him fifty seats. If this was meant to be an accurate estimate, Pearson would have had a majority in Parliament instead of the minority with which he was saddled throughout his term.

Diefenbaker nearly called a snap election on January 31, 1963, on the basis of the ham-handed American press release. He would have done better politically to do so because anti-Americanism would have been a more fruitful issue than the one he had to accept a few days later: defeat in Parliament and the disintegration of his cabinet. A number of people thought then, and still think, that Diefenbaker might have won the 1963 election if he had ordered the Americans to take their damned Bomarcs out of Canada and keep them out. But by this time, Diefenbaker was so hemmed in by the shadows of the monstrous "they" which he saw skulking everywhere ("they laughed;" "they said it couldn't be done") that he was incapable of decision. Harkness and others argued vigorously in cabinet that an anti-American election campaign would hurt the Canadian economy, weaken NATO, and jeopardize Canadian, and North American, defence. Diefenbaker's disregard of these factors — at the same time, he did not dissolve Parliament — persuaded a number of ministers that he had to go.

The cabinet met twice Friday, February 1, and again Saturday; still there was no resolution of the nuclear issue, or of a possible election call. It met again on Sunday morning at 24 Sussex Drive, the prime ministerial house. There was a lot of confused talk, demands by Diefenbaker for loyalty oaths, quitting the room and returning, general and private conversations. What it came down to was Harkness' question: who will bell the cat? The Liberals years later faced the same question with Pierre Trudeau and, like the Conservatives in 1963, ducked it; courage always failed the would-be rebels. But it didn't fail Harkness personally. On that Sunday morning, he said that all the talk was getting nowhere, that he had no confidence in the prime minister, couldn't remain in the cabinet any longer, and was going to resign, period. He walked out. Later, he gave me an hilarious account of this walk:

> During all these days and weeks of discussions, I had a lot of support from other ministers, particularly George Hees and Pierre Sévigny and Leon Balcer, and also Wally McCutcheon. After the cabinet meeting on the Saturday, Hees, Sévigny and I met in Hees' room in the Chateau Laurier, and we were all agreed that Diefenbaker had to go. So on the Sunday morning, I expected some strong support when I announced that I would have to resign. I walked to the door of the room, opened it, and looked behind me to see how many ministers were following me. There wasn't one.

Harkness chuckled. Self-effacing and not noted for his humor, he could tell a joke on himself, especially in the calm relief of having done, like Ralston in 1944, what he considered the honorable thing to do. There are no more ministers like Harkness. None ever resigns on a matter of principle any more. They like the perks too much; a car with a chauffeur is worth a lot of principle.

Harkness announced his resignation the next morning (Bob Needham of the *London Free Press* had scooped us all Sunday night) and informed the Commons on a question of privilege when the House met at 2:30 p.m.: "I resigned on a matter of principle. The point was finally reached when I considered that my honor and integrity required that I take this step." Diefenbaker said: "I find it difficult to understand the decision." Pearson moved a motion of non-confidence in the government and the Conservatives were defeated the next evening, February 5, by a vote of 142 to 111 and Diefenbaker had the last despairing word:

"Mr. Speaker, I shall advise His Excellency the Governor General tomorrow."

8
———

Many Shouted No!

Before he could advise the governor-general, however, Diefenbaker had to make sure he was still the party leader by blocking any last-minute overthrow at the Conservative caucus meeting on the morning of Wednesday, February 6. Only the night before, Social Credit Leader Robert Thompson had said he would vote with the Conservatives and keep them in power if the government were headed by George Nowlan and not Diefenbaker. If Diefenbaker remained, Social Credit would vote against the Conservatives. The latter was the case and now here were the Conservatives with the same problem on their hands: who would bell the cat?

I think the best account of this caucus is that of Harkness. He wrote it in longhand as part of a ninety-page draft of "The Nuclear Arms Question and the Political Crisis which Arose from it in January and February, 1963." The draft was written aboard the SS *Roonagh Head* en route from Quebec to Liverpool between August 19 and 27, six months after the events and based on Harkness' diary kept between the Cuban crisis and his resignation. The straight-faced account of the caucus reads:

Caucus was originally scheduled to be held at the usual time of 11 a.m. Wednesday, following a cabinet meeting, but Diefenbaker evidently heard that the dissident group of ministers planned to put in their resignation at the cabinet meeting and try to force him out. He then switched the caucus to 9 a.m., evidently with the object of appealing to it to support him. George Hees, as chairman of caucus, after calling it to order started on a statement in support of my nuclear position and against an anti-American campaign. Diefenbaker angrily interrupted him and said the caucus was to get the views of the MPs and time should not be taken up by statements from the chairman. Some members shouted in favor of this — others against. George was finally allowed to go on and ended by saying he would resign. Wally McCutcheon and Pierre Sévigny said they would resign also. A good deal of shouting now started and several other ministers who were trying to make statements could not make themselves heard. Diefenbaker got up to speak and order was finally restored. He said it was evident he did not have the support of some of the ministers and members and thus must resign. He said he would go and hand in his resignation to the governor-general and started for the door. Many shouted no, he must not do this and a group of western MPs gathered about him to prevent him leaving. At this moment Senator Alf Brooks rushed up to the front and managed to get the attention of the meeting. He made an impassioned appeal for unity in the party, for the ministers not to resign, and for all to unite behind the prime minister to fight the election. Senator Grattan O'Leary followed him with another impassioned appeal. Further scenes of confusion, and pressure by groups of people on the ministers who had said they would resign, followed — with a good deal of shouting that they should and must change their minds and shake hands with the prime minister. George Hees eventually did this. By that time Wally McCutcheon was at the door to leave — he was forcibly brought back to the front by several members, said he would stay in the cabinet and shook hands with Diefenbaker.

Diefenbaker then said he would stay if he had the unanimous support of caucus to do so. He then asked those who were prepared to support him to stand. I was the only one I could see who did not do so, although I have been told since by Pierre that he did not rise. I was sitting beside Alf Brooks and Grattan O'Leary. They seized my arms and tried to pull me to my feet. I angrily told them to leave me alone, I could not support Diefenbaker and would not stand.

When everyone had sat down Diefenbaker said that with the complete support of the caucus thus indicated he would stay and lead the party in the election — a statement received with loud cheers and clapping. George Hees then attempted to say something, but broke down in tears and could not get it out. I then got up and said I did not want anyone to be under any misapprehension about my position — that I had not stood up and that I could not support Diefenbaker in the position he had taken on nuclear arms and in the anti-American campaign he was proposing.

Diefenbaker then made a sentimental speech about his past political life and the support he had received. He then stated he would go to the governor-general to secure dissolution. Caucus broke up — Diefenbaker and George Hees going out together, and the latter telling the press who were waiting outside the party was united and ready to go ahead and beat the Liberals in the election.

The caucus was more highly charged with emotion than any other meeting of any kind which I have ever attended. It was an outstanding example of the working of mass psychology and the influence of crowd emotion to cause men to agree to a course of action which they knew to be wrong and which they had previously decided against. It was again an example of a failure in human courage when the pressure was extreme. Had the half-dozen or more ministers who had decided to resign had done so, I believe the caucus would have seen the impossibility of the situation and agreed to Diefenbaker resigning. . . .

Wednesday evening Fran and I went to a farewell dinner for the Fultons given by Dick Bell in Room 16 of the House of Commons. It was a very pleasant affair in spite of the stresses all of us had been through. I was sitting next to Grattan O'Leary and he told me I was the only one in the party who had shown real courage and conviction throughout and especially at the caucus that morning.

Harkness had predicted defeat for the Conservatives in the election, though it was far from as devastating as he had imagined. The Liberals won on April 8, 1963, with 129 seats against 95 for the Conservatives, 24 for Social Credit and 17 for the New Democratic Party.

9

Call Me an Airplane

Sévigny couldn't wait for Harkness to go. He issued a press release the following day in which he identified himself as defence minister, an appointment which was in Diefenbaker's purview only. I think Sévigny was testing Diefenbaker, because he had told Harkness his position would be untenable if he were not promoted from associate defence minister. He wasn't, and Sévigny and Hees both resigned from the cabinet the same day, February 9.

With government policy ostensibly non-nuclear now that Harkness had gone, the cabinet still could not make up its mind. In February, 1963, a few days after the government's defeat on the nuclear issue, I went to Zweibruecken, one of the RCAF bases in West Germany, and found a nuclear bomb dump being built at the end of one runway, complete with police dogs to guard the wired enclosure. Starfighter planes littered a hangar floor; they were being refitted to carry nuclear bombs. Was Harkness' policy still at work, though Gordon Churchill was the new defence minister? Who was in charge? Who knew? Diefenbakerland was cuckooland.

Sévigny was probably the defence minister most detested by the military. He was particularly detested by the Royal Canadian Air Force, which Sévigny used as his personal airline. He would order up an RCAF plane to take him from Ottawa to Montreal, alight at Montreal, and say, "Wait for me," as if the plane were a taxi awaiting return of a customer from a short errand. The meter kept ticking — for the Canadian taxpayer. Sometimes Sévigny wouldn't return for three or four days, with the crew standing by all that time, night and day, never knowing when the minister might show up. One time he took a train back to Ottawa without informing the crew.

I once observed the air force's massive retaliation, but carried out oh so delicately. Sévigny was on a trip to Halifax — an official visit, for a change — and took with him his wife, Clu, and the late Bill Dumsday, the reporter who broke the story about the Dionne quintuplets and the chief public relations officer for the defence department. Dumsday was a wise and friendly man who had had to contend with a lot of prima donnas in his life, starting with Dr. Dafoe and going on through to Sévigny, and any number of reporters. Dumsday had invited me along on the trip on the chance Sévigny might generate some news during his visit to the navy. He didn't.

The plane left Ottawa and the steward came round to take drink orders. Sévigny ordered a gin and tonic and I forget what the rest of us had.

"This isn't a gin and tonic," Sévigny barked. "It's rye."

"Oh, I'm terribly sorry, sir," said the steward and went back to the galley. He returned with another drink. Sévigny sipped it.

"I think this is rum," said Sévigny, flustered.

"I'm sorry, sir. I don't know how I could have made such a mistake." Back to the galley. By this time, Sévigny's wife, Bill and I had finished our drinks. Before bringing Sévigny's drink again, the steward took our glasses for seconds. There was a fairly long wait while Sévigny fumed, pretending to read a newspaper.

Back came the steward, serving Mme Sévigny, Bill and me before handing the minister his drink.

"That's not tonic in this," Sévigny said, red in the face.

"I just don't know what's wrong with me today," the steward said, his face as straight as a board.

Dumsday and I looked at each other. Would the steward dare do it one more time? Mme Sévigny loyally pretended she didn't see anything, her head in a book. The steward's safety rested in Dumsday and me as witnesses. We heard him crashing bottles in the galley as a signal that it was going to take him some time to find the tonic. It did, but he finally brought the correct drink. Without ice. Sévigny was about to send it back, thought better of it, and drank a warm gin and tonic.

His torture wasn't over.

There would be steaks for lunch, the steward announced. He was sorry, but that's all he had. Even then, I didn't see what was coming; I didn't believe the steward would press air force revenge any further.

The steaks looked wonderful. Mme Sévigny's, Bill's and mine were, tender as meringue. Sévigny couldn't cut his. He threw his knife and fork down on his plate and stuck up his newspaper in front of his face.

"How was your steak, sir?"

"I couldn't cut it," Sévigny said.

"Oh, I'm terribly sorry, sir. And we put on only four for the passengers. Perhaps I can ask the pilot to give up his."

"No," Sévigny almost exploded.

I kept track of the steward's career for a while afterwards. He wasn't court-martialed, dismissed or demoted.

10

Gerda's Affair

Sévigny and Hees resigned six days after Harkness had walked alone from the cabinet room and four days after the government had fallen. Hees didn't seek re-election until 1965 when he sat sweating on a stage in Campbellford, Ontario, wondering whether Diefenbaker, on the same stage, was going to endorse him as Conservative candidate for Northumberland. Diefenbaker did, in practically the last sentence of his speech, with Hees mopping his face with a huge handkerchief. The reporters on the 1965 campaign had a written-in-a-minute song for Hees:

Georgie Hees is risen today,
Alleluia!
His triumphant campaign day,
Alleluia!
Now in Campbellford he's king,
Alleluia!
Ever more Dief's praise to sing,
Alleluia!

We were wrong. It wasn't ever more, but only as long as it took Dalton Camp to do in Diefenbaker and set up a Conservative leadership convention in which Hees ran against Diefenbaker.

Hees and Sévigny were dragged into the Gerda Munsinger

affair after Prime Minister Pearson called in the Commissioner of the RCMP, George McClellan, and asked him what he had on the Tories.

I admired Mme Sévigny's fortitude during the long Munsinger inquiry. She sat through it all as a spectator and heard Sévigny's testimony that he had a "physical relationship" with Gerda. Later, Sévigny wrote a book called *This Game of Politics*. I happened to be in the Ottawa W.H. Smith store on the day Sévigny was to autograph his book for buyers. Nobody was buying his book, and he sat there, desolate and alone. Suddenly, a woman breezed into the store and proclaimed: "Well, are you Mr. Sévigny? I've heard so much about your book and I want to buy one for myself and one for a friend and I do hope you will be good enough to autograph both of them."

It was Mme Sévigny.

11

The System Permits Procrastination

Paul Hellyer became Pearson's minister of defence and he had only one goal in the portfolio: how to squeeze enough publicity out of it to promote himself into the prime ministership. Pearson quickly cleaned up two defence items, then gave Hellyer his head in the department. The two items were the agreement with the United States, announced August 16, 1963, to equip Canadian forces in Canada and Europe with nuclear warheads, and the extension of that agreement, announced October 9, to allow storage of U.S. nuclear weapons on American bases in Newfoundland.

Hellyer started off well, ordering more integration of support services in the armed forces and more spending on equipment and less on administration. But there wasn't much publicity in those policies. The public generally regards the armed forces in peacetime as high-priced unemployment insurance. And who could argue against integration? It had been tried before, and it was boring. Claxton and Pearkes had spent years cajoling the chaplains into forming a single chaplaincy, though the clergymen exacted their price: a higher rank (brigadier instead of colonel) for their most senior officers. The medical services were not combined until 1959. In 1956, the Army and RCAF waged a struggle for control of ground-to-air missiles. The same internecine battle went on within the Army itself, between the artillery and the electrical and mechanical engineering corps. The air force eventually won. Each service insisted on buying its own type of blankets.

In the late 1950s, the RCAF ignored an order from the combined chiefs of staff to use trained radar operators surplus to army needs and recruited its own — and took two years to train them. It took five years of negotiations before a tri-service school for military bands could be opened in 1963. Without a single administration for the three services, it became necessary to establish more than one hundred tri-service committees at defence headquarters — which put the military right in the swim with the civilian side of government. The military committee system was sometimes even able to surpass its civilian counterpart: the joint telecommunications committee had nine subcommittees, one of them called "joint telecommunications co-ordinating subcommittee of the joint telecommunications committee." The services originally had a single communications link across Canada for all of them. Then each had its own, necessitating committees and subcommittees where none had ever grown before. Air Marshal Hugh Campbell, chief of air staff, once complained that for every committee he managed to abolish two would spring up behind him overnight. But the fault was at the top. The chiefs of staff committee lacked executive authority because each member of it (the representatives of the three services and a chairman) held a virtual veto. It set the pattern for all other tri-service committees.

"The system permits procrastination," judged the 1963 Glassco Royal Commission on Government Organization. As Trudeau was to prove over and over again, it is popular in the civil service because it establishes collective responsibility and nobody ever has to account for individual decision or action. In Ottawa, committees march on, triumphantly. In 1963, the defence department telephone directory listed forty-seven committees reporting to the deputy minister, including: the interservice recruiting committee, the interservice recruiting publicity committee, canteen fund committee, subcommittee on bands, subcommittee on graves and burials, subcommittee on ceremonial, joint services clothing allowance committee, joint services food and nutrition committee, joint services forms control committee, joint services magazines committee, joint services packaging committee, tri-service warehousing committee, and, of course, a tri-service committee on terminology. The number of committees in the defence department is still approximately the same, but they are far more expensive to maintain because they are staffed by officers of higher and higher rank. Most jobs in the armed forces which used to be done by a lieutenant or captain now are carried out by a colonel or brigadier.

As the forces have shrunk in size, promotions have grown, and accelerated. Consider the headquarters structure in 1985 for the armed forces' personnel branch alone: an assistant deputy minister for personnel under a lieutenant-general, an associate assistant deputy minister, a director-general of personnel relations, a director-general of personnel co-ordination, a chief of personnel development, a director-general of personnel research and development, a director-general for recruiting, education and training, a chief of personnel services, a director-general of personnel services, a director-general of compensation and benefits, a director-general of conditions of service, a director-general of dependants' education programs, a chief of personnel careers and senior appointments, a director-general for officers' careers, a director-general for careers of colonels only (because there are hundreds of them), a director-general for careers of other officers, a director-general for careers of administrative officers, a director-general for careers of other ranks, a director-general of manpower utilization, a director-general of civilian personnel, a director-general of reserves and cadets. Each of these directors held the rank of brigadier-general or equivalent, or, in a few cases, the more senior rank of major-general. All this for armed forces numbering about 80,000. When the armed forces numbered 124,000 there were three lieutenant-generals. By 1979, with the forces down to 78,000, there were eight lieutenant-generals.

12

All Those Wanting Promotions, Please Clap

Exposing the proliferation of committees and the accompanying waste did not earn Hellyer many inches in the press or seconds of air time. After all, this was what one expected of the civil service, whether in civilian dress or military uniform. Hellyer needed something much more effective if he were to come to public attention. Pearson had given every indication that he did not intend to stick around more than another year or two and the Liberal leadership race was already on.

Presto! Unification of the armed forces. Knock together those brass heads and with any luck some old fuddy-duddies would oppose one service in one uniform and serve as the straw men for Hellyer's publicity campaign. For a while, it looked like no one was going to take the bait. A few admirals resigned quietly rather than see the navy converted into a green-uniform "water element" of the land, air and sea elements of a single service. Then, to Hellyer's good fortune, Rear-Admiral William Landymore, chief of Maritime Command (the Atlantic and Pacific fleets), refused to resign when asked to do so and Hellyer had to fire him, on July 12, 1966. But Landymore turned out to be made of much tougher material than straw and his forthrightness forced Hellyer into so mishandling the case that in the end the defence minister had to apologize publicly to the admiral.

Hellyer didn't know what to make of Landymore because he was so used to the sycophants around him at defence headquarters. Hellyer demanded loyalty, as of course he had a right to expect, but he meant by loyalty no honest dissenting opinions or even discussion of policies he was going to lay down. Hellyer didn't ask the military for advice. He set out what he wanted and sat back waiting for the plaudits from senior officers. If an officer didn't want to applaud, he said nothing — and found that silence was taken as disloyalty. Some officers with an eye for the main chance provided Hellyer with standing ovations on cue and themselves with fast promotions. The most telling evidence for this is the testimony of Lt.-Gen. Frank Fleury, the army's comptroller-general who "came to the end of my rope" in 1966 at age fifty-two and quit three years before normal retirement age. He told the Commons defence committee that there was so much disloyalty in the defence department that he felt like vomiting on his desk two or three times a week. He said he meant by disloyalty subordinate officers circumventing their superiors, including the chiefs of staff, and dealing directly with Hellyer — with Hellyer's encouragement. It was not difficult to identify the disloyal officers Fleury was talking about. They were the ones whose names, previously unknown, appeared in press releases, often with double promotions, as replacements for more senior officers who had resigned because of disagreement with unification.

In a way, Hellyer was only following Liberal policy. The conversion of the military to political partisanship was in accord with what the Liberals were doing in the civilian departments of government and which Trudeau and Michael Pitfield were to advance further.

Hellyer expected not only the military officers to get on side. He expected reporters covering the defence department to jump onto his unification (and prime ministerial) bandwagon, too. I was his main target of proselytization because I was one of the few reporters covering the department and my stuff went to the more than one hundred daily Canadian Press newspapers — that is, with one or two exceptions all dailies in Canada.

Hellyer wanted only favorable stories about him. Anything else was regarded as treachery. On February 15, 1966, Hellyer had me in for a fatherly talk, though I am older than he. I had to understand what was going on. He had been put in the defence portfolio by "somebody" trying to wreck his career. This hadn't worked, and he didn't intend to go down the political drain like "those others downstairs," an apparent reference to Walter Gordon and Guy Favreau.

During the 1965 election campaign, Hellyer continued, some serving officers had prepared material against him, had it flown to Toronto in a service aircraft and distributed in his riding. Hellyer went on like this for a while, then said that I must be bored silly in my job, and that everybody needed a change. I said I loved my job. He said he could fix me up with a new job. I said I didn't want a new job. He said we had to go "forward together or otherwise." This trailed off into vagueness. Then he said he had a complete file on every story I had written, that I had a good imagination, was skilful at conveying any impression I wanted in the first paragraph and that some of my stories had been concocted.

I denied fabrication; if he had a file on my stuff, he already knew I had made mistakes, including some beauts (see chapter on press). He cited a few stories which he labelled fabrications but when I pinned him down he said that there were no actual inaccuracies but that the stories had left a bad "impression." The conversation dragged on in this vein for a while longer and finally sputtered out with Hellyer bidding me to call him anywhere, anytime. When I left, I was stabbed by the angry glares of high-ranking pro-Hellyer officers who had been waiting for an hour to see him.

13

The Admiral and the Tigress

The unification issue went before the Commons defence committee in early 1967 for hearings which lasted through fifty-five meetings and twenty-three major witnesses, the star being Admiral Landymore, the dissident who never lost his nerve. It takes courage to face, alone, the whole panoply of government power, especially as a member of a group (naval officers) that had been so domineering and arrogant in command that Canadian sailors had mutinied throughout the Atlantic and Pacific fleets in 1949. The officers were so embarrassed by a commission of inquiry into their la-di-da, supercilious behavior that they managed to destroy nearly all copies of the 1949 report and prevent release of the verbatim testimony until 1986. Landymore was not of that type and was generally popular with his men. In return, he wanted to stand up for them and preserve their ranks, uniforms, other trappings and, above all, that special apartness which belongs to every seaman, naval or civilian.

I was in Halifax (my favorite Canadian city) on vacation when the Landymore affair was brewing. I took the opportunity to call and he and his wife were kind enough to ask my wife and me to tea, which turned out thankfully to be rum. Landymore was quiet, sensible and well aware that he was walking the plank. He could see Hellyer's point of view. His wife, suprisingly we thought, was much tougher on Hellyer than he was. If any man's courage ever needed shoring up (and I don't think that Landymore's needed any), she provided more than adequate backing. Not to put too fine a point on it, she was a tigress, and my wife said to me afterwards, "I hope the admiral never wavers for a second or he'll get it, and it won't be from Hellyer."

I give this background because it led to one of my most embarrassing moments. The admiral arrived in his turn to testify before the Commons defence committee on the unification bill C-243. It was February 15, 1967. He sat down at the horseshoe table in the narrow committee room in the West Block and placed in front of him a stack of copies of the speech he was about to deliver. I was sitting at the press table immediately in front of the spectators' chairs. Landymore eye-searched the room for a friend or acquaintance. Then he spotted me. "Dave," he called out from the far end of the room, "would you distribute these for me?" and indicated the stack. I pretended I didn't hear him and struck up a conversation with a colleague. He called again. I tried to raise my voice to drown him out of my ears. A hard finger was shoved into my back and I heard, "Dave, Bill is calling you." It was Landymore's wife, sitting directly behind me in the front row of spectators. Just in case I tried to ignore her, she gave me another poke and said, "Bill wants you." I sloped up to Landymore's place. Hellyer's aides and his senior officers were ranged along the side walls of the room. They began to titter. As I walked back to the press table with Landymore's speech there were open guffaws and stage whispers of "There goes Landymore's public relations officer," and "We know how this story is going to be written." All my press colleagues were grinning and Mrs. Landymore wore a very satisfied look which said, "If you can't rely on your friends, whom can you rely on?"

The nub of Landymore's testimony was that unification was virtually destroying the navy and was politically rather than militarily motivated. "Our servicemen must not become fodder for political cannon," he remarked. But he stretched things, suggesting any defence minister so bent and in cahoots with the chief of Mobile Command (in effect, the Army) could establish a dictatorship overnight.

14

"Up You, Hellyer"

Hellyer maintained that the issue was civilian control of the military. But he, too, went too far by telling the committee February 23 that Landymore had been consistently disloyal to Canada for eighteen months. Grant Deachman of Vancouver, the gracious and witty Liberal chairman of the committee, gently prodded Hellyer into withdrawal of the accusation. By this time, four of the five men who had comprised the top command of the armed forces in the summer of 1966 had all criticized unification before the committee, though all of them had resigned quietly and taken early retirement rather than speak out publicly. A dozen generals, admirals and air marshals had also slipped away quietly with their full pensions, leaving Landymore to fight alone. Only burly Gen. Jean Victor Allard, the army chief, had backed unification among the senior officers. True or not, he was considered a Liberal because in 1953 he had been offered the defence portfolio by Prime Minister St. Laurent.

The Commons committee passed the unification bill's sixty-five clauses on fifty-five formal votes, pausing at the last second for an amendment which removed a provision in the National Defence Act for appointment in an emergency of cabinet ministers for each of the three services. There were no longer three services.

Hellyer had received the publicity he craved in his thirsting for the Liberal leadership. But it did him more harm than good. He came across to the Liberal delegates at the leadership convention in 1968 as a bit of a humorless and plodding autocrat. He missed by a whisker seizing second place behind Trudeau in the early balloting and quickly faded. The Liberals really didn't want Trudeau and if Robert Winters had been more interested — he didn't get into the campaign until very late — the Nova Scotian could have won. The thing I always remember about that convention is Winters' delighted smile and clapping his hands together with the exclamation, "Oh, he's got it," when the final ballot was announced. There was not a shred of bitterness or envy in Bob Winters. I asked him a few days later whether he would serve in a Trudeau cabinet. "Not that man," he said. Trudeau wouldn't allow Pearson to remain in office one more day so that he would have exactly five years as prime minister and assumed leadership of the government April 20, 1968. He began running down the defence department almost immediately.

Hellyer became Trudeau's transport minister, but he couldn't stand having competition around any more than Trudeau could. While Trudeau lopped off cabinet heads as fast as any talent showed above ground, Hellyer thrashed around looking for a new political home, even one created by himself, where he could be leader. He failed ingloriously in his house-hunting and his unification was undone, a stitch at a time until, in 1985, even the old uniforms were brought back.

On July 23, 1985, the armed forces tattoo marking the seventy-fifth anniversary of the Canadian Navy was playing the Ottawa Civic Centre. With enormous fanfare, and a public announcement in case you were blind, the Navy stepped out in blue, the Army in khaki and the Air Force in its own blue. There was a tremendous cheer. In the pause that followed, a man in the crowd shouted, "Up you, Hellyer." The crowd cheered that, too.

15

Reflections from the Moon

Trudeau had no interest in the defence department except its budget and how to cream it for other purposes. One can hardly fault this. It is standard operating procedure for Canadian governments. The first *Canadian Defence Act*, passed in 1868, provided $1,100,000 for defence works. Not a penny was spent for that purpose; it all went to railway construction. The Navy was established in 1910 and a $13 million naval construction program was projected; the government changed and the program was thrown out. In 1932, the RCAF vote was chopped to $4 million from $7 million, forcing discharge of 78 officers and 100 airmen.

Trudeau didn't trust the military, especially with nuclear weapons. Who could blame him, with examples like this: on October 5, 1960, North American Air Defence Command headquarters at Colorado Springs, Colorado, got a blip on its huge radar at Thule, Greenland, indicating that a missile might have been launched over the pole at North America. There was absolute panic among many officers at the headquarters, shouting, rushing outdoors, personal calls to families to take cover. Luckily, Air Marshal Roy Slemon, a Canadian, was in command at that moment. A cool man, he stayed cool, and brought logic to bear: the Thule radar was new and still being broken in; some Soviet leaders were abroad; there had been no incidents, or warnings of incidents, anywhere else in the world. Slemon ordered that no alert be flashed to the U.S. Strategic Air Command to prepare for a counter-strike. It turned out that the Thule radar had picked up not the track of an intercontinental missile but a reflection from the moon of one of its own signals. The story leaked out weeks later (me) but the military managed to prevent any account of the alarming degree of panic which had seized the headquarters staff.

In any case, Trudeau never saw the threat to Canada as coming from Russia. Very early in his prime ministership he made a speech at Kingston, Ontario, in which he envisaged the possibility of a "large rebellion" in the United States which would overflow into Canada and link up with the dissident, militant groups in this country. He was more worried, he said, about the possibility of great riots in Chicago, New York and "perhaps in our own great cities" than about war over the issue of the Berlin Wall. Canada has always feared being swamped by the U.S., economically, politically, or militarily. As late as the 1920s, Canada's main defence plan was how to counter an attack from the U.S. and Pearkes told me that as a junior officer in the 1920s he was once sent to Butte, Montana, in mufti to make a reconnaissance for a possible diversionary attack by the Lord Strathcona's Horse of Calgary into the U.S.

Trudeau took nuclear weapons away from the Canadian military, denied them new equipment, and reduced our NATO contribution in Europe to a corporal's guard. Militarily, we were far worse off than in the Diefenbaker years, but few complained: in peacetime, Canadians have a monumental disinterest in defence matters and Trudeau, in this respect at least, accurately reflected the Canadian attitude. But it meant that we had (and have) wildly expensive, computerized planes to deliver a conventional bomb which could just as easily be dropped by a $50,000 Second War Mosquito fighter-bomber.

Worst of all, Trudeau left us naked in the Arctic. He himself posed the problem accurately enough, but as with so many things he touched, his attention span was narrow and his follow-through limited to pillow-punching. Let us look at our true north, weak and undefended.

16

The True North Strong and Vulnerable

Of all the strange policies to which Canada subscribes, perhaps the oddest is our NATO commitment to help defend arctic Norway against Russian ground attack. We actually participate in snowy military exercises at the top of Norway, though we don't do anything of the kind in our own Arctic. This absurd NATO strategy which contemplates a Soviet land assault down the mountainous, fiorded spine of Norway recalls the Second War period when Americans and some west-coast Canadians became jittery at the prospect of a Japanese overland march through the Aleutians, Alaska and British Columbia. A sane U.S. general observed: "They might get here, but it would be their grandchildren." Canada has agreed to send a battalion of troops to northern Norway in event of attack, and, even more ludicrous, provide it with air support. Why Canada supports such a plan while neglecting any kind of defence of northern Canada might strike one as unfathomable.

But not if you look at it in the historical context; our policy of genuflection to foreign powers on the issue of Arctic sovereignty has been our standard since July 31, 1880, when Britain transferred to Canada jurisdiction over all islands north of the Canadian mainland. We were so lackadaisical about possession and administration of these islands, failing to establish a single police post, that in 1900 explorer Otto Sverdrup claimed for Norway the islands of Axel Heiberg, Ellef Ringnes, Amund Ringnes and King Christian, all west of Ellesmere Island, our most northern territory.

In 1986, the Royal Canadian Mounted Police made public

for the first time its documents on Arctic sovereignty. They show that Canadian policy was consistently panic reaction to foreign action in the Canadian Arctic. For instance:

On October 16, 1920, RCMP Assistant Commissioner Cortlandt Starnes telegraphed Commissioner A.B. Perry, who was visiting Edmonton: "Reported Danish government endeavouring get possession Ellesmere Island. Government anxious police patrol overland take possession first." Starnes recommended against a patrol as hazardous that late in the season, and Perry agreed. An official of the department of the Interior, Wyatt Malcolm, suggested that a dirigible be sent 2,200 miles to Ellesmere from the Imperial Air Station in northern Scotland to drop men and supplies by parachute. An airship, he noted, could cruise 6,000 miles.

The agitation in Ottawa had been caused by the reported plan of Danish explorer Knud Rasmussen for a five-year expedition to Ellesmere and neighboring islands. Rasmussen, who had founded Thule in Greenland in 1910, described Ellesmere as "no-man's-land" and was supported in this view by the Danish government. Frantic preparations were made for a Canadian expedition in 1921 to establish two, and possibly three, RCMP posts on Ellesmere. The government steamship *Arctic* was fitted out at Quebec City and fifteen Mounties detailed for northern duty. Suddenly, the whole thing was called off. Starnes telegraphed Perry, who was in Regina, on May 26, 1921:

Northern proposals completely abandoned. Am arranging for partly utilizing [expedition's] stores to fill Hudson Bay requisitions.... Musical ride one day Belleville June third Minister's instructions. Estimates not yet called. Nothing important. All well.

The Ellesmere expedition that year was scrapped because the Canadian government had discovered, through confidential questioning of the British Geographical Society, that Rasmussen abjured any political motives and that his expedition was purely scientific and bent mainly on tracing Eskimo migration routes. But panic broke out again in Ottawa in 1922 when rumors of American expeditions began to circulate and, especially, when the government found out that a Lieut. Creighton of U.S. Naval Intelligence had been assigned to Alaska for six months. The Interior department mounted another expedition by the *Arctic*, which had been used for years to replenish lighthouses in the St. Lawrence, with J.D. Craig, director-general of surveys in the Interior ministry, in charge. Starnes obtained from the Danish consul-general in Montreal permission for the Mounties to make any necessary purchases in Greenland. The *Arctic* reached the southeast corner of Ellesmere and the RCMP established seven men at a base which Craig promptly named Craig Harbour. Two years later, a post farther north on Kane Basin was established, about the time Rasmussen was completing his epic trip from Greenland to Alaska across the Canadian Arctic.

In 1926, more panic. American explorer Donald B. MacMillan said he was going to establish an airfield on Ellesmere and explore the northern islands with airplanes supplied by the U.S. Navy under command of Richard E. Byrd. The Canadian government determined that it would require MacMillan to seek Ottawa's permission to explore Ellesmere, but backed off when the Americans declined to apply for it. Rasmussen got in a nasty dig by saying that he had been required to promise that he would not dispute Canadian sovereignty over any territory he reached on his expedition and asking pointedly: would Canada demand the same stipulation from MacMillan, representing a much bigger country than Denmark?

Canada did not; and it is embarrassing that fifty-nine years later, in 1985, the Americans declined to seek permission for the U.S. Coast Guard ship *Polar Sea* to traverse the Northwest Passage. Canada granted unsought permission retroactively anyway. In 1986, when three U.S. submarines surfaced at the North Pole, external affairs told the House of Commons lamely: "It is government policy not to comment on the movements of Allied warships that may transit Canadian waters." The subs were there to help check the effectiveness of the Americans' Arctic Ocean submarine detection system, operated mainly from Alert and using devices buried in or under the polar ice hundreds of miles offshore. The equipment is all American.

On June 1, 1925, Interior Minister Charles Stewart had made the jingoistic statement that Canada claimed all lands north of its mainland between Greenland and Alaska, right up to the North Pole, but the Canadian government purposely never brought the claim officially to the attention of the U.S. Weather prevented MacMillan from establishing an airfield on Ellesmere, but Byrd's planes made reconnaissance flights over it. MacMillan rubbed it in when he found that the *Arctic*'s radio had broken down; he offered to send any Canadian messages from Etah, his Greenland base thirty-five miles from Ellesmere.

Sovereignty over the Arctic islands began to fade as an issue in 1930 when Norway gave up its claim to Axel Heiberg and three adjoining islands in return for Canadian payment of Sverdrup's exploration expenses in 1898-1902 (The *Chicago Daily Tribune* said, "The Canadians want more ice."). But the U.S., for one, has never conceded Canadian sovereignty over the Northwest Passage, and the *Polar Sea* treated Canadian insistence on formal permission with the same polite disdain as MacMillan and Byrd had shown in 1926.

17

Stars and Stripes over Canada

During the Second World War, the U.S. built in Canada three staging routes for aircraft, as well as the Alaska Highway. The northwest staging route comprised airfields and landing strips along the highway and the Mackenzie River; the Hudson Bay route included airfields at The Pas, Fort Churchill and Southhampton Island; the northeast staging route included bases at Mingan, Goose Bay, Fort Chimo and Frobisher. Canada and the U.S. formally agreed in June, 1944, that the U.S. would give up the bases to Canada within a year of the war's end. The war ended in 1945 but in 1947, rather than giving up any bases, the U.S. was expanding them. In 1948, the U.S. commander at Fort Chimo, Quebec, refused to accept Canadian money from Canadian officials staying at or passing through the base; he insisted on U.S. currency. Canada had accepted this. Canadian government finance officers were issuing U.S. funds to Canadian officials going to Fort Chimo. A stop was put to the practice in November, 1948, but only after a complaint was received by then External Affairs Minister St. Laurent from Jacques Rousseau, director of the Montreal Botanical Garden, who had been en route to the Arctic through Chimo with the Royal Canadian Air Force. About the same time, the Canadian defence department received from the United States Air Force detachment at Frobisher an information bulletin on which was stamped: "This information is furnished upon the condition that it will not be released to another nation without specific authority of the Department of the Air Force of the United States, that it will be used for military purposes only and that the information be provided substantially the same degree of security (secret) afforded it by the national Military Establishment of the U.S."

The American patronization of Canada continued in 1949. American servicemen were based at Edmonton, Fort Nelson and Whitehorse to maintain planes flying between the U.S. and Alaska, and the U.S. was still operating bases at Fort Chimo, Frobisher and Mingan. Canadian officials were summoned to Washington August 25, 1949, to review the activities of the U.S. Air Force in Canada. On January 7, 1952, RCMP Commissioner L.H. Nicholson wrote to C.M. Drury, deputy minister of defence, to ask to be informed of U.S. military exercises in the Canadian north. The U.S. exercise Totem Pole had been held in the Yukon in 1951 without anybody telling the Mounties in advance. Nicholson also asked to be informed about the construction of large American defence installations in the north, such as the radar station at Cartwright, Labrador.

Canada finally began to stir into activity in the Arctic and by the mid-1950s the Royal Canadian Air Force had three squadrons — about fifty planes — operating there, mainly on photo-survey and reconnaissance. It maintained a big air base at Resolute on Cornwallis Island. When the Russians occupied ice islands close to Ellesmere and supplied them by air, the RCAF knew about it right away and kept tabs on them. An RCAF plane photographed a damaged Badger bomber on the Russian drift station North Pole 6. The Badger was the Soviets' chief medium-range bomber and the RCAF photos provided even the factory number on the fuselage as well as accurate dimensions for NATO intelligence.

In the early 1950s, a few scientists of the Defence Research Board, the research arm of the Canadian military, and notably Trevor Harwood of the Arctic section, kept urging the Canadian government to push higher into the Arctic by building airstrips on Ellesmere to support exploring and scientific expeditions and thereby solidify claims of sovereignty. But they faced the mammoth indifference of the government and the defence department.

Documents released in 1986 by the Public Archives show that in April, 1953, the United States sought Canadian approval to expand the landing strips at Alert and Eureka on Ellesmere and to build a new strip at Clyde River on Baffin Island to accommodate jet fighter planes in event that its big base at Thule was ever knocked out of commission by weather or war. The RCAF said that the U.S. should be free to go ahead because the U.S. base at Thule was the only one it (the RCAF) needed in the high Arctic. A furious Harwood wrote that the only RCAF bases in the Arctic had all been built by the Americans: Resolute, Southhampton Island, Frobisher, Chimo, Churchill, Eureka, Mould Bay, Isachsen, and Alert. Wasn't it time that Canada built an airfield on Ellesmere to meet Canadian needs? Harwood proposed an airstrip at Lake Hazen, south of Alert at 82 degrees north. Dr. J.J. Green, Harwood's superior at the Defence Research Board, vainly tackled the RCAF himself on the issue. He wrote a memo dated January 27, 1954, which is surely one of the most astonishing documents in the annals of Canadian Arctic sovereignty. This is Green's memo in its entirety:

> I have again taken this question up with the RCAF in order to cover the points raised by Mr. Harwood. The viewpoint within the RCAF still indicates that they have no requirement for an alternate landing strip to Thule and the demonstrated need which Mr. Harwood has discussed is an American one. The points raised by Mr. Harwood regarding the RCAF falling heir to strips and bases that were all initiated and built by the Americans are conceded, but, again, within the RCAF, the view is held that the RCAF requirement for these bases is not a firm one.
>
> Again, it is feared within the RCAF that the provision of still another landing strip in the Arctic will increase the

supply commitment and possibly the Shoran [navigation aid] commitment of the RCAF.

Despite the foregoing, it is recognized that, based on past performance whereby the RCAF has fallen heir to such bases and also from the point of view of Canadian sovereignty, there might be an argument for Canada to participate in the selection of a site for an alternate to Thule. However, since such action would not be based on an RCAF requirement, it was thought that the matter should be discussed by the Chiefs of Staff. It was the understanding within the RCAF that the Chiefs of Staff were not anxious to increase the number of landing strips in the Arctic, since in wartime it would be necessary to provide defence for them.

The RCAF view prevailed with the department and the government and the U.S. got to Hazen first. In 1955, the U.S. Air Force landed on the ice at Hazen (the lake is fifty miles long and seven wide) to explore possibilities of landing strips for B-47 nuclear bombers and KC-97 air tankers. In 1956, the U.S. Air Force landed there again, taking along two Canadian military officers as observers. The American survey team found three suitable landing strips for bombers and tankers.

Harwood was not deterred by official Canadian lethargy. He kept plotting how to put a Canadian expedition into Hazen, and finally succeeded by seizing on the 1957 International Geophysical Year. The government wanted to make a big splash during this world-wide scientific extravaganza and, presto, here was a ready-made project from the Defence Research Board. Moreover, the Russians were becoming worrisome with their aircraft landings on the ice in the Beaufort Sea, in a latitude more than 500 miles south of Hazen. (Canadian government offices clipped reports of these landings from the *New York Times* and stamped them "secret".)

The IGY expedition, called Operation Hazen, took twenty Canadian scientists to northern Ellesmere. The project extended through the winter of 1957-58 and the summer of 1958 and proved so successful that Harwood was able to keep teams on Ellesmere into the 1960s. The U.S. Air Force followed closely the activities of the Canadians at Hazen. On January 16, 1958, Col. William

A. Trippet, chief of the U.S. Air Force's central co-ordinating staff in Ottawa, wrote to the chairman of the Defence Research Board that all Hazen information should be sent to seven U.S. military commands, including Strategic Air Command and the 8th Air Force. (On another occasion, U.S. Northeast Air Command told the chairman that the Board's observer on a U.S. team in the Canadian Arctic would be issued American clothing but, "if you perfer, your own clothing may be worn.")

In 1958, an international convention on the continental shelf authorized a coastal state such as Canada to exercise exclusive sovereign rights over its part of the shelf, or for 200 miles from the shoreline, whichever the greater. Canada ratified the convention in 1970 but it took four years before the Trudeau cabinet decided to apply Canadian law to the shelf. And it took another twelve years before the required legislation (application of the Criminal Code, the Canada Labor Code, etc.) was presented to Parliament. By that time, the oil drilling rigs and ships were departing the Canadian Atlantic and Arctic shelf because of the drop in world oil prices. One government department, Fisheries and Oceans, cared so little about Canadian sovereignty even in Canadian territorial waters (twelve miles from the coast) that in 1978 it arranged with Russia for transshipment points off Newfoundland for Soviet fishing vessels and supply ships without notifying the defence department, coast guard, or RCMP. So desultory is our surveillance that these three organizations didn't find out about the arrangement with Russia for two years.

Most of the Defence Research Board's Arctic work of the 1950s and 1960s has been abandoned. No new airfields have been built on Ellesmere and the scientists have largely withdrawn. There is talk of a tourist camp at Lake Hazen for rich Americans. The military has pulled back so far that "northern" winter exercises are now held at Camp Petawawa, Ontario, 120 miles west of Ottawa, Camp Wainright, Alberta — or in Norway. There used to be 800 Canadian servicemen at Churchill; now there are none. Today, the Russians make more training flights over our high Arctic than we do. As far back as 1968, the Canadian defence department conceded that Russian bombers were flying close to the northern coasts of North America twice a week — and that accounted for only the detected flights. Now we try to make a "sovereignty flight" over the high Arctic about once a month, depending on whether the electronically-temperamental Aurora patrol planes get off the ground. In an economy drive, the defence department cut back on spare parts for the Aurora and now some of the planes have to be cannibalized to keep the others flying. In 1985, during the *Polar Sea* incident, the government announced construction of a huge icebreaker for Arctic duty. It also announced, in December, 1986, that a naval modernization program had jumped in cost to $1,625 million from the 1983 estimate, "based on conceptual (but still not defined) capability options," of $923 million. Broadening your concepts, you might call it.

Despite our own *laissez-faire* policy in the north, Canada was quick to approve U.S. plans for the new North Warning System along the line (70th parallel) of the old distant early warning radar line. (The entire $600 million capital cost of the DEW line was paid for by the U.S., which has also paid all maintenance costs since 1957. The only embarrassment about this ever felt by the Canadian government occurred in 1956 when Canadian reporters visiting the Canadian Arctic — in an American military transport plane, of course — found the Stars and Stripes flying over Canadian bases, or, rather bases in Canada).

In September, 1986, the Canadian Arctic Resources Committee, a non-profit organization, published a report by two Arctic veterans showing that Canadian defence in the north is still being tailored to American, not Canadian, needs, and that Canadian sovereignty has lost rather than gained ground. Brig.-Gen. Keith Greenaway, a former associate of Harwood's and one of the world's foremost Arctic navigators, and Brig.-Gen. Clay Beattie, former commander of the northern (Canadian) region of North American Aerospace Defence Command, say that location of the North Warning System will not afford radar detection and interceptor control over the Northwest Passage, let alone Ellesmere and the other islands in Canada's Arctic archipelago, and that surveillance of the high Arctic will be left to American airborne radar planes based at Thule and in Alaska. They added in their article, "Offering Up Canada's North," in the fall, 1986, issue of *Northern Perspectives*, published by the Resources Committee:

The situation is clearly prejudicial to Canada's claims to sovereignty. Although token Canadian representation might be permitted, or even encouraged, the net result would be to concede responsibility for surveillance over disputed waters to the United States.

Greenaway and Beattie argue that the North Warning System should be built right at the top of Canadian territory, at Mould Bay on Prince Patrick Island, Isachsen on Ellef Ringnes Island, and Alert on the north coast of Ellesmere. There are already airfields at all three bases. These locations could give Canada (and the U.S.) earlier warning of attack and afford opportunity to intercept launch bombers and cruise missiles over the uninhabited, rather than inhabited, parts of this country. Greenaway said in a conversation with the writer that radars on the outer rim of Canada could well force the Russians back to the drawing board to re-design their cruise missiles to carry more fuel for necessary longer range. Detection and interception of these missiles could take place well out in the Arctic Ocean instead of over our Arctic islands. But, Greenaway said, the government appears willing to sacrifice better defence and Arctic sovereignty on the grounds that it might be more expensive and logistically more difficult to put radars and fighter planes in the high Arctic than to base them 1,200 kilometres south on the old DEW line sites, now thirty years old.

Defence Minister Perrin Beatty rejected the criticism out of hand. The North Warning System's placement will improve warning and protect Canadian sovereignty, he said. Appropriately, Beatty made this statement in Washington, where he was visiting U.S. Defence Secretary Caspar Weinberger.

To conclude this chapter on defence, let's have a look at Trudeau's use of defence funds as summed up by C.R. (Buzz) Nixon, deputy defence minister from 1975 to 1982, in a letter to Auditor-General Kenneth Dye January 21, 1985, complaining about Dye's harsh treatment of the handling of military expenditures. Nixon is writing about the big construction project, mainly a language training school for the military, at St. Jean, Quebec:

Turning now to the St. Jean Megaplex, it would have been helpful for you to have recalled in your report that at the time the Megaplex decision was taken, the capital funding in the Department of National Defence was abysmally low, but the shortcomings and equipment deficiencies of the Canadian Forces were almost endless. Under such circumstances, would it have been reasonable priority decision making or good defence management, seeking value for money, to have given the St. Jean project the highest priority? Certainly not.

The high priority given to the St. Jean project arose because in 1974-75 the mammoth construction projects in Montreal for Olympics '76 were coming to an end, giving rise to high levels of unemployment in architectural firms and in the construction industry. In the light of that situation the government made it apparent to the Department of National Defence that a major construction project reasonably close to Montreal would be well received, providing it could be undertaken quickly and generate significant construction employment. These conditions attached to the approval of the St. Jean Megaplex, forced the project to be managed in a "fast-track" or sequential way under which fully detailed drawings of the project were not completed before the construction commenced, thus complicating project management and creating greater risk of error.

And so was Trudeau defence policy made.

PART FOUR

SPIES: The Secret World

I was sitting on a shaded bench in Strathcona Park in Ottawa one day at the tag end of summer when suddenly that old yearning for the secret world came over me. But only for a moment. I know that I'm well out of it.

Dave McIntosh

1

I Spy

The reason that the feeling came over me at all was that I found myself staring at the Russian embassy, which sits at the northeast corner of Strathcona Park, and remembering that I had been a frequent visitor there many years before. I had a pretty active life in intelligence and, without divulging any national secrets, except perhaps accidentally, I would like now to reveal — within my oath, of course — my role in a number of international incidents.

I won't dwell on my dangerous wartime exploits, which consisted mainly of reporting to the squadron intelligence officer after every flight over occupied Europe. This officer never took a note, retaining all such classified information in his head; indeed, he managed to maintain such a casual air that he never looked up from his dirty book or magazine while I gave breathless details of signal fires and other illuminated communications from the Maquis, the French resistance. One summer night in a small town northwest of Paris, somebody tore aside the blackout curtains, leaned far out of the upstairs window bathed in light and waved frantically to me going by in a Mosquito fighter. This was breaking all the rules about showing lights. I decided the gesture must be a trap and didn't report it.

I arrived in Ottawa in 1953 as a reporter covering, in particular, defence and foreign affairs. This took me into the very buildings — one could get in, then — where the secrets, if we'd had any, would have been stored, so a Mountie was assigned to check me out.

I knew he was checking me out because he came to my door, thinking it was my neighbor's, and asked all kinds of personal questions about me. Speaking in the third person, I gave a modest appraisal of myself generally (so as not to arouse suspicions) but a very high security rating, especially on heterosexuality, moderate drinking verging on teetotalism, and excellent credit at several recognized banks.

Those were the years when the Cold War was at absolute zero. In the line of duty, I accepted all invitations to Soviet diplomatic events, nearly all of them at the embassy. Those soirées were so chilly that they severely tested my self-ascribed moderation approaching abstention. But I had to be discreet. I knew that the Russians knew that I was at the nerve-centre of defence and foreign policy.

Unassisted, I devised a system of disinformation combined with a test of the reliability of our own military officers. One night at the embassy, after some red-caviared crackers and four sodas, I confided to the Soviet naval attaché that Canada was developing a tri-element (code name: TE Mark I) winged and tracked weapons carrier which could fly at mach 2, travel on land at 140 miles an hour, and dive deeper than any known submarine. I made sure that a Royal Canadian Air Force group captain, also a guest, was standing close enough to overhear. Sure enough, the next day I received a call from one of my secret sources at the defence department that the group captain had immediately reported me to Air Marshal Roy Slemon, chief of air staff, on the grounds of treason. I never heard what the Russians did with my disinformation, but I imagine they were burning up the wires to Moscow that very night.

2

There Have Been Some Changes Since Lenin

The Mounties obviously appreciated my volunteer work because one day I got a call — it sounded as if it were being made through a handkerchief — inviting me to an interview in an old brick building downtown.

"What about?" I asked.

"Not on the phone," the caller hissed.

I was shown into a huge, ill-lit room containing a small table and two folding chairs. Here I was, in the heart of the secret world. The occasion lost some of its glamor, however, when I discovered that my interrogator was not the commissioner of the RCMP but a corporal.

"We know you go to a lot of Russian embassy parties," he began.

"Parties?" I exclaimed. "Those are working sessions for me."

He waved away my remonstrance and went on: "Have you picked up any rumors about the KGB?"

"KGB?"

"Yes, KGB. It's the Soviet secret service."

"Oh, you mean Ogpu," I said.

The corporal rolled his eyes at the ceiling, drummed his fingers on the table and finally said: "There have been some changes since Lenin." He dismissed me a moment later. I noticed that he hadn't taken a single note in his little black book. No doubt there was a bug under the table.

There was a gap of several years before I decided to resume my secret life.

I arrived in Cyprus in 1964 to cover the United Nations peace-keeping operation. (Canada's Royal 22nd Regiment played a very big part in it at the start.) Both the United States and Russia used Cyprus as a Middle East listening post and I saw right away that there were more spies in the island than China-watchers in Hong Kong. (I had made close observations during a one-hour stopover in Hong Kong in 1950.) The U.S. Central Intelligence Agency had so many agents in Cyprus that it had to take over an entire hotel to accommodate them and establish the downtown Date Club as a meeting place for its off-duty personnel. The KGB, for its part, occupied an entire row of villas.

I decided that all this spying was a detriment to UN peace-keeping and that I would bust it wide open. I pondered for a long time how best to do this. I suddenly realized that the best way would be a story for all the Canadian newspapers which I represented. As far as I know, not a single newspaper, Canadian or otherwise, ever used my exposé blowing the cover of the CIA and KGB at one and at the same time. It was quite a while before I got over this.

3

The Israeli Intelligence Taxi Service

I arrived in Israel on the eve, literally, of the Six-Day War in 1967, still as a Canadian Press reporter covering war and diplomacy, the two sides of the same coin.

What luck. The taxi driver from Lod airport at Tel Aviv offered to be on hand throughout my stay to drive me anywhere. A chauffeur, how befitting a foreign correspondent, I thought, though it was much too warm for a trench coat.

The Israelis in effect won the war on the first day. That is one of the problems with Israel; its very brief wars leave its generals unemployed and they go into politics. At the evening press briefing at the end of the first day, there were loud bursts of applause from the back of the room at each announcement by a colonel. I looked around. Among the applauders was my taxi driver.

"Hey, there's my cabbie," a colleague said, pointing to the man sitting beside my driver. Israeli intelligence was driving all the journalists.

I went back to Israel a few years later, still as a reporter. When we reached the hotel, the taxi driver asked whether he could give me a lift anywhere the next morning.

"Are you with Israeli intelligence?" I asked cunningly.

"Yes," he said.

Well, I didn't have to sweat it out of him.

He had been an Israeli agent for twenty-two years, he told me, and the most devastating thing that had ever happened to him was that he had once been given the code name Ronnie. "Can you imagine a spy named Ronnie," he said sheepishly.

I didn't want to take a chance on acquiring a name like that so I decided when I got home to get out of intelligence — always subject to emergency recall, of course.

I stayed clean, up to the summer of 1983, when the old yearning for the secret world came back. Just how important had my role been in national security during the Cold War? Under the access to information and privacy acts, I'd find out to what use the Mounties had put the results of the secret interview with me about the KGB.

Under date September 8, 1983, the RCMP informed me:

> Please be advised that this request would fall under our RCMP-P130 Security Service records bank. The governor-in-council has designated our Security Service records ... as exempt from access under Section 18 of the Privacy Act. We cannot comply with your request nor can we confirm whether or not such information exists concerning you. This is necessary to preserve the integrity of this information category.

Just as I thought: information so vital that not even its existence can be admitted, not even to its source.

4
___

A Fistful of Betrayal

If you think my experiences in the secret world are a little Kafkaesque, consider those of a real spy, Igor Zergevich Gouzenko, the Soviet embassy cypher clerk in Ottawa who defected in 1945 with twenty-two documents which blew a Russian-run espionage ring in Canada.

Gouzenko had more trouble with Canadians than Russians in trying to defect. Not only did the *Ottawa Journal* turn him away (twice) when he tried to hand over his fistful of betrayal. So did the RCMP. It took Gouzenko a strenuous three days to reach a safe house.

The transcripts of the 1946 royal commission secret hearings into the case were not made public until the 1980s, and then not all of them. No wonder. They give spying a very bad name. Here are a few of the Keystone Cops routines disclosed on the microfilm of the transcripts cached in the Public Archives of Canada:

- Fred Rose, MP, one of a dozen traitorous Canadians, was first given the code-name "Fred" by the embassy spy network run by Col. N. Zabotin, ostensibly the military attaché. Moscow had to suggest a less revealing cover and Rose was re-coded "Debouz."

• Zabotin's apparatus had trouble contacting "Bagley" (Edward Wilfred Mazerall) because, the colonel informed Moscow, "his wife doesn't want him to galavant around at night."

• Coded telegrams to Moscow (on blue paper; incoming were pink) were sent by Canadian National and Canadian Pacific telegraph.

• At least four of the Canadian spies kept self-incriminating diaries and notebooks which were found in their homes.

Gouzenko was a trained encoder and decoder when he arrived in Ottawa from Moscow in June, 1943. Beginning in 1944, Moscow kept trying to recall Gouzenko (reasons unknown) but Zabotin, a keen judge of loyalty, insisted that his cypherman stay in Ottawa. When Gouzenko decided which documents to make off with, he turned up the corners for quick and easy identification before he put them back in the safe in Room 14 of the special double-steel-doored wing of the embassy.

The Russians had a predilection for code-names starting with B. As well as "Bagley" there were "Brent" (L.C. Rogov, Soviet air attaché and paymaster for the Canadian spies), "Back" (David Gordon Lunan), "Badeau" (Durnford Smith), "Baxter" (Angelov, secretary to and NKVD watcher of, Zabotin), "Berger" (Steinberg, a U.S. scientist), "Bacon" (a Canadian operative who was acquitted), and "Ballantyne" (never identified). A meeting of "Back" and "Bacon" would have been interesting.

At the end of the hearings, there were a whole lot of code-names left over without any real names attached to them: "Green," "Gol," "Galya," "Gini," "Gisel," (the Russians liked G, too) "Albert," "Jack," "Paul," "Tounkin," and "Mr. Ross." Zabotin was "Grant" and Gouzenko was "Klark," no relation to Clark Kent. "The Professor" was a professor, Dr. Raymond Boyer, Canadian scientist, and "The Economist" was Krotov, the embassy's commercial attaché. Canada was "Lesovia," land of forests. "Brent" sometimes called himself "Jan," apparently just on whim. Emma Woikin was "Nora" but "Emma" was the code-name for a U.S. propellant. There were two "Henrys," one in Toronto, the other Gouseev, a doorman at the embassy. Korschkov ("Chester"), one of the embassy drivers, selected one of the mail drops, the washroom of the dentist's office where he was having his teeth fixed.

5

The Top Secret Lending Library

When a Canadian operative met British atomic scientist Allan Nunn May ("Alec") in London, the meeting was arranged, appropriately enough, in front of the Canadian High Commission on Trafalgar Square. The password was "How's Elsie?" and the counter was "She's fine." Richard Hannay couldn't have done better.

The Canadian government and bureaucracy made Soviet spying pretty easy. The 1928-1940 files of the passport office were kept in a room in the basement of St. George's church in downtown Ottawa. There was no custodian and the key was kept by a file clerk in a desk in another building to which at least 30 people had access. Before that, the files had been kept in a building at the experimental farm. Documents classified "most secret" and "top secret" could be taken out on loan from the National Research Council library. One Canadian traitor took out a secret paper on airborne radar and had it at home from June 25 to August 13, 1945.

A Canadian Army colonel on Zabotin's recruitment list turned out to be "a very kind-hearted man" who didn't have any useful knowledge. "We didn't even give him a code name," Gouzenko told his interrogators.

When Gouzenko finally left his apartment with wife, son and documents and the *Ottawa Journal* wouldn't listen to him, he went to see Justice Minister Louis St. Laurent the next day, Sept. 6, 1945. St. Laurent wouldn't see him. Gouzenko then tried the RCMP naturalization bureau. The Mounties sent him packing, saying he might try a magistrate's office on Nicholas St. if he wanted protection. Gouzenko watched from the crack in the door of a friendly neighbor's apartment as four Russian drivers and doormen tried to break into his apartment and grab him. The neighbor bicycled to fetch the local police, who gave Gouzenko sanctuary.

PART FIVE

PEACEKEEPING

Remember, men, we are fighting for this woman's honor, which is probably more than she ever did.

Groucho Marx in *Duck Soup*

1

Welcome to the Peace Garden

He sat, as he did most evenings, in a little wicker chair on a balcony clinging like a swallow's nest to the side of the 12th-century Bellapais Abbey. The hot Cyprus sun was falling like a bomb into the Mediterranean and already a cool breeze was coming in off the sea two miles away. The only sound was the tinkling of the bells of a herd of homeward-bound sheep on the steep hill far below the abbey. At two nearby cafés, the men of the village, including the priest, sat in silent contemplation of the purple-pink sunset.

"Ah, peace," sighed Costa Kollis, the custodian of the abbey, a squat man with wiry arms, a crew cut, and deep tan. "What the world wouldn't give for the peace of Bellapais."

It was the fall of 1969 and the wish didn't seem so crazy then. The race war between the Greek and Turkish Cypriots had simmered down to an occasional exchange of erratic rifle shots; the Egyptians and Israelis were shelling each other off and on across the Suez Canal but there was no immediate threat of their war's renewal; and the insane massacres and counter-massacres in Lebanon were still a year or two away.

I had been coming to the Middle East since 1956 when Britain and France embarked on empire's last and bitter hurrah in the Suez Canal on the arrogant European assumption that the "wogs" could never run the canal which they had nationalized. ("We are not at war with Egypt," Anthony Eden told the British Commons on November 4, 1956. "We are in an armed conflict.") Israel drove across the Sinai Desert to Suez in a week. Enter the United Nations, at the urging of St. Laurent and Pearson. Canada was off again on its favorite foreign policy kick: peacekeeping.

Cyprus had been on my Middle East reportorial itinerary since 1964 when I accompanied the Royal 22nd Regiment from Quebec to Nicosia. The regiment interposed itself between Greeks and Turks in two of the nastiest sectors, Nicosia and the Kyrenian Pass, and succeeded marvellously in keeping the two apart. (I asked a Greek gunman once how the Greeks and Turks could tell each other apart so that they could at least aim at the proper enemy. He replied, "How do you English- and French-Canadians tell each other apart? Like you, we just know.") It was because of the Canadians' presence in the Kyrenian Pass that I could drive a few miles east from there to Bellapais for a beer and chewy goat's cheese under the Tree of Forgetfulness in the village square and then watch the sunset with Kollis.

"You can't get those colors in a photograph or on a color television set," he said. I had seen a lot of magnificent sunsets at home but I allowed that his was at least as magnificent.

"The dawns are just as good," Kollis said. "I'm here nearly every morning at 4 a.m. to see them." He had me there.

Kollis was born in the village of Kazaphani one mile below the abbey. He worked for the Cyprus antiquities department and his pride was the abbey. "And how I miss St. Hilarion's. I haven't been able to go there for three years. I used to sleep there too, you know." He was speaking of the mountaintop castle and monastery three miles west in the Kyrenian range occupied by Turkish Cypriot guerillas. Kollis was a Greek Cypriot.

He dismissed the island's troubles as something the abbey would outlive. "The abbey will last forever," he said without qualification. "Sometimes I stay here at night and sleep in the cloister, it's so peaceful." Nearly every morning, soon after dawn, Kollis was busy at the abbey planting flowers and grafting trees. With one graft, he had lemons growing from a bougainvillaea, or was it bougainvillaea from a lemon tree? Another Canadian visitor, Peter Ward, had brought him zinnia seeds from Canada. Kollis' green thumb had coaxed shoots above ground in two nights and one day. The zinnias have flourished, but paratroopers came from Turkey in 1974 and occupied the northern half of Cyprus and Kollis died of a heart attack not long after.

2

———

Jaw-Jaw is Better than War-War

Suez was not by any means the first Canadian peacekeeping venture. As early as 1948 we had put a small contingent in Kashmir and become part of a larger United Nations observer group established at the end of the first Israeli-Arab war. A Canadian observer, Col. Flint, was killed on Mount Scopus outside Jerusalem by artillery fire. In 1950-53, we lost five-hundred killed in the UN police action in Korea. (Some of our boys became wealthy by smuggling jewels on the "pearl run," the air force supply route between Tokyo and Tacoma, Wash.) In 1954 we became entangled in the non-UN Canada-India-Poland truce supervisory commissions in Viet Nam, Laos and Cambodia and watched the United States slowly vanish into the same bog which had trapped the French in Indochina. (Some of our boys made a lot of money, jeeping opium and heroin from the hinterland to American soldier-entrepreneurs in Saigon who smuggled it home in bodybags containing corpses of fellow servicemen.)

Canada never had any illusions about its peacekeeping role in Viet Nam; it got into it in the first instance only to save face.

Viet Nam has never known democratic government, or any semblance of it. It was ruled by emperors for centuries until the French conquered Indochina in the 19th century. The French were pushed out by the Japanese in the Second World War but restored by mainly British arms in 1945. For Viet Nam, war — civil war — went right on after 1945. In 1954, the French were defeated disastrously at Dien Bien Phu. The Americans assumed the French role, though anti-communist rather than colonial, until they fled ignominiously two decades later. So much for capsule history.

At the 1954 Geneva conference which divided Viet Nam at the 17th parallel, Canada was represented because the subject of Korea was also discussed, to no avail. Pearson as our external affairs minister let it be known that Canada was willing to help in the Indochina situation. But it was nonetheless a shock for the government when, on July 21, 1954, a five-paragraph letter signed "Anthony Eden, V. Molotov" arrived in Ottawa. The letter was an invitation from the then British and Russian foreign ministers — Britain and the Soviet Union were co-chairmen of the Geneva conference — for Canada to participate with India and Poland on three international truce supervisory commissions for Viet Nam and neutral Laos and Cambodia. Hoisted on its own mouth, the St. Laurent government reluctantly agreed — after dithering for an entire week.

Canada played the peacekeeping game scrupulously fair and square. On the one hand, it bared the tactics of communist North Viet Nam in preventing refugees from moving to South Viet Nam. On the other hand, it withheld from South Viet Nam planned medical aid, including ten 200-bed hospitals and a children's rehabilitation centre, because the military junta of South Viet Nam insisted that Canada issue a concurrent statement indicating that it supported the junta's conduct of the war. Canada and the United States have long had a working agreement between their military air transport commands to help each other out when they have unoccupied space. But the Canadian air force was careful not to carry, even as far as Honolulu, American servicemen bound for Viet Nam — or even their baggage.

In 1954-55, about one hundred and seventy Canadians served on the three Indochina truce commissions. Most of them were soldiers. A decade later the number was down to ninety (sixty-five of them soldiers) as the peacekeeping role became more and more ludicrous. Canada accurately predicted that the communists of North Viet Nam would keep coming and coming until they won the war; that the American bombing of the North served only to spur Hanoi to greater effort; that U.S. economic and military aid would never be sufficient to save the South. Canada told the U.S. as much. All the U.S. did was get mad and take it out on the messenger.

Canada was on the point more than once of withdrawing from the commissions. But it stayed on in the tenuous hope that the commissions might some day be used for peace negotiating instead of truce (in reality, war) observing. The commissions were the only groups in touch with all the parties involved. Canada even sent a special envoy, Chester Ronning, to Hanoi twice to sound out the North Vietnamese on negotiations. The U.S. State department ungenerously announced that Ronning had failed and after Ronning's return from his second mission in 1966 the U.S. began bombing Hanoi and Haiphong.

Such experiences didn't deter Canada from Churchill's dictum that jaw-jaw was better than war-war, even when war-war went with jaw-jaw. Successive Canadian governments sent peacekeepers to Suez in 1956, the Congo in 1960, West New Guinea in 1962, Yemen in 1963, and Cyprus in 1964.

On April 7, 1968, the day after he was elected Liberal leader, Trudeau indicated that Canada might be getting a little tired of so-called peacekeeping. It couldn't always act as policeman for the world, he said.

But a few weeks later, the peacekeeping bug got him, too. He told United Nations Secretary-General U Thant that Canada would not "shirk her role" in any peacekeeping force established for Viet Nam.

Only the year before, U Thant had presided over the death of the UN peacekeeping force in the Sinai Desert. It had started out eleven years earlier on the banks of the Suez Canal.

3

With Only the Sand between Them

UN troops for Suez were funnelled through Naples and supplied from there, mainly by the Canadian air force. I kept taking taxis from Naples out to the airport to gather what information I could and one day on the airfield actually bumped into a UN information officer, a Dane. I said that if I could call him it would save me a taxi trip or two a day. He handed me his card. I spent all the next morning vainly trying to reach him by telephone. I finally gave up and resumed my taxiing to and from the airport. A couple of days later, I ran into him again and told him I'd been unable to get through to him on the Naples phone system. "Oh, I'm sorry," he said, "that's my telepone number in Copenhagen." That's the way, in my experience, the UN has always operated. Luckily for this UN force, a Canadian, Gen. E.L.M. Burns, was the commander and the Canadian military was in charge of the transport and communications.

Finally, the day arrived for me to fly to Egypt (the day arrived because my boss, Gillis Purcell, sent me a cable saying "Why are you still hanging around in Naples?") and Jim Lynch, the

Toronto photographer, an Arab oil lawyer, and I got on a great big plane in Rome (we were the only passengers) and went to Cairo, dragging in all the way from the coast at a few hundred feet above the desert and at little more than landing speed; this was to prevent us being mistaken for a bomber, which I thought was a good idea.

The best thing about the trip was the lawyer. He was very well connected with the Egyptian external affairs department and straightaway asked us to a party at his apartment, which included a ballroom. Jim and I went. The lawyer had invited some senior external affairs people and I got a cool and calm, almost subdued, appraisal of the Middle East situation from an Egyptian point of view, something, I found out later, which was extremely hard to come by. Jim shot all kinds of pictures of the lawyer's family, which pleased his wife, and Jim was the type of guy who, when he said he'd be sure to send them the pictures, did. We roomed together in the Semiramis, an old colonial hotel with high ceilings, enormous bathroom fittings and a verandah, and which we called, cleverly, Half a Ramis. It was especially lucky that we had met the Cairo lawyer, because Burns wouldn't talk to the press. Neither would Herbert Norman, the Canadian ambassador in Cairo. And neither would Canadian King Gordon, the UN information officer.

The UN force was on the Suez Canal, about sixty miles east of Cairo. There were no cars for hire. Every morning, three or four of us piled into a taxi with a bag of oranges and professionally ordered the driver to take us to Ismalia on the canal. Every Cairo taxi had a shimmy, like the dancers. As we reached forty or fifty miles an hour, we went through a buffeting zone like a jet fighter approaching the speed of sound. We all made very funny remarks about the Sweetwater Canal and spent the day kibbitzing with the UN troops, mainly the Canadian truck drivers, trying to pick up scraps of information. We returned at nightfall, the most harrowing part of the daily ride. Drivers approaching each other at night feared being blinded by headlights and worked out a simple solution; when within one hundred yards of each other, both switched off their headlights at the same time and the two cars slid by in the dark, each's presence felt by a sudden gust of air. For the first few trips, we kept shouting at the driver to keep his goddam lights on. It did no good. We finally gave up and sat with eyes closed and fists clenched (just like on a plane), waiting for the gust of air to tell us we had passed safely one more time and praying for a full moon in the coming nights.

We filed our stories (five copies) with the censor. Buck Johnston of the *Toronto Star* cabled 1,500 words a night at fourteen cents a word. Canadian Press frowned on such lavish expenditures and I might cable as many as one hundred words now and then. Mostly, I smuggled my articles aboard a Canadian air force plane at Abu Suwehr, north of Ismalia, for mailing in Naples. This avoided censorship but, more important to Canadain Press, fourteen cents a word. After our filing routine we had dinner at a restaurant and trailed back in the blackout to the Semiramis, where Gen. Burns also had a room. He had two Egyptian guards outside his door. One or both of them were usually asleep.

I had to disabuse myself of some standard Canadian misconceptions about the Arabs. They were not, for instance, thieves and mendicants; they did not speak to me by screaming in my face; all the educated Egyptians spoke at least three languages — Arabic, French and English — and, the most important point for a reporter, their side of the argument with the Israelis made as much sense as the Jews'. The attitude of North American Jewry, or, at least, its official spokesmen, that the Arabs have no argument, and are not even entitled to one, is one of the great stumbling blocks to any Middle East settlement, given that one is possible at all. I shall come back to this point later because I have personal experience of it. In the meantime, I have always felt as safe in Cairo as in Tel Aviv, and a great deal safer than in most cities of the world.

Israel withdrew from Sinai, re-scorching a scorched earth, and the Yugoslav members of the UN force were the first to insert themselves between the Egyptians and the Franco-British invaders based on Port Said at the northern (Mediterranean) end of the Suez Canal. On a sunny afternoon, Buck Johnston, Jim Lynch and I decided to go for a walk along the main road on the west side of the canal. First we went through the Egyptian lines; there was an occasional explosion followed by the screaming of some poor wretch who didn't know or hadn't been told the location of Egyptian land mines. We passed through the Yugoslav line, the commander giving us a big smile and a wave. Then across no-man's-land to the Anglo-French forward posts. The Brits were not amused. An angry Tommy said he should have shot us for making monkeys of them. This hadn't occurred to us; we were just out for a stroll to check on the ceasefire, which was holding up well, thank heaven. I didn't walk so jauntily on the way back; I could feel that Tommy peeering through his sight at my back and the skin between my shoulder blades twitched.

Eventually, the UN force moved across the Sinai to the Egyptian-Israeli border and patrolled it faithfully for eleven years — to no purpose, it turned out. Pearson was under no illusions about the force. At the Bermuda summit conference in 1957 (Dwight Eisenhower, Harold MacMillan and Louis St. Laurent) Pearson held one of his frequent off-the-record discussions with Canadian reporters, including John Walker of Southam, Harold Greer, myself and others. Pearson said the UN peacekeeping operation in Egypt would never work because Israel would not allow any part of the UN force on its territory. He accurately predicted that the moment Egypt wanted the force out, it would have to go. In 1967 U Thant, secretary-general of the UN, took the same attitude despite the protestations of Paul Martin, by then our external affairs minister. Egypt and Israel were left with only the sand between them.

It was the sand, I guess, which drove many Canadian soldiers out of their wits. Certainly it was the sand that killed many, too, because it had drifted over forgotten land mines all over Sinai. The Canadians in effect ran the force and, besides, took on a very big share of the desert patrolling by jeep and small plane. It was so hot that all the work was done in the morning and if a man didn't have a hobby beyond making moonshine his days were very long and boring to the point of mental breakdown. The leave centre then (in the 1960s) was, if you can believe it, Beirut, at that time the most beautiful and most affluent city in the Middle East.

As a reporter covering the defence department, I used to go to Sinai every other year or so to see how the Canadians were faring at their rotten job. With one or two notable exceptions, no Canadian diplomats ever went near them. It was always the military, usually majors and captains, who visited the Bedouin

sheiks in their ragged tents and unblinkingly swallowed the pro-
ferred delicacy, a sheep's eye, in aid of keeping the desert as
peaceful as possible. Our foreign service officers remained stead-
fastly on the cocktail roundabouts of Cairo and Tel Aviv, shud-
dering at even the thought of a scrap of ill-cooked goat's meat
in a remote tent where one couldn't even find, for goodness'
sake, a soda siphon. Canadian soldiers provided the only medical
care the nomad Bedouins had probably ever had. The children
were continually kicking over kerosene lamps in the tents and
being severely burned. A Canadian jeep took them to the Canadian
hospital where they were cared for until they were recovered
enough to go back to the desert, which sometimes entailed a
long hunt to find the parental tent which had moved in the
meantime.

4

Yellow Smarties for the Runs, Green Ones for Boils, and Red Ones for Headaches.

The Canadian soldier in the field has always been an impressive
figure: a scrounger, a bitcher, a make-doer, a rebel who obeys
reasonable orders, an innovator, and, above all, a funny and
compassionate man. Perhaps I can illustrate all or most of these
attributes with an account of a visit to the Canadians in Sinai
in 1963.

Their base was at Camp Rafah near the border with Israel
and not far from the Gaza Strip. On a jeep tour of Khan Yunis
in the Strip, our vehicle fluttering the UN flag was stoned by
Palestinian street boys, the sons of Arabs who had fled, or been
forced to flee, Israel in the 1948 war. Out of town and back
among the orchards, my guide said, "Only one stoning. Last week
one of our jeeps was stoned seven times. They must be starting
to like us." And he laughed. "Does anybody ever get badly hurt?"
I asked. "Naw, and I guess it makes them feel better. It's called
peacekeeping."

The Canadian barracks at Rafah were like Canadian barracks
at Camp Petawawa, Ontario, or Camp Shilo, Manitoba. In the

mess hall, there were salt pills to prevent dehydration and instructions not to forget malaria pills. (The Canadian peacekeepers in Cyprus took their malaria pills religiously for more than a year before they found out there hadn't been a case of malaria on the island for more than fifty years.) I was given an honorary membership card for the Bedouin Golf and Country Club (which I still treasure) and played a round the next day. The Canadians had built the course in their spare time, that is, in the afternoon heat, and it was of course entirely of sand. The greens were called browns and the ball left a tiny rut in the sand, necessitating a raking after the passage of each group. Tee and fairway shots usually plunked bounceless into the sand, so that every shot, in effect, was a bunker shot. Never, never, put your hand down a hole for a ball; you would most likely be bitten by a scorpion. Egyptians did the caddying and halted frequently on tee, fairway or green to take out a carpet, kneel, and pray. The Canadians suspected that the Egyptians were taking advantage of them, having discovered that Canadians seldom interrupt another person's prayers, in- or ex-cathedral.

Out into Sinai at dawn, we stop at a barbed-wired enclosure with watch tower, a Canadian UN outpost. There are scores of waiting Arabs sitting in their bedraggled robes all around the post. They seem to be expecting somebody. Soon a corporal appears and goes among them, gravely handing out different colored pills to eager hands. All the pills are candy Smarties. "What the hell," he says later with a grin, "We have no medicine and there isn't a doctor for miles. They seem to like the treatment. Yellow Smarties for the runs, green ones for boils and red ones headaches. At least they don't hurt them, which is more than you can say for some of our pills at home." Wraith-like, the Bedouins vanish back into the desert, some smiling and waving. In a moment, they are gone among the dunes. Only the Canadians in the tower can see them now, and perhaps a tent or two far in the distance.

We deliver water, food, mail and orders and are off again into the sand toward El Quseima. (The Yugoslavs don't even have the comfort of an anchor like Rafah and are stationed out in the middle of Sinai and all the way down to the Gulf of

Aqaba.) The jeep sticks as much as possible to the same track for fear of leftover mines, but there is at least one diversion. The Canadians have found a particularly steep and high dune down which it is possible for the jeep to slide, like the final swoop of a roller-coaster. By noon, with the temperature about 120 degrees, we reach a watering hole were there is a cluster of Bedouins, camels and goats. The Canadian soldiers greet the Bedouins like old friends, laughing, clapping them on the back, employing the interpreter they have brought along only on occasion because nearly all the communication is by sign. In the afternoon, there is a special treat for me. In a long wadi, we park and wait for a few minutes, a Canadian Otter plane lands and takes me up for a long flight all over Sinai. I have claimed ever since that I know Sinai like the back of my hand.

I make the obligatory visit to the barracks of an afternoon, the heat so intense that even the flies are standing still. One soldier has devised an elaborate sound system which he tinkers with daily. Another is taking a correspondence course in televison maintenance. Another has paid to bring in an instructor every afternoon to teach him Arabic. Another writes a constant stream of letters. A few are lying on their bunks, hands behind head, staring at the ceiling. "They won't last long," my guide says. "They have nothing to fall back on to fill the time; they'll go round the bend, in a quiet way, and be shipped home. They just lie there wondering whether the wife is having it off with somebody back home, or why did I get a posting like this, or screw the goddam Army, or whatever. I know. I used to do that, but I went to Beirut on leave and looked at the girls at the St. George's and I went to Cairo on leave and discovered the Pyramids and took up Egyptology."

In the hills behind Sharm el Sheik at the southern tip of Sinai, across the narrow strait from Saudi Arabia, the Canadians find a human skeleton, a remnant of the 1956 war and well preserved in the dry heat in an area so windless that it is said a man's footsteps can be followed in the sand a decade later. A cigarette is put between the finger bones and a small sign erected: Beware of Smoking. In Cyprus, on a lonely patch of sun-beaten gravel, the Canadians dig a tiny grave and put up a wooden headboard which says: Sex. The women of Cyprus are not the women of Beirut.

In faraway Ottawa, peacekeeping is all the rage. Pearson wins the Nobel Prize for peace for his part in establishing the UN force in Sinai and rides it (though he really doesn't need the conveyance) into the Liberal leadership in 1958. Little UN peace-keeping operations pop up all over the world — in West New Guinea and Yemen, for instance. Prime Minister Diefenbaker and his external affairs minister, Howard Green, grab off Gen. Burns as their peace and disarmament negotiator. Paul Martin becomes external affairs minister after the Liberal restoration and tries to emulate Pearson's Nobel Prize by twisting every arm in sight to establish the UN force in Cyprus.

5

Oh What a Lovely War

At Christmastime, 1963, the Turks and Greeks had begun but-chering each other, the favorite method being to murder a lonely shepherd and dump his body down a well. Nothing would do but to have another group of blue-capped UN no-shoot-'ems get between the two sides. Martin was so enthusiastic about the venture that the Canadian advance party for the UN force was in the air en route to Cyprus before a formal arrangement was worked out at UN headquarters. But he pulled it off, and there the UN peacekeeping force still sits, more than two decades later. Ottawa became so caught up in its self-praise for saving the world that it organized an international conference on peacekeeping techniques. Even one communist country showed up, Yugoslavia, Canada's old Sinai friend.

In Cyprus, the Royal 22nd set up on the green line in Nicosia and in the northern mountain range and the gunfire gradually died away. But the old racial hatreds, mistrusts and feuds did not. They stayed, like the rusty barbed wire, teetery stone for-tifications, tattered sandbags and tiresome roadblocks made of discarded oil drums. The press operated out of the Ledra Palace Hotel, in the Greek sector and only a step from a Turkish roadblock. Behind this roadblock, the Turkish Cypriots ran a small information office in a vacated apartment where they handed out daily bogus pictures of children being shot and bayoneted by Greeks. (The Greeks used the same fake photographs, on much glossier paper, but the perpetrators were, of course, Turkish.)

It was a grand little war to cover, less dangerous than the days of "Murder Mile" (Ledra Street within walled Nicosia) when the Greek terrorists (freedom fighters) gunned down the British in their fight for independence — less dangerous because the boundaries were now defined. The Greeks held most of the island and the UN, in effect, was protecting the Turks in their enclaves, almost all in the northern end of the island.

After a leisurely patio breakfast, the reporters individually headed out of the hotel parking lot, made a quick run along the green line, and drove to the known trouble spots: St. Hilarion's Castle, Morphou and, farther west along the north coast, Kokkina, a poverty-stricken, rocky outcropping where many Turks lived in caves. There was usually some random and sporadic shooting in the hills behind Kokkina, enabling us to report "pitched battles," or, if there was no shooting at all that day, "fierce skirmishes." Whatever was going on, we were never late for lunch in Kyrenia at the Harbor Club, a superb restaurant run by an Englishman who looked and spoke like Trevor Howard. We sat in treeshade and looked down at the bowl of a harbor with its medieval fort, sipped our drinks, ate red snapper, sipped more drinks and left about 3:30 p.m., giving us time for a quick call at the Canadian outpost in the Kyrenian Pass before getting back to the Ledra Palace for a quick cable and quick shower before the cocktail hour and our daily grilling for information by officials of the Canadian external affairs department who would not, of course, deign to gather it themselves in the field.

The Ledra Palace was the best hotel I have ever known. (It has since become military headquarters for the UN.) It was large-roomed, wide-corridored, high-ceilinged, bright, airy, the staff accommodating without being obsequious, the food, drink and service unparalleled. The night porter, Zavas, was the key man in our operation. For a reasonable retainer (reasonable because he was collecting from each and every one of us), he tipped us off to any pitched battles or fierce skirmishes which occurred out of business hours, supplied the Greek and Turkish press releases under our doors at dawn, ordered picnic lunches in the rare cases where our morning expeditions wouldn't let us make the club in Kyrenia for lunch, and kept up a constant stream of rumor and gossip about President Makarios, the numbers of American and Russian spies in Nicosia, the most likely lodging houses of clap, menu changes at the better restaurants, availability of sports cars at the rental agency, the new Cyprus wine crop, and whatever your question was. He was a one-man news agency, covering international, national and local events all on one broadcast band.

The Greek and Turkish Cypriots never shot directly at one another, unless one side was unarmed. They used to extend their rifles around corners of buildings and pump off a couple of random rounds. They could seldom bring themselves to peek afterwards. This made it more dangerous, though. Not being knowledgeable about firearms, they waved them about carelessly. One of the grisliest shootings I saw, in a Greek village near Kokkina, was completely accidental; two men were horsing around in an outdoor café, one had a shotgun and he shot his friend right up the rectum. This happened when the Greeks were holding a few of us reporters at a roadblock on the way back to Nicosia from Kokkina and there was an awful moment when it was not clear that the shooting was accidental. I was driving that day with Charlie King of Southam in his snappy sports car and we left a few moments later. We climbed the hill out of the village and at the first bend found ourselves looking straight into a bazooka. "Listen to this," said daredevil Charlie, and deliberately backfired the engine just as we came abreast of the bazooka and the man crouched behind it. I went limp, and drove myself after that, snappy sports car or not.

In the early days of the UN operation in Cyprus, there was a fair bit of shooting around the Ledra Palace at night because it was on the green, or so-called ceasefire, line. The management pulled the drapes in the bar so that it wouldn't be an obvious target, but this kept out the cool evening breezes and the scent of the climbing hibiscus. We urged the management to open the drapes on the grounds that, given the marksmanship of the shooters on both sides, we would be less likely to be hit if we were in plain view. This was done. The only warlike incident I can recall in the hotel was my sudden return to my room one lunchtime (why I wasn't in Kyrenia, I can't imagine — my car must have been disabled) and found a Greek guerilla shooting out of my window toward the Turkish side of the green line with a sub-machinegun. I told him to get the hell out of my room and he did, quickly and meekly. I complained to Stavos, one of the porters, who said he had done his best; he had told the guerilla to use somebody else's room.

As the years passed, and the UN periodically threatened to pull out if no progress toward political settlement was made, attitudes hardened to the point where one UN official claimed "negative success," meaning no fighting between Greeks and Turks, but no anything else, either. The wily Archbishop Makarios wanted enossis, the union of Greece and Cyprus, with himself as president of the combined state. But the Greeks in Athens went too far, brought down Makarios, put a group of extreme army officers into power, and brought on Turkish military invasion in 1974. The Turkish Cypriots comprise fewer than 20 per cent of Cyprus' population, but now they hold 40 per cent of the land through military occupation from Turkey. In 1983, northern Cyprus declared itself an independent Turkish Cypriot republic but it is recognized by Turkey only. A whole generation of Cypriots has grown up since the inter-communal butchery of 1963 and it has been even more expertly taught than its predecessors to hate. In Cyprus, education is miseducation.

6

Another Shot at the Israelis

The Canadian soldier never had a high opinion of the UN, though it was a far stretch from the absolute contempt of the Israeli citizen. His self-mockery as a no-shoot-'em UN combatant turned to derisiveness after 1967, however.

Egypt had been gearing up for years for another shot at Israel. In May, 1967, it ordered the UN out of Sharm el Sheik and closed the strait it commands to Israeli shipping. It moved troops into Sinai and told the UN to get out of the way. Canada protested and Egypt ordered the Canadian contingent out of Egypt within forty-eight hours. Lucky Canadians. An efficient air force evacuated our angry, shamefaced soldiers through El Arish, the big airfield near Rafah. Back and forth the big Hercules transport planes flew between El Arish and Cyprus. Other UN contingents were floundering around in Sinai without their Canadian-run base and communications. Still, the Egyptians did not strike. Israel let the Egyptian troops sit in the ferocious desert heat for another week, then struck with its tank army.

I had flown to Cairo by KLM via Istanbul, the only air route apparently acceptable to the Egyptians. Again, as in 1956, there were only three passengers, this time a French-language CBC reporter and Bert Plimer, a CBC cameraman. There was no possible way of getting any news because the Egyptians wouldn't let us go to Sinai (even when I rattled off all the memorized names of the places I had been in the desert, including wadis and watering holes) and I quickly persuaded Jack Scott of the *Toronto Star* to fly to Cyprus from where we could quickly get to Israel. Off we went, in a low-slung Russian plane, and put up at the Ledra Palace where I was greeted as a big tipper (this was never reported to Canadian Press). Scott liked the Ledra Palace as much as I did. Too much. I couldn't drag him away from the pool and the poolside bar. Finally, on June 3, I told Scott ("Why are you in Cyprus?" Purcell had cabled), "I'm going to Israel tomorrow whether you come or not." "Slave driver," said Scott, accepting a fresh drink from the waiter. But we caught the Sunday plane to Lod airport in Tel Aviv and remarked on arrival how nice and quiet it was. The war broke out the next morning.

There is nothing like an air raid warning to get you up and dressed in the morning. But the Israelis had not set off the sirens to warn of an air raid. It was just a convenient way to tell everybody that the war had started. And it was over, in effect, in three hours on the Monday morning, June 5, 1967.

It took no longer than that for the Israeli air force to wipe out the air forces of Egypt, Jordan, Syria and Iraq. In the case of Egypt, the main opponent, the Israelis flew west at low level, sometimes on one engine to save fuel, over the Mediterranean well beyond Alexandria, the cut straight south over the desert, then east to catch the Egyptian air force asleep and aground at dawn. They decimated the Egyptian squadrons on twenty-five airfields as far south as Luxor. Seven Egyptian army divisions were left without cover in the Sinai and the Israeli tanks swept through them to Suez in three days. The Jordanian army then was pinched off in the West Bank and the Israelis tidied up everything Saturday with a frontal assault on the Golan Heights overlooking the Sea of Galilee which could easily have taken them into Damascus. All the world's military colleges should be located in Tel Aviv, said a Canadian army attaché.

At the end of the first day of the war, Monday, the reporters gathered at the press office for a briefing by a colonel. The officer was cool and dispassionate and didn't resort to any of the jokes we heard so often later, such as: "We Israelis are very peaceful. We have a piece of Egypt and a piece of Jordan and piece of Syria."

Immediately after the Six-Day War, I went to Cyprus to file stories which I couldn't send from Israel, which has press censorship all the time. For me, the most ominous story of the war was in the UN hospital in Cyprus; the Israelis had killed fourteen unarmed members of the Indian contingent of the UN in the Gaza Strip and wounded twenty-four others. Members of the 1st Sikh Light Infantry had been in convoy from Camp Rafah to Gaza on the first day of the war when they met some Israeli tanks on the road. The convoy pulled off the road and stopped. Three tanks went by. The fourth stopped and opened fire from a few feet on the unarmed Indians. It rammed its gun through the windshield of a jeep, decapitating the two men inside. Eleven were killed. Three others died in the Israeli shelling of the UN headquarters in Gaza. The dead were cremated in Egypt, the wounded flown to Cyprus.

I obtained the information from the Indian commander, Col. M.S. Brar, by interviewing the wounded in the Austrian-run UN hospital, and by confirmation with UN staff evacuated from Sinai. When I got home to Ottawa, I received several poison-pen letters from persons I took to be Canadian Jews. One signed his name: he was a colleague in the parliamentary press gallery. James Hornick of the *Toronto Star* complained to Purcell but my boss stood by me. The incident shook me because it showed clearly how far some North American Jews will go to vilify anyone who even hints at a suggestion of criticism of Israel. Such vilification had deeply hurt my friend, Rev. Al Forrest, editor of the *United Church Observer*, who had tried to present the Arab as well as the Israeli side of the everlasting Middle East confrontation.

The odd thing about all this is that the Israelis themselves do not bear such attitudes. So far, Israel is a keen democracy, so democratic, in fact, that extremists like Meir Kuhane can be elected to the Knesset. (While Kuhane was preaching expulsion of all Arabs from Israel, former school teacher Jim Keegstra was being convicted in Canada for preaching hatred of Jews.) The nasty things about Israel, such as complicity in the slaughter of Beirut Palestinians and the deaths by beating of two Arab kidnappers after their capture, are dug out by Israeli newspapers. But official Jewry in North America makes out any criticism of Israel to be anti-Semitism.

7

A Nice Place to Visit, But ...

During the '67 Six-Day War (there was a story at the time that Israel stretched it out that long so that it would not go into the history books as just a skirmish) I was staying in the Dan Hotel, a sort of down-home place compared with the office-like Tel Aviv Hilton. Every night, a Cleveland doctor was buying drinks all round and exhorting the Israelis to faster and wider blitzkreig. What wonderful people, what a wonderful country, he would exclaim, raising his glass again. We all felt that, I guess; at least I do every time I'm on the winning side.

A woman Israeli soldier asked him: "But are you going to stay here after the war?"

The doctor walked away and was not seen again in the bar.

Young Israelis were sick and tired of American and Canadian Jews who lavished money on their state and came occasionally as lauding tourists but who would not settle in the Jewish homeland, built at the cost of lives and suffering of so many European Jews and of the sabras, the Israel-born. That problem remains. That's why Israel has to bend so much energy trying to get Jews out of Russia; it knows it can't pry them (six million strong) out of Canada and the U.S.

When I returned to Israel in 1969, I took great delight and comfort in passing most of my Tel Aviv evenings sitting at an outdoor café (any outdoor café) on Dizengoff Street and watching Israel on parade in front of me. It made me feel good. Old people, many with their concentration camp numbers visible on their arms, shuffled along, smiling, glancing from side to side, taking everything in. They never again had to be afraid of the battered door in the middle of the night, the cattle car to the crematorium.

I remarked one evening on the obvious contentment of the old people to a young Israeli sitting near me.

"How could they?" he snapped.

It was a common reaction among the young: how could six million Jews, no matter how unprotected and vulnerable, have allowed themselves to be herded like sheep to the gas ovens. The young Israeli, a proud fighter, found it incomprehensible. He was embarrassed by, if not ashamed of, the Holocaust. Moreover, the young Israeli was not so much a Jew as a member of a national state. I mean by that that he did not pay much regard to religion, though he had to observe the religious laws. As a member of a national state created in recent affliction and war, he was a prime recruit for jingoism. And jingoism, combined with lebensraum, is what he got from some of the Israeli leaders.

The problem with Israel is that it is becoming another Middle East country. Many Israelis and many Jews in North America see this clearly and are dismayed. The annexation of territory, the detention without trial of Arab residents, the artillery shelling of hapless, anarchic Beirut, can all be carefully and cogently explained politically and militarily. But they are no part of the Zionist principles which governed the founding of Israel.

Israel has been trapped in its own military success. It can strike anywhere it pleases any time it pleases without fear of military retaliation. But official terror does not produce peace or even acquiescence. It produces only counter-terror. After the Six-Day

War, when Israel found itself no longer the underdog, the tra-
ditional greeting, shalom, meaning peace, took on a note of urgency. What must Israel do to achieve peace? The Arab armies and
air forces had been conquered. The Palestinian fedayeen had been
rooted out and killed as soon as they had infiltrated. But more
took their places. They kept coming. Was it always to be this
way? Must Israeli children and their children be brought up in
this eternal nerve war? The answer lies in the solution of the
Palestinian problem, and that becomes more difficult year by
year. The treatment of its minorities is central to a democracy.
Sigmund Freud said: "A culture which leaves unsatisfied and
drives to rebelliousness so large a number of its members neither
has a prospect of continued existence nor deserves it." Israel as
the conqueror faces the same problem (in reverse) as the pre-
Israel Jew, as expressed by essayist Paul Johnson: "No intellectual
society can flourish where a Jew feels even slightly uneasy."

For nearly forty years, Israel's Jews (now 3.5 million) have
been fighting for their lives and country against a mostly hostile
Arab world of 160 million. They have won four of the five wars,
the fifth (Lebanon) ending in a no-win in 1985. They doubtless
can go on winning, though to what advantage is difficult to discern.
And one loss could be their undoing. Israel has answered the
military question over and over again: it can protect itself. But
now there is a moral question, which is much more difficult.

When I was first in Israel, the country was in the middle of
the wave of Jewish immigration from North Africa and west
Asia, particularly Morocco and Iraq. These (Sephardic) Jews
became in general the street-sweepers and toilet-bowl-cleaners for
the Ashkenazic or European Jews, mainly from Russia and
Poland, who ran the government, armed forces, industry, the
professions and the kibbutz. There was a sharp cleavage in Israeli
society, still there but decreasing through political and economic
assimilation. Israeli intolerance for the Sephardic Jew in the 1950s
and 1960s now has settled on the Arab within Israel. There are
more than two million Arabs living in Greater Israel — that
is, including the occupied West Bank and Gaza Strip. In the
annexed and occupied territories, the Palestinian Arabs live under
a different law than the Israelis; they have few, if any, rights
and resisters can be deported or jailed without trial. And the
so-called "Oriental" Jews from Africa and Asia, without demo-

cratic background and formerly oppressed by Arabs, now are the majority among Jews in Israel and more likely than their fellow countrymen to favor confrontation with the Arab world, near or far. The Jewish victim of racism is becoming the racist, the oppressed the oppressor.

A homeland for the dispossessed Palestinians (there are between three and four million of them altogether) is usually referred to as the Palestinian problem. It really is the central Israeli problem. The Jews know what it means to be dispossessed and some day, somehow, the problem will be solved. The greatest hope for a solution is that Israel remain, as it is now, a living parliamentary democracy which sees its own faults and failings more quickly and unerringly than any outsider (like this one) ever can.

8

Lebanon is Grief and Revenge

I recall especially one visit just before the main civil war (as opposed to earlier and smaller ones) broke out. I wrote at the time (October, 1969): "The high life goes on in Beirut as if nothing were happening. But a cruel prospect for Lebanon is civil war or assault by Israel — or both." It turned out to be both.

What was happening was that Lebanon's army and police had lost control of the southern part of the country. The fedayeen, or guerillas, or commandos as they liked to call themselves, were then the effective government of Jordan, though they hadn't assassinated King Hussein in sixteen attempts (he assassinated them instead soon after). In Egypt and Syria, the fedayeen were under the thumb of those governments. In Lebanon, the issue was in doubt. Lebanon stayed out of the 1956 and 1967 wars with Israel on the grounds that it just wanted to live in peace. But about half the Lebanese are Moslem and about half Christian. Most of the Christians wanted Lebanon to stay neutral, but many Moslems believed Lebanon should do more to help the Arab cause and therefore supported the presence in their country of the fedayeen, mostly stateless Palestinians. The green-clad gunmen of the Palestinians were the freedom-fighters (to Israel, terrorists) just as the Hagannah and Irgun Zvei Leumi were the Jewish freedom fighters during the British mandate in Palestine up to 1948.

On the road from Beirut to Saida, the car carrying a driver and me was stopped at a Lebanese police roadblock and searched for arms. The roadblock was a few miles north of Saida and was the limit of Lebanese government control. The driver, a Christian, was reluctant to go farther, but did so at my urging. He became frightened in a narrow alley in Saida when a green-clad carrying a Czech submachine gun got into the back seat. "I am a commando," he announced proudly. Those were his only non-Arabic words. More fedayeen gathered around the car and I asked to be taken to their leader (honest, that's what I said). I was told curtly to go back to Beirut and get a letter of introduction. I protested that I was already Johnny-on-the-spot. "Jewish spies," one of the fedayeen said, "go back or we will shoot you." I wasn't alarmed. He said it in Arabic and my driver didn't translate for me until we were on our way back, never having been taken to the leader.

I returned to the Phoenicia Hotel and went to the downstairs bar to watch the swimmers underwater through a wide window behind the bartender. But it was so nice outdoors that I walked to the oceanfront St. George's and to the actual barstool where Kim Philby used to sit during his days of treachery in Beirut. The next time I saw the Phoenicia it was on television and it was full of shell holes.

The Viet Nam and Sinai experiences took all the political joy out of peacekeeping and peace supervising. By 1981, when another peacekeeping mission was being mounted in Sinai, the Canadian government could hardly bring itself to admit that it had been asked to participate.

Allan McKinnon, former Conservative defence minister, asked in the Commons November 2, 1981, how many Canadian troops might be involved, and for how long.

Defence Minister Gilles Lamontagne asked Mr. McKinnon to submit his question in writing "and I will prepare an answer."

Thus peacekeeping died in Canada with a crisp, "Put it in writing, Mac."

PART SIX

THE PRESS

I'd rather have my facts all wrong than have no facts whatever.

Ogden Nash

All for One, and Everybody for Themselves

The Parliamentary Press Gallery in Ottawa is a place of cheerful back-stabbing. There is also lots of inadvertent falling on swords. I have done both there.

I think my own best example of the former was to wait one evening until the entire gallery had trooped down to the Chateau Laurier for a giant seafood freebie to spring a story that the defence department had a contingency plan to send troops to Viet Nam for peacekeeping. The story was accurate enough, though it didn't mention that the department had similar plans for a lot of other countries. But Viet Nam was topical. The enjoyment was sitting with a double rum in the gallery awaiting the return of colleagues called away from their feasting by frantic office orders to deny or match my story — very difficult at that hour of night.

The best (or worst) example of falling on my own sword was my attempt to beat the government to the announcement that it was going to buy one hundred Arrow interceptors from A.V. Roe Ltd. I beat the government to the announcement by about seven hours. Unfortunately, the announcement was that the Arrow program was being cancelled. "Well, there's McIntosh," Diefenbaker said with relish when opening his press conference to announce the Arrow's death. "Out on a limb and sawed it off behind him."

Douglas Leiterman, editor-producer for the ostensibly independent Public Affairs TV of the Canadian Broadcasting Corporation, wrote to Defence Minister Pearkes on a CBC letterhead:

I feel impelled to write to you this morning and congratulate you on the decision on the Arrow. Only those of us with some meagre knowledge of the situation you faced can imagine the courage it took to make that decision. In three years of military reporting, when the department was in other hands, I had begun to lose faith in the system. A well-meaning but single-minded bureaucracy seemed to hold the upper hand over the people's elected representatives, and the public seemed to be willing to accept any kind of nonsense in place of a policy.

Your incumbency, like Duncan Sandys' in Britain, has shown that a forward-looking defense policy is possible if leadership is forthcoming. You can be confident, I believe, that Canadians will give you their continued support.

And you must have smiled, as many of us did, at your once again confounding the pundits!

The gallery is fiercely competitive despite its habit of running in packs after the same story, no matter how trivial, on the same day. It doesn't dig out as many stories on its own as it used to, but neither does it roll over and play dead for the government. But that is probably no more than a reflection of the public's attitude, surveyed officially as long ago as 1971 (by ill-starred Information Canada), that more than half of Canadians never have any faith in what government — any government — says.

When I was sent to Ottawa by Canadian Press in 1953, the gallery was a tightly-knit group of newspaper and news agency reporters which barred radio and television from membership. I could never understand clearly the reason, if any, for this black-balling, but I think it had to do with upsetting the cosy arrangements reporters had with cabinet ministers for the imparting and receiving of news. Radio and television would force ministers to go on the record and they would therefore be much more circumspect in their confidences. The gallery members sensed only too accurately that their jobs were going to be made more difficult but I don't think we even suspected how fast the politicians would seek the warm embrace of the broadcasters who, with a few notable exceptions, were practitioners of the soft question to the point of pulling the forelock. Example: "Would you say, Mr. Minister, that this is an excellent policy for the Canadian public?"

Parliament and government were as tightly-knit as the press gallery. We were all jammed in the one building, the Centre Block of the Parliament Buildings, with the exception that the prime minister and external affairs minister also had offices in the adjacent East Block. All the cabinet ministers, the opposition leader, and all other MPs were right at hand. Apart from the prime minister, it was not difficult to see ministers, who did not sit behind protective banks of assistants as they do today. Some ministers courted certain reporters. At that time, the Liberals had been so long in power that reporters for Liberal newspapers such as the *Toronto Star* and *Winnipeg Free Press* simply took it for granted that they would be favored with ministerial scoops, and they usually were. When Diefenbaker came to power in 1957, Conservative newspapers, especially the *Ottawa Journal* and *Toronto Telegram*, had sweet revenge. Diefenbaker saw Dick Jackson of the *Journal* and Pete Dempson of the *Telegram* nearly every Friday. This tended to make it tough on the rest of us, though I never had it as tough as I had covering the British Columbia legislature and government against Jack Webster, wizard reporter and superlative confrontationalist. I have always regarded ministerial talks with the press, whether with one reporter or several, as an essential part of government. Certainly the press release and television commercial do not do the job. I don't recall exactly when ministers started to go into hiding but it was probably soon after Trudeau came to office. He terrified his ministers as he did his purported friends and his cowering underlings. But the trend was there anyway because most politicians had discovered that they could get on television nationally with one or two soapy sentences which conveyed deep concern for a problem, but no information.

2

Bring on the Cameras, If You Dare

The Parliamentary Press Gallery could not hold out long against the radio and television hordes and we allowed them membership, ungracefully, in 1959. An underlying current of animosity lingered for a time. I recall one incident when we had dutifully gone out to the airport in Ottawa to witness the arrival of Engine Charlie Wilson, Eisenhower's secretary of defence. In the middle of the customary airport statement in front of microphones, Jim Oastler of the *Montreal Star* whirled around and hung his hat over the lens of the CBC televison camera. There followed some pushing and shoving and muffled shouts and I was shouldered aside by a Mountie to whom I wittily remarked, "Sure, one government agency helping another." We finally accepted the radio and television representatives (we still couldn't bring ourselves to apply the word reporters to them) mainly because among the early arrivals were some extremely able men, including Sam Ross of Vancouver, who established a western radio news network, and Tom Earle of the CBC. Television's greatest asset was Norm DePoe of the CBC who day after day summed up the affairs of Parliament and government clearly, crisply, briefly and fairly. And he did it live on camera without notes and, what the rest of us envied most, he could do it half-bombed.

DePoe says in his unpublished memoirs that the "medium distorts the message." He railed against such contrivances as a National Film Board clip of a prairie combine shown at the reporter's every mention of wheat. He would probably have been shocked to find that television has not changed; at every mention of energy we see the revolving dial of a gas pump, at every mention of inflation the cash register of a grocery store. But DePoe took the CBC away from its heavy reliance on Canadian Press, to the point where, as DePoe put it, "If the story wasn't on the CP wire, it couldn't have happened." If a special report were required, the CBC commissioned a newspaper or magazine writer to do it. That way, it wasn't the CBC saying what it was carrying. In 1985, eighty-two of the 331 members of the press gallery were from the CBC.

CBC wasn't the only organization which relied heavily on Canadian Press. The newspapers did, and do, because it is their own co-operative agency, each member paying according to its circulation and area of population. Canadian Press was supposed to supply the basic coverage of Parliament and government and the Supreme Court, rewriting the press releases and supplying running copy on the House of Commons. CP has three centre seats in the gallery immediately behind and above the speaker's chair in the House. During the question period, which usually opens the session, CP reporters left the chamber at intervals of ten minutes or so, oftener if the story was hot, ran to their office down the corridor and immediately wrote the news for quick transfer to the teleprinter and swift passage across Canada.

I can remember my first question period very well. I didn't have the slightest idea what was going on. I could hear fuzzy statements but didn't know who was making them or what was being said. There was no PA system then, and no translation. Some ministers, embarrassed by a question, or in total ignorance of the subject, deliberately dropped their voices so that we couldn't hear. This meant that we had to wait for the "blues," the first-draft verbatim (well, almost verbatim) transcript of Commons proceedings. The main purpose of the blues was to allow MPs to make changes before the published record appeared the next day. Changes in facts and meanings were not allowed; the alterations were supposed to be cosmetic, that is, confined mainly to grammatical tuning.

The most delightful change I can recall was made by Ellen Fairclough, the first woman cabinet minister and probably the brightest minister of the Diefenbaker government. Judy LaMarsh had just completed a speech. Mrs. Fairclough said she had found the speech "Gerry Waring," a reference to a friend of Miss LaMarsh who was a member of the press gallery and wrote speeches for her. Not comprehending the sally, the Hansard reporter changed "Gerry Waring" to "very wearing." Mrs. Fairclough was damned if she was going to let her remark be lost forever and when she got the blues she changed the phrase back to her original "Gerry Waring" and that's the way it appeared in the published record the next day.

3

It's Not Easy Feeding MPs

Unless there was some debate of note, the press gallery in the Commons was deserted after the question period except for the presence of two reporters, one from Canadian Press and one from British United Press, later United Press International, still later defunct. I spent many long, weary afternoons and evenings up there chatting with Ron Nickerson of BUP. It became so boring sometimes that one or the other of us would shout "Shame" at some particularly outrageous remark by whomever had the floor and a number of times we got into Hansard this way. Unfortunately, our names could not be attached in Hansard to these outbursts, which brought rebukes from the speaker's chair once or twice, and posterity will never know that it was Ron and me speaking. We never matched Dick Jackson of the *Ottawa Journal*, though. Late one evening when a bare quorum was dozing in the chamber, Jackson slipped into the back row on the opposition side and sat for ten minutes without ever being challenged. He finally left out of boredom.

At that time, we had access to the MPs' lobbies, government and opposition. The main purpose was to be able to buttonhole an MP, usually a minister, to expand on some statement in the House or answer our tidying-up questions. This privilege was seldom abused, and hiding in a lobby phone booth to eavesdrop on private conversations occurred infrequently. We often sent in messages by the pages to ask an MP to come out of the House to see us. An MP who didn't want to talk with us had only to remain in his seat in the chamber.

I soon discovered that reporters used opposition MPs constantly as a conduit for information. The practice was called "feeding." A reporter would feed an opposition MP a question on which he was seeking information which he couldn't pry out any other way. The MP used the question in the question period, the reporter poised in the gallery above to write down the ministerial answer, if any. Cabinet ministers could and often did duck questions, but it was harder to do so in the Commons, making chances of getting a reply better there than anywhere else. The MP concerned was usually willing to play along if he was helping his hometown newspaper and, what the hell, it was the opposition's duty to ask questions. The trouble was that the reply, if it came, was available to all other reporters unless question and answer were both worded so obliquely that only the principals could understand. Well, I decided to get in on the game, and I approached an opposition MP to put a question to a cabinet minister. I forget the question, for a reason that will be clear in a second. I was a rookie, and I chose a rookie MP to pose my question. Little did I realize what a rookie he was. "Mr. McIntosh of The Canadian Press has asked me to put this question to the minister of ..." He never got any further because of the laughter. The MP sat down in confusion. I slipped under my chair in the gallery above, cursing the MP, myself and especially my crimson face. It was years before I tried again. I went to Harold Winch of the New Democrats (who deserved to be, and should have been, premier of British Columbia), a very experienced parliamentarian. He laughed and said, "Do you want me to say that Mr. McIntosh has asked me to ask this question?" I blushed again for the umpteenth time since my original gaffe. I thought everybody had forgotten.

We achieved a lot more success using opposition MPs as information pipelines in the Commons committees. Often a reporter who specialized in a few fields knew more about a subject under discussion in a committee than the opposition MP did. This is no reflection on the MPs, who were scattered thin among several committees and had no time to bone up on all the topics coming up. In the cramped committee rooms, a reporter could sit along a wall directly behind an MP or two, and either whisper questions to them, or hand them notes with the scribbled questions. MPs generally were very discriminating. They wouldn't accept just any question. It had to interest them for one reason or another or enable them to score a political point against the government. It used to drive us to distraction when an MP, on a keen line of questioning leading to our desired answer, was diverted by a red herring thrown out by a clever minister or bureaucrat. Frantically, with urgent whispers and swift notes, we would try to get the MP back on track. The government side was quite aware of what was going on, of course, and I think we reporters were the real cheeses in this cat-and-mouse game. Looking back on it, I suspect that both government and opposition MPs were leading us on a hot trail and then deliberately sidetracking us into frustration at the last second in return for all the ills they constantly suffered at our hands, mainly the ill of misquoting them, or, worse, ignoring them. C.D. Howe never actually said, "What's a million?" That was our interpretation of what he said.

Which reminds me: George Welsh of Amherstburg, Ontario, was the last surviving member of the Stanley expedition that found Dr. David Livingstone in Africa. When he died at age ninety-five in 1943, he was still insisting that Henry Stanley did not say, "Dr. Livingstone, I presume," but "Dr. Livingstone, I believe." The world ignored him.

4

"May I Call You 'Sir,' Mr. Minister?"

Coverage of Parliament has changed. Hardly anybody attends the House of Commons, even for question period. Reporters watch television monitors in their offices. And the final ignominy is that newspaper reporters carry tape recorders and hold out their little microphones to record, at the ministerial and opposition scrums after question period, the very same words that radio and television broadcasters are taping. To me, the most embarrassing sight on television, and it occurs almost nightly, is the silent, unquestioning newspaper reporter with arm extended recording, in excruciating boredom, the rehearsed answers to rehearsed questions put by radio and television to cabinet ministers and opposition leaders. It is even more embarrassing than the broadcaster recording a ministerial statement who glances at his watch and shuts off his recorder and retreats because he has the requisite fifteen seconds on tape.

Some of the questions put by broadcasters are hard to believe even when you hear them with your own ears. Example: when Communications Minister Marcel Masse was informed November 28, 1985, that the RCMP was not going to bring charges against him for supposed campaign fund irregularities, the CTV reporter asked him: "Are you pleased that the RCMP is not bringing charges against you?" If only Masse had had the presence of mind to say something like, "Certainly not, I should have been charged." But then television would have thrown it out. It doesn't like anybody one-upping a medium which must work on the basis of scheduled events. Spontaneity is not wanted; wide-eyed viewers might come to expect it occasionally.

The scrum is not new. The main difference is that newspaper

and news agency reporters used to ask the questions. More than thirty years ago, the cabinet used to meet in the Privy Council chamber in the East Block (this was before today's forty-member cabinets) and the press gathered in the narrow corridor outside between it and the prime minister's office. The prime minister had no choice but to run the gauntlet of questions, though he didn't always reply. We closed in around him and began firing. St. Laurent was extremely courteous but seldom gave us any replies that amounted to anything. I was convinced that his idea of what constituted news would by a two-page mimeographed sheet issued by the Liberal party two or three days a week. I saw him lose his temper only once in these corridor scrums. Al Donnelly of Canadian Press asked him three times (the reporter had been ordered to get an answer no matter what) why the government had restored to his former position a senior federal bureaucrat in Saskatchewan who had resigned to run for the Liberals in an election and been defeated. St. Laurent turned red as a beet and his moustache sprang straight out from his lip and the reporter was told to mind his own business. St. Laurent was not one to crack jokes with the press. Diefenbaker was pretty free and easy but he protested to Canadian Press one day after CP reporter John Leblanc said, "C'mon, Dief, don't give us that horseshit."

Such familiarities were rare, even as a joke. Charlie King of Southam was the only reporter I knew who regularly called cabinet ministers (though not the prime minister) by their first names. Jim Oastler of the *Montreal Star* and Diefenbaker were personal friends, but the relationship had to change drastically the moment Diefenbaker became prime minister: no more evenings at each other's homes, for instance, and Oastler called Diefenbaker "Mr. Prime Minister" as the rest of us did. At a cocktail party or some other informal occasion, an old hand in the press gallery might address Pearson as "Mike" but this was considered uncouth, if not disrespectful to the office. Most of us had been brought up to address our elders by their surnames. We used "Mr. (or Madame) Minister" because ministers liked it. It is a necessary phrase today because there are so many ministers that few reporters can recall all their names.

The East Block melée after every cabinet meeting, especially with television cameras present, gradually brought on its end during the latter days of the Pearson government. Some of us used to take up stations outside the west door of the East Block, but there were at least three other exits for the prime minister to give us the slip. The cabinet moved its meetings to the Centre Block and the scrum moved with it, growing bigger, more confused, and producing less and less information. A room was set aside in the basement under the Commons for television and radio interviews. The camera sometimes strayed from the minister being interviewed to show another minister or opposition spokesman lining up to deliver his rehearsed comment in thirty, or preferably fewer, seconds.

The good newspaper reporter had to rely on none of these cosmetic news trappings, of course. He popped in and out of ministerial offices every day all day, just to keep in touch if for no other reason. Most ministers were readily accessible for quick questions, though appointments were usually required for a full-dress interview. Sometimes the visit itself was more revealing than the minister's reply to a question. I had dropped in one day to ask Justice Minister Stuart Garson a question about some aspect of the Gouzenko case. He was in the middle of a reply when we heard J.W. Pickersgill talking to Garson's secretary as he prepared to walk into Garson's office. Quickly, Garson ushered me out of the other door (one of the great assets of ministerial offices in the Centre Block). He practically pushed me out. It was obvious that he was very scared of Pickersgill, then secretary to the cabinet, a civil service position. In the Trudeau era, Michael Pitfield was to affect cabinet ministers the same way. Some cabinet ministers exercise more power than other cabinet ministers, but few exercise as much as some civil servants.

5

Working for the Fifth Estate

There is no trick to reporting. It simply comprises straightforward questions. The first one is, "What is your name?" The second, most important of all in a country as wide as Canada, is "Where are you from?" These two questions suit social and political life, and plain good manners, as well as newspaperdom. Paul Martin, my political hero, used these two questions incessantly. Sometimes he reversed the order and his first question in almost any place where two or more people unknown to him were gathered was "Is there anyone here from Windsor?"

I used a variation of this question all the time I was covering the military because I knew that if I named in my story one person from each region of Canada, the story would have to be carried on CP wires right across the country. I was always taking down names and hometowns, especially overseas. In a barrack, or on a flight line, or in a ship, I would always scan my list and make sure I had representatives of all regions. If I didn't, all I had to do was call out, "Anybody here from Alberta?" Or Prince Edward Island, or wherever. It never failed. After every trip, I tried to make a point of writing the brass to praise everybody I had met, especially the pilots in the RCAF, my wartime service, for getting me there and back safely. One day, a pilot told me a letter I had written in such circumstances had won him a promotion. He and another pilot had equal qualifications and my letter on his file had tipped the balance. Knowing such power to be in my hands, I wrote even more letters, even more fulsomely, but I never provoked another promotion that I know of.

There was an easy way for a CP reporter to make sure of getting his story in the big dailies. Drop it on them just before their deadline so that their own reporters in Ottawa would have no time to run checks. I had the deadlines of the Toronto and Montreal dailies fairly well memorized for this purpose, because no self-respecting CP staffer was interested in making just the small papers: CP was often their only service. The proper test was to get a story into the big dailies. Besides, that was usually the best way to attract head office attention. The trouble was that it attracted even more head office attention if the story proved wrong.

The reporters on the big dailies, good men and women all or they wouldn't have been in Ottawa, regarded CP as upstart. They wanted CP to provide its so-called good, grey, standard coverage of Parliament and leave the digging and exclusives to them. But no CP bureau chief in Ottawa would accept this, and they assigned reporters to individual beats which usually comprised two or three departments and odds and sods such as certain crown corporations and other agencies. One result of this was a lot of stories emanating from "informed sources," usually civil servants who couldn't be named because they'd never speak to you again. CP's head office in Toronto would sometimes want to know for its information who the "informed sources" were, and we'd have to name them privately. Later, this became a standard procedure: filing as a message the names of sources after the stories which quoted them unnamed. Some of us at CP Ottawa thought this was too risky; the names could easily fall into the wrong hands, that is, the deskmen on newspapers who would promptly tell their reporters in Ottawa. So we used fictitious names as sources. My own personal favorite was "Colonel Maurice Code, chief of communications." I don't know whether anyone in Toronto ever twigged, but nobody ever questioned the colonel's good name. As the years passed, I didn't forget to give Code regular promotions, to brigadier and then major-general.

Canadian Press had to cover the Senate because Senator Rupert Davies was the owner of the *Kingston Whig-Standard*. The moment he looked up from the floor of the Senate and saw the press gallery empty he rushed out and telephoned CP's general manager to report that there was no CP reporter present to take down the senators' distilled and verbalized sober second thoughts. When CP was short-staffed through illness or too much going on elsewhere, it sometimes took a chance that Senator Davies was ill or out of the chamber for some other reason and left the CP seat vacant. But, more often, it grabbed anyone, usually the copy-boy, told him to put on a jacket and tie, carry a notebook and pencil and sit in the Senate press gallery until relieved, or until the Senate adjourned, or until hell froze over.

One of the toughest assignments was calling a minister at home at night. Ministers used to list their numbers in the Ottawa telephone book just like real people, and there could be no begging off that you couldn't find the number. Nearly all of these calls were ordered by the chief deskman in Toronto (who had never made such a call himself) to obtain confirmation or denial of or comment on some event in Timbuctoo or Zanzibar or sometimes even in Canada. The only good call I remember was the one made in 1957 by John Bird of CP to Pearson to inform him that he won the Nobel Prize for peace. (Pearson said, "O my God" and CP censored it to read "O my gosh.")

I had to call Pearson at home one night when he was external affairs minister to obtain his comment on some obscure happening at the United Nations. He was having a dinner party. When he came to the phone and found out it was a reporter he said sharply, "Not now," and hung up. I didn't blame him. I would have been a lot ruder.

Another CP reporter once had to call Defence Minister Brooke Claxton in the middle of the night. The reporter got him out of bed, and Claxton said, "I'm never going to speak to you again," and he didn't. I was covering the defence department at the time and thank heaven it wasn't I who had to make the call. We kept protesting that we were throwing away any goodwill we might have, not to mention sources of information, by making these night calls on the whims of ignorant deskmen. But head office was unrepentant in its pursuit of news night and day. Ministers finally solved the problem for us by unlisting their numbers.

6
———

Notes from an Air-Conditioned Room

I always found local color important in a story, especially overseas. It lent an air of authenticity which the story otherwise might lack. For instance, I always applied adjectives to the first commentator every reporter encounters on arrival in foreign parts — the taxi driver or, less often, the hotel bartender. In my stories from Europe, the taxi driver or bartender was usually a wartime German paratrooper or Lancashire merchant seaman. In the Middle East, these gentlemen were always "giant" and Nubian, Senegalese, Berber or Masai. Other people met on the road might include the carpet salesman from Smyrna, the ouzo merchant from Delphi or the dealer in smoky topazes from Kandy (or Pusan, Peshawar or Balbek).

Foreign words scattered judiciously here and there like rose petals also lend authenticity. *Khamsin* (sandstorm) was a must in stories from Egypt, as was *jihad* (holy war) in anything from

Lebanon and *shalom* (peace) from Israel. I always tried to obtain small guidebooks on the local flora and fauna so that I could throw in a reference to a baobab or jacaranda tree or a gecko lizard: "Outside my mosquito net, an orange-tailed gecko snapped the bugs off the walls and ceiling." A lot of the time abroad, I was reliving my boyhood years with the pulp magazines where giant Nubians armed with *bundukis* (Swahili for rifles) snatched white maidens in gossamer blouses from under the baobab tree and made off on camelback through the *khamsin* shouting, "*Jihad.*"

There is one type of foreign story which is always popular with reporters. Most of these stories are set at poolside and contrast the iced drink served by an immaculate waiter with the gunfire down the street between two rabbles. This was a favorite of mine in Cyprus. I never kept a Cyprus example of this kind of story but I just happen to have one here from Buliji, Pakistan, written January 9, 1971:

Prime Minister Trudeau drove in a Rolls-Royce Saturday to this little village of shacks made out of mud, stone, burlap, lath and tree branches.

He came to inspect a nuclear reactor which Canada has built for Pakistan at a cost of $48 million.

Outside the cement fence topped by broken glass and barbed wire, pitifully thin children squatted in the dust and waved as the Rolls-Royce drove by.

Inside the fence, the beautifully-dressed children of 30 Canadian families played on a thick green lawn.

On the lawn were set out chairs under gay umbrellas and tables with little cakes protected against the random fly by colored cheese-cloth.

The Pakistani waiters stayed behind a high cloth screen until ordered to appear with tea for the guests.

Pakistani officials also attended the garden party but they did not have their wives or children and sat at tables by themselves. There was no mingling of Canadian and Pakistani reactor technicians though Dr. H.I. Usmani, head of the Pakistan Atomic Energy Commisssion, said in a welcoming speech that Canadians and Pakistanis at the reactor site are one big happy family.

The reactor, scheduled to produce power this summer, sits beside the Arabian Sea in a bleak landscape of salt flats and scrub growth 25 miles west of Karachi.

A small boy was tending goats which, however, ran in and out of shacks.

A weary camel driver escorted his groaning beast which bore a load of bales.

A woman dressed in rags beat her laundry — more rags — beside a stinking slough of green slime.

A few hundred yards away inside the reactor compound the teacups tinkled in merry conversation and Canadian wives in miniskirts shook hands happily with a beaming Mr. Trudeau.

Potted flowers had been set along the clean roadway and pretty tablecloths blew in the breeze from out a cloudless sky. The temperature was about 80.

Mr. Trudeau said it was a great experience for Canadian children to know another land.

Then he drove in the Rolls-Royce through the gate and past the village where even hardy palm trees were dying. A small dark girl stood beside an emaciated donkey and waved at the big car. Down the road was the Canadian compound, a walled area in the desert with lawns and ferns and air conditioners protruding from newly-painted houses and apartments.

Such stories of contrast are easy pickings in a poor country, especially when the reporter knows he can write them back in his air-conditioned hotel room with a drink beside him and a variety of sandwiches en route by room service. Nonetheless, the depth of poverty in most of Asia and Africa is startling and depressing for a Canadian on first experience. I remember driving with Pete Thomson of the *Montreal Star*, a newcomer to Asia, from the airport in Islamabad, Pakistan, at dusk. People were squatting in the dust in front of fires trying to keep warm. Dung to be used as fuel was drying on the walls of their shacks. Pete stared for a long time, then said, "Jesus, I didn't think it was going to be any worse than Nova Scotia."

I had felt something like that (though I would have said Manitoba, where Pete comes from) when I first saw Asia in 1950 at Pusan, Korea. It was a double shock because my Aunt Elsie had lived and worked in Japan in the 1920s and '30s and had told us about her beautiful vacations in Korea. She had also been to Angkor Wat in Cambodia and scattered about her home in Stanstead were pieces of softstone sculpture — heads, but mostly arms and hands, which she had picked up off the ground there. They all melted in the fire that killed her.

7

Drumbeating for the P.M. and the Truth Squad

The Trudeau visit to Pakistan referred to here preceded the 1971 Commonwealth conference in Singapore where the chief topic was British arms sales to South Africa. What was required, as at all Commonwealth meetings, was a watered-down declaration to which all members, including Britain, could subscribe without giving way on any point at all. It all seemed terribly important at the time, and we ran into an age-old problem in reporting. The declaration was settled at the last moment and we had only a few minutes to write the story before scrambling for the airport and Trudeau's armed forces plane on which we were all travelling. We were informed by Ivan Head, Trudeau's foreign affairs specialist who had been a participant in the negotiations, that the Canadian prime minister had saved the conference at the last moment by supplying the key words of compromise for the Commonwealth statement. There was no way we could check this with any other delegation and we all filed quick "informed-sources" stories in line with what Head had told us. We had to take Head on trust despite the obvious political drum-beating for Trudeau. I had no problem accepting Head on these grounds, and had many times before. He always struck me as an honest man. Most reporters covering that conference felt the same way but there was some questioning among us of the principle of playing jingo on the uncheckable word of one informant, no matter how highly placed.

Bryce Mackasey became notorious for walking into labor-management disputes which his deputy, Bill Kelly, had solved five minutes before and marching out with the news that Mackasey had done it again, yessirree. Claims to last-minute saves have become general though few can even remember the subject, let alone the saving play, two weeks after the event.

Questioning the source took a strange twist in the Diefenbaker-Pearson contests. Tony Westell, then with the *Globe and Mail*, contended that a lot of Diefenbaker's statements were not true. He carried around with him dossiers of background information and, when he deemed it necessary, corrected in bracketed paragraphs what he considered misstatements of facts by Diefenbaker. The trouble was that these corrections, to keep up with Diefenbaker, became so convoluted that they themselves became interpretations of what had been said and not the actual words. And the stories became so confusing the reader was at a loss to know what to make of the whole thing. I thought this was ridiculous: just put down accurately what the man said; it was up to the political opposition to deny or correct. I came to see that, despite its reputation for dullness, Canadian Press was the backbone of all reporting in Canada: don't sit in judgment; just set out the facts in order.

The Liberals themselves got sucked into the trap of interpretation when they set up their "truth squad" (another brilliant Keith Davey innovation) to follow Diefenbaker around and issue corrections of his alleged mis-statements. Diefenbaker had the squad laughed out of the campaign halls: "Would the squad like to come right up front where it can hear better instead of skulking at the back of the room?" "Why, there's the truth squad. Let me read what it said after my speech last night." And there would follow some outlandish fiction by Diefenbaker who would say at the end, "Let's see what they have to say about that." The squad lasted only a few days and withdrew in disarray with the nonsensical claim that it had forced Diefenbaker into a new regime of speaking the truth and its duty was therefore done.

8

"I Often Read Your Stuff"

One of the delights of going to wars, revolutions and Commonwealth and NATO meetings was meeting, or at least seeing, the stars of the newspaper world: Jack Scott, James Cameron, Homer Bigart, Art Gavshon, Scotty Reston. I first saw Reston in the press room in Tel Aviv at the start of the Six-Day War in 1967 and he obviously found stardom an encumbrance. There were three or four Israeli public relations officers gathered around his desk asking whether there was anything he needed, an interview with so-and-so, another coffee, more paper. He was not only embarrassed in front of colleagues but couldn't get a story written. I suggested from a nearby desk that if one of the attendants dancing on Reston wasn't doing anything he could get me a coffee. I got a long, cool look and no coffee. My CP friend, Joe MacSween, once told me that Red Smith said to him at first meeting, "I often read your stuff." Joe said he felt great even though he realized there was no way Smith could ever have seen his dispatches.

9

Exit Eva

I don't think anybody ever handled the press, including its stars, as well as Trudeau did. He held us in contempt as his intellectual inferiors, which was generally true enough, but more than that I think he held himself in some contempt for playing us like fish, that is, unworthy catches. In his early days, he had us cavorting around him like schoolboys around Mr. Chips. Patrick Watson, for instance, was actually simpering in a famous CBC television interview with Trudeau, who must have been a bit ashamed himself because it was all so easy. (Watson himself is honest enough to say that he is still embarrassed by this soft interview.)

For myself, I recall babbling to Trudeau that I was also a Quebecois and the same age. (A little later, it turned out Trudeau had lied about his age and I was really two years younger than he — a great relief.) But a small incident in the 1968 election campaign jarred me out of any adoration for Trudeau. He was leaving Kelowna, B.C., airport on a bright morning and the local Liberals had arranged an honor guard to the airplane steps of pretty teen-agers in cheerleader costumes. Trudeau kissed each one, each one swooning, but deliberately ignored one girl. He danced up the steps, leaving her in tears. He pretended to spot his oversight, went slowly down the steps as she waited in agony, then kissed her and went aboard the plane.

Trudeau's handling of the press is best illustrated by his attendance at the Commonwealth conference in London in January, 1969, less than a year after he had become prime minister. Trudeau did not make a splash at the conference, but he made a splash socially, which gave us something to write about. One of his dates was a high-priced jet-setter named Eva Rittinghausen, introduced to him earlier at Murray Bay, Quebec, by Renaud St. Laurent, the former prime minister's son and to whom, apparently, Trudeau never spoke again.

Eva couldn't keep her mouth shut. Here are some tidbits from a radio interview:

Q: You are quoted as saying it was love at first sight on both sides?
A: I did not say at first sight . . . . Maybe it's more like interest from both sides . . . . We found out we have so many things in common like sports, yoga, swimming, diving and to some extent I'm interested in literature where of course he's very well ahead as we all know. And I love to wear turtleneck sweaters as well.
Q: What about marriage?
A: Well, it never came up. And I don't know what he has in mind at all because I do know that I'm not the only woman in his life at the very moment . . . . I'm sure there are two or three others involved, or interested in being married to him.
Q: Is he the marrying kind?
A: I do think, yes.
Q: He's 49 now . . .

A: Yes, it doesn't matter... it's a wonderful age.

Q: Do you have any reason to think you are more than just another woman?

A: I know I'm very well aware of my strong personality and maybe where I have more than any other female is that I know how to capture people, if not the audience.

Q: How have you managed to avoid entanglements before Mr. Trudeau came into your life?

A: I happen to have been very ambitious all my life long, so it was very hard. Not just any man could please me and it is just the enthusiasm, the ambition that is so strong in me that it would have to be someone very special I should show interest in.

Q: What do you find very special about Pierre Trudeau?

A: Well, the first thing that appeals to me is that he is a man who we all know doesn't commit himself. He makes you speak and he makes you show to him what you have to offer and then he may respond. Certainly his smile and charm, but especially I admire and adore in him the courage he shows.

Q: You are not concerned that these interviews you are giving to the press will interfere with your friendship? The prime minister has been quoted as saying in the *Daily Express* that no friend of his would talk to the press.

A: I did not know about this. You are telling me this a little bit late.

Exit Eva.

The Commonwealth meeting ended and Trudeau was holding a press conference and not saying anything worth a damn about it because the subjects hadn't really interested him. He knew that back home there had been editorial questioning of his lack of participation. Suddenly, he turned the tables on us. Our behavior, he said, had been "crummy," the way we had hounded poor little girls about his private life. Radio reporter Paul Taylor was so taken aback he said, "Is this on the record, sir?" Trudeau stared at him in amazement. It was on the record in spades, and the Canadian public adored it. The press has never understood that the public view of the press is every reporter, photographer or cameraman who ever blocked public view of the Queen (or Trudeau).

After the 1971 Commonwealth conference, Trudeau was asked whether our behavior had improved since its "crummy" state in 1969. Yes, he replied, "and I might say I'm rather grateful for that."

We lapped it up.

When I left the press gallery and went to work for a government commission, then a department, I was once asked for advice on how to handle the press. I set out a few basic rules:

- Don't take the press too seriously; all its programs and columns are gone forever in hours, minutes or seconds.

- If you aren't prepared for certain questions, don't fret; more often than not, the reporter won't know the question to ask.

- If the reporter catches the major points you were trying to make and gets them down more or less accurately, count yourself lucky. If he spells your name right, you're a winner.

- If you have something untrivial you think the public should know, call up the press and tell them; don't issue a press release.

- Don't leave press relations to subordinates; accept all press phone calls immediately or call back as soon as you can.

- Don't try to cover up a goof. Tell the whole ghastly mess in one go; otherwise reporters will come back day after day for more details and your trauma will be merely lengthened. Dump the works once. There's far less splatter that way.

None of this advice was ever taken, of course.

PART SEVEN

GOVERNMENT BY CIVIL SERVICE

If a project isn't worth doing at all, it isn't worth doing well.

Old Saw

1

"The Process Is the Product"

This McLuhanism was not coined by Marshall McLuhan, late Canadian theorist on communications and sometime adviser to Prime Minister Trudeau. It was the inspiration of Jim Davey, one of the few unTrudeaumaniacal persons Trudeau had on his staff in the early days and who unfortunately died in a fall from a ladder. Davey used the expression to cover a specific set of circumstances: federal-provincial constitutional talks. It meant that as long as the provinces and Ottawa were talking — and talking and talking — about a new constitution, the talkathon was at least as beneficial for Canadian unity as the achievement of a new constitution itself. He was proved right in the long run because when a new constitution was finally gained in 1982, the provinces were allowed to opt out generally or specifically. Quebec did so generally right away; Saskatchewan did so specifically in 1986.

Though the "process is the product" was designed to define a single field of government endeavor, it came, as the Trudeau years waxed and waned, to stand for all of government. There was no product except the everlasting process of government: the widening committee system, interminable discussion following lengthy discussion, option piled on option, conference on conference, commissions royal and common, task forces with little tasks and no force, and decisions, if any, so fuzzy as to be open to the individual interpretations of all the participants. Keep talking until the problem, if anyone knows what it is, disappears or is forgotten: the great (and sometimes highly successful) Canadian solution.

The process, invented, enthusiastically endorsed, practised and encouraged by the civil service, has resulted in effective take-over of government in Ottawa by the civil service, 560,000 strong and growing despite purported freezes and layoffs. In 1985, the government announced, with the usual fanfare, that it was going to cut the civil service by 15,000, or less than three per cent, in five years. But at least 12,000 retire or leave the civil service every year; a cut of 15,000 could be achieved in fifteen months simply by not replacing the departees.

2

Who's Running this Country Anyway?

It used to be said that one of Parliament's essential problems was how to control the bureaucratic machine, including the executive (government) which directs it. That is no longer a problem because the bureaucracy has long been out of parliamentary control. It is now out of the control of the executive.

All this seemingly began innocently enough. Parliament could not handle — and was not and is not supposed to handle — all the technical details and administrative judgments involved in legislation. More and more, legislation had to be confined to broad objectives and it was left to government and bureaucracy to make all the necessary regulations and exercise discretion. In many cases, Parliament had to go beyond this and create special boards, commissions, crown corporations and similar agencies to supervise enormously technical subjects, such as transportation, radio and television, atomic energy, foreign aid. The relation of government, let alone Parliament, to such agencies became more and more remote until these scores of bodies took on lives of their own outside public control but, you may be sure, gobbling up public money. More than thirty years ago, a very great Canadian parliamentarian, C.G. (Chubby) Power, warned that the civil service in drafting regulations was creating presumptions in favor of government departments in their relations with individual citizens, thus shifting the onus of proof to the individual. Power said at that time that ministers (and he had been one) in daily touch with the civil service tended to accept its advice rather than that of political friends or followers and the result was often illiberal if not undemocratic legislation.

Harold Laski once wrote that "everyone with the least acquaintance with government cannot but be aware that there is a give and take between every minister and his staff officials which makes the latter unseen partners, as it were, in the purpose he seeks to implement." Ministers now are for the most part so obscure that they have become the unseen partners in government by civil service. The only time they lose their obscurity is when public blame has to be attached for wrongheaded or badly executed policies. Nobody had heard of Barbara McDougall, minister of state for finance, until in 1985 she had to carry the can in Parliament for the collapse of two regional banks caused by the enormous bungling of the Bank of Canada and of the regional banks' executives. The civil service — in this case the Bank of Canada — accepted no blame at all. It pointed at everybody but itself, reaffirming the basic civil service philosophy and practice of non-accountability.

The civil service is secure. It has tenure, the highest civil service salaries in the world, and somebody else to take the blame for its blunders. The corollary used to be that ministers would receive the praise for beneficial policies well executed. But such policies now are so few, if detectable at all, that the corollary seldom if ever applies any more. The highest principle for a deputy minister used to be to make his minister look good. But his governing principle now is to make himself look good in the eyes of the central agencies — mainly, the prime minister's office, the privy council office (it is almost impossible now to differentiate between these two) and the treasury board. They, not the cabinet, are the route to more promotions and more money.

I submit that we would be better off if we returned to the old patronage system of the government appointing all civil servants. The government already pleads the necessity of "outside" patronage in the senior ranks of the civil service as a means to inject new outlooks and fresh talents. If this is good enough for the upper crust, as it is now (the prime minister directly controls 2,000 senior appointments), it should be good enough for the underlings. Indeed, there is a good example from the last general election how well this works. In 1984, one hundred and ten thousand temporary civil servants were appointed by the political parties to enumerate the voters. They did so without fuss or complaint. The enumerators were paid on the basis of productivity: forty-eight cents for each enumeration for the first two hundred names, seventy-two cents a name after that. No overtime. No Thursday-to-Tuesday weekends with pay. No fancy expense accounts: a maximum $18 for incidentals, such as bus fare. No committees. No special courses in Las Vegas, Banff or Monaco, just $18 maximum for a training session. The enumerators were nominated by the candidates who ran first and second in the last previous election. Returning officers accepted the nominations. The whole operation was quick, smooth and value for money.

Why not run the whole civil service this way? We used to, and it was lean and cost-conscious. It had to be, because the servants could be dumped at any time, and often were. But the best ones rose and good ones stayed and that led to our assumption (no longer defended, let alone assumed) that we had the best civil service in the world.

Well, there were drawbacks, certainly.

Samuel Thompson, editor of the *Toronto Daily Colonist*, recounted in an 1884 book a story about William Lyon Mackenzie, printer and reformer. When he arrived in Montreal from Scotland in 1820, Mackenzie got a job as chain-bearer on the survey of the Lachine Canal. "A few days afterwards, the surveying party, as usual at noon, sat down on a grassy bank to eat their dinner. They had been thus occupied for half an hour, and were getting ready for a smoke, when the new chain-bearer suddenly jumped up with an exclamation: 'Now, boys, time for work! We mustn't waste the government's money!' The consequence of his ill-timed outburst was his prompt dismissal from the service." (That reminds me: historian Donald Creighton wrote: "William Lyon Mackenzie's career as a journalist probably encouraged his tendency to invective and disorderly verbosity.")

On July 28, 1860, Chauncy Bullock, revenue officer for the district of St. Francis, Canada East (Quebec), wrote to the Commissioner of Customs, R.S.M. Bouchette, describirtg one of his officers, Thomas Williamson, as a "useless tax" on his office and an "unmitigated public disgrace" because of "idleness, dissipation and stupidity." Then Bullock added: "I did not intend to ask for his dismission from the public service. I was only anxious to relieve this port from a useless and disgraceful incumbent."

On January 10, 1945, George Pickering, collector of Customs at Prince Albert, Saskatchewan, wrote to his superintendent in Ottawa: "Re: report of staff — Form H. MacLeod, Roderick has been rated as passable as he appears to regard his position as merely a sideline, accepting Customs entries and passing them without proper checking, causing much additional work in the department at this port."

In 1975, the Treasury Board created a "temporary assignment pool" for middle-ranking civil servants unloaded as unwanted by other departments. At November 30, 1984, there were forty bureaucrats in this pool drawing annual salaries of between $50,000 and $80,970. Some of them managed to be farmed out temporarily to jobs which included "task force co-ordinator, review of national defence activities," "co-ordinator of the management plan sector and corporate planning, External Affairs," and "advisor to the federal co-ordinator on urea formaldehyde foam insulation."

At Confederation, the federal government controlled all appointments in the civil service from, in an official phrase of the time, "the highest to the lowest." A recommendation by your local MP, especially if he were on the government side, was tantamount to a job. In 1880, a royal commission on the civil service was told the government departments had tried to use examinations to test the qualifications of applicants for government positions but that the only qualification that meant anything was an MP's recommendation. Some of the most enjoyable reading I have ever found in government documents are patronage letters by Prime Minister John A. Macdonald. Allow me to cite a couple, because Macdonald could see clearly and state candidly the buffoonery in many aspects of patronage.

On July 18, 1884, Macdonald wrote his minister of Customs, Mackenzie Bowell, from his cottage, Les Rochers, at St. Patrick, near Rivière du Loup, on behalf of Capt. Charette, whose schooner *Andora* had been seized for smuggling liquor. Macdonald said: "I send them [the affidavits] to you so that you may if possible have mercy upon the owner of the schooner and let him off as your conscience will allow."

Six days later, Macdonald asked Bowell not to hire Asher Farrow, a member of Parliament: "Remember Asher will never run again as M.P. and only thinks now of his family and not of the party.... Farrow already has had more than his share of the loaves and fishes."

3
———

You Can't Fire Me — I'm a Civil Servant

Another drawback to the old patronage system was that few ministers or MPs were willing to concede that they had backed a wastrel for a government job, so that laziness, incompetence and drunkenness were usually dealt with by transfer rather than dismissal. But this holds today. The only change is that the backer of the wastrel is a civil servant instead of a politician. Many transfers can be carried out only by concurrent promotion. That is why so many incompetents rise in the civil service until, to everybody's astonishment and dismay, they are at the top of the heap. Trying to fire an incompetent is much more trouble that fobbing him off on an unsuspecting department. Written recommendations on behalf of a civil servant seeking another job should be, but often aren't, treated with the highest suspicion. The grievance procedure has defeated many civil service employers who have tried to get rid of undesirables. There was the Toronto case in 1982 of a postal employee who was dismissed on the grounds of bank robbery, but was reinstated when he showed that he had participated in the robbery outside his post office working hours, that is, on his own time. In January, 1986, the public service staff relations board reinstated a civilian cook fired after conviction for theft from an armed forces kitchen. The cook explained that he had been coaxed into the theft by a female cook at the same base who promised him sex in exchange for groceries.

4

___

Upper Town and Lower Town

Ottawa was originally a lumber town with the owners living in their mansions in Upper Town and along the river and the millworkers and raftsmen crowded into Lower Town. When the civil service arrived in 1866, the bureaucracy joined the lumber barons in Upper Town. The working stiff and civil servant bore each other a restrained animosity. One of my favorite accounts of the division between rich and poor in Ottawa is contained in Jack London's *The Road*. London was riding the freights across North America when he hit Ottawa in the fall of 1894:

> Let me put it on record right here that Ottawa, with one exception, is the hardest town in the United States and Canada to beg clothes in; the one exception is Washington, D.C.... At eight sharp in the morning I started out after clothes. I worked energetically all day. I swear I walked forty miles. I interviewed the housewives of a thousand homes. I did not even knock off work for dinner. And at six in the afternoon, after ten hours of unremitting and depressing toil, I was still shy one shirt....
>
> At six I quit work and headed for the railroad yards, expecting to pick up something to eat on the way. But my hard luck was still with me. I was refused food at house after house. Then I got a hand-out. My spirits soared, for it was the largest hand-out I had ever seen in a long and varied experience. It was a parcel wrapped in newspaper and as big as a mature suitcase. I hurried to a vacant lot and opened it. First, I saw cake, then more cake, all kinds and makes of cake, and then some. It was all cake. No bread and butter with thick firm slices of meat between — nothing but cake. I suppose I was an ungrateful tramp, for I refused to partake of the bounteousness of the house that had had a party the night before.

An illuminating view of how the civil service set itself apart from Canadians generally is contained in the resolution of a Canadian Legion convention in 1934. It criticizes the failure of veterans who were federal civil servants to join the Legion after it had defeated a government plan to eliminate their disability pensions and stoutly defended veterans preference in civil service hiring. The Legion's magazine commented:

> It has to be regretfully recorded that thousands of ex-servicemen in government jobs whose pensions had been saved through the vigorous resistance of the associated veterans, led by the Canadian Legion, promptly forgot all about the Legion once the battle was won for them.
>
> As a measure of ordinary gratitude, one would have expected the civil servants to join the Legion, even if for no other purpose than to ensure that the rights which the Legion had secured for them might be enjoyed by others of their former comrades in a position of less security than they themselves.
>
> Self-sacrifices and efforts on behalf of those in secure and sheltered employment, while in preserving for them their pensions intact, failed to extract from them any gesture of appreciation or thanks.

5

Another Slurp at the Trough

The patronage system in the lower ranks of the civil service continued well into this century despite a 1908 act of Parliament proclaiming the merit principle as supreme in civil service hiring. When the Liberals were returned to power in 1926, Postmaster General Peter John Veniot dismissed three hundred and fifty postmasters across the country and replaced them with Liberal appointees. When the Conservatives complained, Veniot had only to remind them that he had been dismissed from his civil service job in exactly the same way after the Tory election victory in 1911. Well into the 1930s, entire sections of the civil service outside Ottawa were reserved for ministerial appointment. Any civil servant accused by an MP of political partisanship was automatically dismissed. Despite this, complaints about patronage appointments were far fewer than those about the difficulty of getting rid of deadwood.

In recent years, patronage appointments, whether to the Senate, bench, diplomatic corps, deputy ministerships, crown corporations, commissions or boards, were generally accepted with little more than a shrug or raised eyebrow. (A line in the Saskatchewan musical play *Paper Wheat* had it that Canadians would never know Ottawa was there except for the occasional scandal). What suddenly made patronage offensively odorous was the Trudeau-Turner cramming of the Liberal trough in June and July, 1984. Poor old Turner, sabotaged by Trudeau, who despises him. Turner didn't even see the swiftly-approaching disaster: the light at the end of the tunnel is usually the train coming at you. Even the unspeakable Bryce Mackasey was given another slurp at the trough, though it was short-lived; before he could even get to his appointment as ambassador to Portugal he was replaced by the equally unspeakable Lloyd Francis, the former speaker. (Speakers are usually looked after in this way. Diefenbaker wouldn't appoint Roland Michener to anything because he so disliked Michener's wife, Norah; it was left to Pearson to make Michener ambassador to India.)

It wasn't the usual poor quality of the Trudeau-Turner patronage that upset the voters so much as the quantity — 225 appointments by Trudeau in his last month in office (the usual number is 300 to 400 a year), and a dozen by Turner in his first few days. One nice touch, whether by wit or gall, was the appointment of a Liberal MP to the Livestock Feed Board. If the troughing had been spaced out in the normal way, few would have noticed except the appointees. But it was a method Trudeau could use to undermine the naive Turner. As a public expense, patronage appointments are relatively cheap. The much costlier patronage is represented by tax remissions, tax loopholes for the rich, and such official scams as the scientific research tax credit. Brian Mulroney, in his early months at least, confined his patronage to appointments. There were lots of them, but what the hell, the Conservatives had been the "outs" for so long he could hardly be blamed, and he used some non-Tory graspers like Stephen Lewis and Dennis McDermott to deflect attention from the flood of Conservative appointees. Mulroney didn't become prime minister to preside over the liquidation of patronage.

6
———

That Was Then ... This Is Now

The civil service always had an influence on government simply by being there. But until the Second World War, when it tripled in size, it was still a fairly compact group (at Confederation, the three Parliament Buildings housed the Commons, Senate, the governor-general's office and all government departments) which was well aware how difficult it was to raise tax money and therefore counted the pennies. Here's an example from a memorandum written May 29, 1942, by G.N. Bunker, chief inspector of Customs and Excise, to the Customs man at Dorval airport, Montreal:

> With reference to the drinking cups for the Waiting Room, since the Department of Transport has decided to do away with this service in lieu of the drinking fountain in the main waiting room, I can see no reason why this Department should provide the required cups. It will, therefore, be necessary for passengers to wait for drinking water either until they have cleared Customs or until they board the plane.

And thus were federal budgets balanced.

The beginning of the switch in roles between government and civil service can, I think, be traced to the 1930s when O.D. Skelton, the deputy minister of external affairs, subverted Prime Minister R.B. Bennett's policy that Canada live up to its League of Nations obligations, including economic sanctions. Skelton opposed sanctions and was the major obstacle in Bennett's attempt to fulfill what he saw as Canada's international commitments. Mackenzie King, who succeeded Bennett in 1935, was a willing listener to Skelton and Canada opted out of all League undertakings (it wasn't the only one, by any means).

External affairs has always considered itself a law unto itself. This shows particularly in its snobbery. In 1966, Canadian veterans of the 1941 Hong Kong disaster returned to Hong Kong for a twenty-fifth anniversary memorial service. External arranged the accommodations: all the former officers were to stay in a posh downtown hotel; all the former non-commissioned ranks in Stanley barracks, the very place where they had been held as prisoners-of-war for three and a half years. That kind of thing is still going on. When Hong Kong veterans went back in 1985 to mark the fortieth anniversary of their release, External held a reception for the official party and excluded all the Canadian veterans who had paid their own way to Hong Kong. It required a public report by Auditor-General Kenneth Dye to put a stop in 1985 to $750,000 worth of publicly-paid memberships in an exclusive Hong Kong club for members and families of External's staff there. Up to then, no minister had been powerful enough to halt such blatant misuse of public funds.

External has always felt part of the Liberal establishment. It came to it naturally, I suppose, when Pearson was the deputy minister for ten years and then the minister for ten more and prime minister for another five after that. When Diefenbaker was prime minister, External systematically tried to subvert any policy to which it thought Peason would object. It accommodated itself in time to Trudeau but it tried to sabotage the Joe Clark ministry. We have former External Affairs Minister Flora Mac-Donald's testimony for that. She said in an article written in 1980 that she was entrapped by civil servants in her own department into blocking any change in the previous government's policies. That was because those policies were devised and implemented by the civil service, not the government; the policies were not politically partisan so much as civil service status quo. Miss MacDonald went to some pains to detail how entrapment worked: breathless corridor encounters demanding immediate decision; memos long and numerous; submissions for cabinet produced at the last second and with only one option, the civil service position. Her deputy minister was Allan Gotlieb who, as soon as Trudeau was back, arranged his appointment as ambassador to Washington. Gotlieb turned out to be one of the worst informed ambassadors in the history of our diplomatic service. He and his wife, Sondra, (his public temper tantrums were even worse than hers) invited the very best people to their high table but were so busy talking about themselves that they neglected to inquire about what was going on in Washington.

There was always easy, almost foreordained transmigration of Liberals from civil service to government benches, even from civil service to government benches and back to the civil service. C.M. Drury was deputy defence minister, held Liberal cabinet portfolios from 1963 to 1975, then went back to the civil service as chairman of the National Capital Commission until 1984. J.W. Pickersgill was secretary to the cabinet, a cabinet minister, and chairman of the Canadian Transport Commission. Mitchell Sharp was deputy trade minister, a cabinet minister in the Pearson and Trudeau ministries, then pipeline commissioner (for a non-existent pipeline). Pierre Juneau was a civil servant as chairman of the Canadian Radio and Television Commission, communications minister in the Trudeau cabinet (briefly, because he couldn't win a Commons seat), and returned to the civil service, first through the National Capital Commission and then through the CBC. Lionel Chevrier held the record: minister of transport; president of the St. Lawrence Seaway; back to cabinet as justice minister; back to the civil service as high commissioner in London. Liberal cabinet ministers Edgar Benson, Jean Marchand, Gérard Pelletier, Bryce Mackasey, Léo Cadieux, Paul Martin, Barnett Danson, Don Jamieson, Roger Teillet, Jack Horner, Jean-Luc Pépin, John Munro and others got cushy government jobs; others went to the Senate and the bench. Ministers like Pearson, Trudeau, Maurice Lamontagne, Jacob Austin and Martin O'Connell had been civil servants. (I can't recall a single member of the Diefenbaker cabinet who ever got a federal government job, cushy or otherwise.)

There is another tradition building up among Liberal appointees: clinging to high-paying office despite illness so severe that the office cannot be properly filled. Cases include Bora Laskin as chief justice of the Supreme Court of Canada, Jules Léger, governor-general, and Drury at the National Capital Commission. There is a stable of Liberal historians always available to tilt Canadian history Liberalward.

7

No Public to Serve but Itself

As late as the 1950s, and even into the early 1960s, the government was run by the government. Cabinet sat around a big table in the East Block, decided on a policy, and instructed the civil service to put it into effect, pronto. The only civil servant present was the clerk of the privy council, i.e., the secretary to the cabinet, and he (never a woman, yet) was there to record the decision. That's all changed now. Cabinet ministers still sit around a table — in tiers, because there are so many of them — but their agenda comprises policies and papers drawn up by bureaucrats who, to ensure implementation of their self-programmed programs, sit right at the same table, sometimes flanking the minister-chairman, including the prime minister. In the 1950s, the Liberals came to rely more and more on the civil service for ideas. The civil service could hardly be blamed for seizing the opportunity; it took over the apparatus as well as the policy-making. Allow me to cite a few examples here:

Politicians, gritting their teeth, accepted the six-and-five program in 1983-84 restraining pay increases to those percentages. Not the civil service. Largely through upward reclassifications and promotions, incomes of federal civil servants grew by an average 9.5 per cent in 1983 to $8.2 billion from $7.5 billion in 1982.

Crown-owned de Havilland Aircraft of Canada Ltd. lost $236 million in 1983 and began to lay off workers. The twelve senior executives of the company helped themselves to bonuses totalling $115,000. The government appeared powerless to block these self-gifts. Indeed, it defended them in the House of Commons.

The Ottawa mandarins are paid $110,000 a year, about $25,000 more (in Canadian terms) than their American counterparts in Washington. Each year, they award one of their number $5,000 of the taxpayers' money for "distinguished achievement."

Auditor-General Kenneth Dye says that the advisers who told Trudeau to refuse him access to cabinet documents on the Petro-fina takeover were still in the privy council office working for Prime Minister Mulroney, who also denied Dye access to the papers. Dye has gone to court to try to get them. The inference is that it is not government but the civil service which wants the Petrofina deal hidden forever. Deputy ministers have a long history of opposing attempts by Canada's auditors-general to dig out information on public spending.

Michael Pitfield, when secretary to the cabinet, didn't even bother to call the cabinet minister concerned, let alone seek his approval, when he shuffled the minister's deputy to another post. In his brief reign, Prime Minister Clark managed to fire Pitfield, but he had to give him $100,000 in severance pay to do it. When Trudeau came back in 1980, so did Pitfield. He tried like hell later but couldn't find a job in the private sector and had to settle for a Senate appointment. Then he put in a huge bill for overtime as clerk of the privy council. The treasury board paid him a handsome, if not the full, amount, though nobody has been able to find out how much. Only one politician ever stood up to Pitfield: Allan MacEachen. When Pitfield protested appointment of a defeated Cape Breton Conservative to a government board, MacEachen told him sharply: "When you've been elected in Cape Breton, come and talk to me."

The Canadian Transport Commission until 1987 had no one but a former Liberal cabinet minister as president: Pickersgill, Benson, and Marchand. The commission is supposed to regulate, among other enterprises, Air Canada, but between 1973 and 1984 no fewer than 107 members of the commission and their "travelling companions" accepted annual and trip passes from Air Canada.

The armed forces offer good career pickings. In four months between March 31 and July 31, 1982, while the number of military remained unchanged, the number of major-generals increased to 33 from 24, the number of brigadier-generals to 84 from 75, and the number of colonels to 1,356 from 1,277. On July 31, 1982, there were 43,548 non-commissioned officers in our armed forces compared with 23,528 privates. On January 1, 1986, there were 50,944 non-commissioned officers and 15,631 privates. At this rate, there will be no privates at all by 1994.

Despite so-called decentralization, veterans affairs is the only department headquarters to have been shifted out of Ottawa. Others haven't moved because the bureaucrats can't bear to be away, even for a short period, from the seat of power, perks and pay. They might be overlooked or, worse, forgotten. Indeed, the deputy minister of veterans affairs still has his office in Ottawa. It took years and $28 million to relocate veterans affairs in Charlottetown, but the department still has, in Charlottetown, a man who holds the post "director general corporate planning, national capital operations."

In 1975, the National Capital Commission, a crown agency, sent scores of its employees to see the movie *The Towering Inferno* at public expense on the grounds of promoting fire safety. The public purse was not reimbursed.

The National Library listed among its "major acquisitions" in 1985-86: "Melhorn, Lise. *My God, Ain't She Long.* Toronto; Transformer Press, 1984. Portfolio contains 3 sets of connected paper dolls cut from sheet of paper. Limited edition of 25 signed and numbered copies."

In 1985, more than half of all appointments in the federal civil service (54.3 per cent) were made without competition for the jobs. Nearly all appointments are internal, and the public is rarely advised to apply, let alone compete.

At April 1, 1982, the population of the Yukon was 23,000. At the same date, there were 3,510 civil servants in the Yukon, 2,203 territorial and 1,307 federal. The Yukon may be the first entity to attain the Canadian millenium: a public service with no public to serve but itself.

Membership in the Privy Council is generally confined to cabinet ministers, past and present. Three civil service secretaries to the cabinet, Gordon Robertson, Michael Pitfield and Gordon Osbaldeston, all Liberal appointees, are members of the Privy Council. Marcel Massé, who was secretary to the cabinet under Joe Clark, is not. Walter Dinsdale, northern affairs minister in the Diefenbaker government, told Peter Stursberg in an interview recorded for the Public Archives of Canada that Robertson, when his deputy minister, subverted nearly every policy he tried to introduce. Two months after the Liberals' return to power in 1963, Robertson was promoted secretary to the cabinet.

Enough examples for the moment. Let's look at the mechanics of civil service control of the government.

8
_____

Let's Have a Committee

Pearson placated a restive civil service, starting with seaway workers, with enormous wage increases in the mid-1960s. The civil service became one of the best-paying occupations in Canada, including medicine, law and plumbing. Not only were civil servants given tenure as entrenched as that of university professors, but also the right to strike. What a combination: you can hardly ever be fired but you can strike for higher pay. Apart from the post office (no wonder: the post office has eighteen vice-presidents) there are few civil service strikes. The employees don't want to miss a single day of that good pay.

The lucrative Trudeau years began. He introduced, to delighted response from the civil service, what became known as the "collegial" system. The word is in none of my three dictionaries but it means, basically, "let's have a committee." You name a subject in Ottawa, there's a committee for it, from the tiniest branch in a government department up to and including the cabinet. All options are considered, then reconsidered. Anyone with the remotest connection with a subject must be consulted, interested or not, and, of course, by committee meeting, never by a single telephone call or letter. The civil service loved it because the more committees the more people and the more people you have working for you the bigger the purported responsibility and the quicker the promotion and the fatter the paycheque. The civil service expanded in the late 1960s and 1970s at a rate of ten to twelve per cent a year. Liberal Works Minister Jean-Eudes Dubé (later part of the Liberal stuffing of the federal court) put it all in a nutshell when he proclaimed to the Ottawa construction industry, "Put up the office buildings. We'll fill 'em up." Very few fought the multiplication of the civil service. One was the late Robert Andras when he was president of the Treasury Board. Douglas Fullerton, government economist, declared (into the wind): "Fire a third of the civil service and double its efficiency."

In the middle and higher echelons of the bureaucracy, promotion and salary increase came every eighteen months to two years, or oftener. The Trudeau-Pitfield system was to keep the mandarins on the move with the result that bureaucrats sang and danced their way through a position just long enough to pick up more salary but not long enough to learn anything about the job. Fast moves enabled the senior civil servants to escape accountability: "Don't look at me, I just got here," or "Don't look at me, I'm not there any more."

Accountability is listed last in the Treasury Board's 1983 "Principles for the Management of the Public Service of Canada." It says:

> Managers are held responsible, and hold their subordinates responsible, for their performance within a system of accountable management that contains the following elements: mutually agreed objectives and priorities which are defined and stated as clearly as possible in view of the complexity of the environment, and which are expressed in terms of a contractual understanding which ensures an obligation and commitment to the achievement of expected results within available resources; the assignment of authority and resources commensurate with expected results; a performance measurement, evaluation and feedback system that keeps both managers and subordinates aware of progress towards expected results; means of ensuring that employee performance is appraised on the results achieved and that rewards or sanctions follow equitably from such appraisal.

That's the entire instruction on accountability; there is no glossary with it.

Perhaps we might give a couple of examples of how accountability works, first in the case of a film produced by the National Film Board and, second, in civil service conflict-of-interest instructions.

9

Docu-Bull: Rewriting History, NFB Style

In 1982, the publicly-financed National Film Board released a film called *The Kid Who Couldn't Miss* and labelled it a documentary about Billy Bishop, the famous Canadian World War One flier who shot down seventy-two German planes.

There were more than 3,000 letters of protest about the film and the Board quietly shelved it for a year waiting for the heat to die down. It didn't. The Manitoba branch of the Royal Military College Club (Bishop attended RMC) did an exhaustive study of the film's more than thirty errors in fact, other groups such as the Royal Canadian Air Force Association launched protests and finally the veterans affairs committee of the Senate held an inquiry.

The central point of the protests was that the film described Bishop as a cheat and liar. It ascribed to a long-dead Walter Bourne, Bishop's mechanic, a fiction that the WWI ace had faked a raid for which he won the Victoria Cross by landing his plane, shooting holes in its tail to simulate action, and returning to base claiming three German planes destroyed. To dispose of this point, the following exchange took place on November 28, 1985, in the committee between Senator D.D. Everett and Paul Cowan, director of the film:

> Everett: And you agree that Bourne never made those statements?
> Cowan: Yes.
> Everett: These were statements that were put into his mouth?
> Cowan: Yes.

Two successive cabinet ministers charged with responsibility for speaking for the National Film Board washed their hands of any responsibility for the film. On May 14, 1984, Liberal Communications Minister Francis Fox told the RCAF Association: "I must reiterate that it would be inappropriate for me to intervene in the internal affairs of the NFB. This is not to say that I do not regard your complaints as meriting serious consideration." Fox's Conservative successor, Marcel Masse, told the same association November 16, 1984: "I must also state that it would be inappropriate for me to intervene in the internal matters of the NFB.... I must also decline your request for a meeting between you, Mr. Macerola (or his representative) and myself as I feel it would unduly question the integrity of the NFB, and the appropriateness of their decision not to change the content of the film."

François Macerola, NFB commissioner, wouldn't accept responsibility for the film either. He refused to talk to any of the protesters. Most requests to him for meetings were not even acknowledged. Prof. A.R. Kear, president of the RMC Club which had done the critique on the film, put on the Senate committee record his 1985 letters to Macerola on May 27, July 22 and September 11 to which he received no reply at all. Finally, after the Senate decided to examine the affair, Macerola wrote to Kear October 22 that he couldn't meet the club because the film was a "subject of deliberations" by the committee. On April 15, 1985, Cowan also refused to meet club members to discuss his film.

Macerola and Cowan then tried to avoid testifying before the committee. The commissioner had the Board lawyers (he himself had been a Board lawyer) try to beg off but Parliament's lawyers informed them that Macerola and Cowan could be subpoenaed if they did not appear willingly. The senators had to wring from Macerola a concession that as a parliamentary body the committee was entitled to question him. Even at that, Macerola held that the committee could ask about the general principles on which the Board operated, but not about an individual film. The senators ignored him.

I won't take you through the whole sorry performance of Macerola's flight from accountability. In the end, he announced that every print of the film would be recalled and relabelled as fiction ("docu-drama") instead of documentary, but insisted with ill grace that the change really didn't mean anything, and Cowan chimed in that the film was just as "true" as it had ever been. Senator Finlay MacDonald quoted to Macerola a 1964 statement to the National Film Board by its founder, John Grierson:

I have come to remind you that you are all employees of the Government of Canada. You are still civil servants using tax money and working for the benefit of the people of Canada. This is not a playground. It has come to my attention recently that the Film Board more and more is becoming infiltrated with arty-tarty types who intend to use the facilities which it offers for their own private purposes. There will come a time, and mark my words it will come, when the limit of public tolerance will be transgressed and the activities of the Board will be severely curtailed.

In 1985, Deputy Prime Minister Erik Nielsen's task force on government expenditures proposed a $20 million cut in the National Film Board's annual budget of $63 million. This recommendation, like all others by the task force for heavy cuts, was ignored by the civil service.

10

Conflict of Interest: The Popular Choice

The "Conflict of Interest and Post-Employment Code for the Public Service" issued by the federal government through the treasury board in October, 1985, is outwardly very stern. For instance:

Employees must, within 60 days after appointment, make a Confidential Report to the designated official of all assets other than exempt assets as described in section 20 and of all direct and contingent liabilities, where such assets and liabilities might give rise to a conflict of interest in respect of the employee's official duties and responsibilities. Assets and Liabilities subject to Confidential Report:
Section 22
(a) publicly traded securities of corporations and foreign governments and self-administered registered retirement savings plans composed of such securities;
(b) interests in partnerships, proprietorships, joint ventures, private companies and family businesses, in particular those that own or control shares of public companies or that do business with the government;
(c) farms under commercial operation;
(d) real property that is not an exempt asset;
(e) commodities, futures and foreign currencies held or traded for speculative purposes;
(f) assets that are beneficially owned, that are not exempt assets and that are administered at arm's length;
(g) secured or unsecured loans granted to persons other than to members of the employee's immediate family;
(h) any other assets or liabilities that could give rise to a

real or potential conflict of interest due to the particular nature of the employee's duties and responsibilities; and (i) direct and contingent liabilities in respect of any of the assets described in this section.

And so the rules go on for eighteen pages. However, the confidential report which the civil servant actually signs is a pussy-cat. It contains this popular choice: "I do own or possess assets and/or I have responsibilities identified in Section 22, but my owning or possessing such assets, or my having such liabilities, does not give rise to a real or potential conflict of interest relative to my official duties and responsibilities."

Here's an actual conflict-of-interest case:

Mr. G. was office manager at Senneterre, Quebec, for the federal employment department. A forestry company supported by more than $550,000 in federal and Quebec job-creation funds ran into trouble and Mr. G. was ordered to try to sort out the company's problems. Mr. G. worked with the company for four years and was eventually installed as president while continuing his federal government job. He put himself and his wife on the company payroll and made many trips, including two to Paris, to drum up business for the company. The department eventually got wind of what was going on and fired Mr. G. However, on appeal, the Public Service Staff Relations Board reinstated him on the grounds that though he had violated the department's conflict-of-interest regulations, the department had let Mr. G. sink into the conflict through lack of supervision.

11

Drowning in a Paper River

The civil service takeover of government by drowning ministers in a river of paper includes these major elements:

- There are 300 meetings annually of cabinet or cabinet committees.
- Nearly 1,000 memoranda are discussed in these meetings. They are not one-page documents, but may easily run to 100 single-space foolscap pages swimming in gobbledegook.

- The memoranda are prepared by civil servants, who brief all ministers, including the prime minister. (When Mulroney took office in September, 1984, his first briefer was not a politician but Trudeau appointee Gordon Osbaldeston, clerk of the privy council.) Civil servants are present at all cabinet meetings. Civil servants take the minutes. They write the 750 annual decisions by cabinet.
- There are committees of deputy ministers which correspond to cabinet committees, and some of them meet weekly, as often as the cabinet. There is even a co-ordinating committee of deputy ministers which meets weekly. There have been, at one time, more than 100 interdepartmental committees at the level of deputy minister or assistant deputy minister.
- Interdepartmental consultation has completely hornswoggled any initiative by a single department or a single minister. In December, 1983, Ian Clark, then deputy secretary to the cabinet, wrote in a memo for his civil service colleagues:

It should be emphasized that the existence of the deputies committees does not affect the right of any Minister to bring any proposal he wishes to his colleagues. A Minister can sign a Memorandum to Cabinet that completely ignores comments made by officials in other departments and in the central agencies. A Minister could, if he wishes, insist that a Memorandum be put directly into the Cabinet system without any officials outside his department seeing it. However, the other side of the collective decision-making coin is that the Minister's colleagues have the right to know how the proposal will affect their portfolio interests and they can equally insist that a decision not be taken until these issues are clarified. Such clarification usually requires consultation among the officials reporting to the respective Ministers.

In other words, boys, we've got 'em coming or going.

Few, if any, policy ideas come from ministers now. They're too busy reading policy proposals by civil servants and sitting around at cabinet meetings dotting i's and crossing t's on documents prepared by the civil service, but deferentially bearing ministers' signatures. Then Resources Minister Alvin Hamilton is believed the last cabinet minister ever to present to cabinet a policy (roads to resources) not prepared by the civil service. That was in 1958. Most government documents now are so wordy that the chief occupation of some civil servants is to read them and mark in yellow crayon only the important sentences to save the time (and patience) of ministers trying to scan them. Often there are only one or two yellowed sentences in half a dozen pages. In the vital cabinet committee on priorities and planning, the deputy minister of finance is as much a fixture as the chairman, who is the prime minister. Before meetings of this committee, the prime minister is briefed by the privy council office. His briefing book usually consists of a three-inch-thick binder with all the pertinent documents and a briefing note of up to a dozen pages on each agenda item prepared by the privy council office. In other important cabinet committees such as economic and regional development, and foreign and defence policy, the minister-chairman is flanked by his two senior officials. Key departments such as finance and treasury board are also represented by civil servants. In the cabinet committee of treasury board, the minister-chairman and his ministerial colleagues sit on one side of the table and the civil servants on the treasury board sit on the other. Guess which side has more information.

There are standing committees of deputy ministers and they more or less mirror the committees of cabinet. Some meet weekly, some twice a month, some less frequently. These committees hear reports on pertinent cabinet decisions and on the "atmosphere" of cabinet meetings which have dealt with subjects of concern to the appropriate deputies. Proposals by departments requiring cabinet approval or other action are discussed at the meetings of deputies and advice is given on issues which should be covered in cabinet submissions. In other words, everything is co-ordinated in advance before cabinet ministers ever get a look at the issue. The deputies maintain, of course, that they only advise, never decide. But they have been, for instance, the chief assailants of the auditor-general of Canada for allegedly questioning policies instead of sticking to auditing. The civil service smarted so severely under the constant exposure of its follies by the auditor-general that it easily persuaded the Trudeau government to establish the department of the comptroller-general. This department in effect intercepts and tries to cover up civil service financial blunders before they can reach the stern eye of the auditor-general, with attendant publicity. In 1983-84, this department had 170 employees and their average annual salary was $70,000. The civil service is keen on keeping the auditor-general away from the field of policy because it is generally responsible for the policies in question. The fight between the auditor-general, who reports directly to Parliament and whose reports therefore cannot be watered down before they reach Parliament, and the civil service rages on, vehemently.

12

Writing Their Own Tickets

The connection between the civil service and the Liberals did not go unnoticed by the Conservatives all those years, of course. The Clark government in 1980 vowed to erase 60,000 civil service jobs in three years. Nothing happened, and when the Conservatives got back in they promised to eliminate 15,000 jobs in five years, an indication that they caught on quickly that it is unwise to fool around with the real government. Stories about Tory "hit lists" in the senior civil service evaporated one by one and almost the entire Liberal-appointed mandarinate remained in place. Instead of tackling the bureaucracy directly, the Conservatives instead tried the tactic of setting up another to fight it. Ministerial executive assistants were transformed into chiefs of staff with more salary and, presumably, more power. But the civil service made short work of most of them because the chiefs of staff were mostly newcomers to Ottawa or inexperienced in such jobs and they had to go cap-in-hand to the regular bureaucrats for information.

In Ottawa, accurate data is precious in the daily struggles for power and prestige. The civil service is armed to the teeth. Mulroney also has tried (vainly) to fight the bureaucracy by enlarging the prime minister's office beyond even its Trudeau-inflated size. It's the old story: too many chefs spoil the gruel. By contrast, on the Monday morning after Mulroney was elected Conservative leader, Pete Thomson and I were talking on the sidewalk in front of the Chateau Laurier when Mulroney emerged with Senator Jacques Flynn. There were no taxis available and the Conservatives had sent no car. Mulroney set off on foot. Who would subscribe to a party that can't even organize a ride for its new leader?

It has been shown repeatedly, mainly by the auditor-general, that the civil service is 20 per cent overclassified in their jobs. In other words, one-fifth of the civil service is overpaid, the extra cost being $125 million a year. The Treasury Board has been promising for years to do something about it and in 1985 Jack Manion, secretary of the Treasury Board, said the review of classification procedures — not the classifications themselves — would be completed in two years. Even at that, one of the civil service unions complained that the government was breaking a promise that job classification would be part of union bargaining.

While still in opposition, Mulroney proposed that deputy ministers in the most senior jobs, such as finance and trade, be required to testify before a parliamentary committee on their qualifications and their views on a broad range of economic and social affairs. He even suggested that their appointments would have to be ratified by the committee. When he became prime minister, new deputy ministers of finance and trade went unquestioned by committee.

Civil servants are mostly still able to write their own tickets.

Timothy Porteous had been in the Liberal trough since 1966 when he was an executive assistant in the office of the minister of industry. He later went to Trudeau's office and then to the Canada Council in 1973, becoming director in 1982. In 1985, after twenty years of Liberal welfare, he called a press conference to complain that he was being "terminated" by the Mulroney government. It had offered him, can you imagine, a subordinate job in the Canadian consulate in Los Angeles.

When Simon Reisman was appointed special ambassador for free-trade negotiations with the United States, at $1,000 a day, he insisted on retaining his directorships in two Canadian companies — George Weston Ltd. and Bombardier, Inc. — which have a stake in the outcome of the negotiations. Under pressure, he announced May 23, 1986, that he was relinquishing the two directorships. Reisman would be chagrinned to know that his daily fee has been surpassed by the $1,600-a-day paid to a consultant from Touche Ross by the National Capital Commission.

In July, 1985, the cabinet increased the top annual salary ranges of four prominent appointees: to $475,00 from $380,000 for Wilbert Hopper, Petro-Canada chairman; to $455, 000 from $370,000 for Edward Lakusta, Petro-Canada president; to $325,000 from $245,000 for Dr. Maurice LeClair, chairman of Canadian National Railways; and to $160,000 from $114,260 for Lawrence Hanigan, chairman of VIA Rail.

In October, 1983, Trefflé Lacombe, a member of the Public Service Commission, said the government must find solutions to the frustrations of civil servants confronted by a sharp drop in promotion opportunities. At the time, unemployment stood at 1.5 million.

The Public Service Commission has a history of saying out-of-touch things like that. Consider this quote from its 1983 annual report marking the seventy-fifth anniversary of the so-called merit principle in the civil service:

> The Commission's ultimate goal is to continue to encourage the current evolution toward a staffing approach that is better adapted to the needs of the Public Service and the expectations of Canadians, while meeting the requirements of the public interest, impartiality and merit. This will greatly strengthen the confidence and mutual trust that already exist between the Public Service and the Canadian people.

Here's another from the same report: "The merit principle guarantees the competence of public servants, but it is not an absolute concept."

13
―――

Give Me Job Security and Hold the National Unity

I think it is worth looking at the Commission's jelly-like role in the Parti Québécois referendum on the partition of Canada in 1980.

Late in the 1979 federal election campaign, the Commission got the wind up about civil servants participating, or seeming to participate, in the goings-on. It sternly warned that it had the power to dismiss federal employees for contravening Section 32 of the Public Service Employment Act. Section 32 does permit a federal employee to attend political meetings, contribute money to a political party and — if granted leave — to be, or seek to be, a candidate in a federal, provincial or territorial election. But it also bars the employees from engaging in work for or against a candidate. In the words of the Commission, no employee "shall engage in, work for, or on behalf of, or against, a political party." Well and good.

Now we come to the PQ referendum on taking Quebec out of Confederation. The Public Service Commission didn't find the issue as clear as it did for an election. A referendum wasn't quite the same as an election, see? Working for a political cause was not quite the same as working for a political party, now was it? Dancing on the head of a pin, the Commission went haring off to the justice department for a legal opinion. Together, the two came up with this: "... as the law now stands it is possible for federal public servants to engage in some referendum activities without violating Section 32. ... Federal employees must recognize that there may well be partisan party work going on during the campaign. Therefore, the Commission considers it appropriate to advise federal employees to take special care and use their own discretion to ensure that any activities they undertake do not actually engage them, as such, in partisan party activity. Furthermore, the Commission must also emphasize that in general, federal employees, in deciding whether to become involved and, if so, in deciding what the specific nature of that involvement might be, should at all times be conscious of their obligation not to engage in activity which might adversely affect their ability to perform their functions in the federal public service in an effective and credible manner. The foregoing consideration should be of particular importance to senior federal employees, especially those involved in policy advice to the government." When in doubt, "employees are advised to consult with their deputy heads."

The object of this wishy-washy directive was to protect the job of the civil servant, not the unity of the country. The Commission in effect gave the partitionists in the federal civil service

— and there are still thousands of them — a free hand to subvert Confederation while staying on the federal payroll, and while Trudeau and his colleagues were fighting energetically against the PQ. Of course, the Commission ruling (or non-ruling) also gave federalists in the civil service a free hand to support federalism. What could be more democratic?

The PQ government of René Lévesque had a split-personality relationship with Ottawa. It preached independence from Canada but at every opportunity took all the money it could from federal coffers. Jocelyne Ouellette, PQ works minister, said it all: "If they [the feds] offer us money, of course we'll take it."

The Quebec situation easily sorted itself out despite all the fire and brimstone. Quebec got the basic rights it wanted: to speak French at work as well as at home, and, like all other Canadians, to go to Florida in the winter.

The Trudeau cabinet in 1978, two years after Lévesque's election to office, took off on something it called the "federal identity program." Huge signs, often installed lopsidedly, were put up outside federal buildings to say they were federal buildings. There was a campaign to name places after famous Canadians, though the Canadians always seemed to be former Liberal cabinet ministers, as in Pearson International Airport, not much of an identification for a foreign tourist planning a trip to Canada. There was a big jag on repainting federal vehicles, but this program began to idle when the cabinet determined that the colors of the political parties could not be used. This ruled out red (Liberal), blue (Conservative), and green (NDP). Brown was also made out of bounds because it was too earthy, though this seemed to deny grass roots. "A government that is not visible cannot be answerable," proclaimed a Treasury Board administrative policy manual on the federal identity program in 1982.

14

Spending as a "Federal Activity"

The euphemism is part of civil service life. One of my favorite examples was that of C.M. Drury when he was chairman of the National Capital Commission. He always changed the phrases "federal spending" or "federal expenditures" to "federal activity." (A former Liberal cabinet minister, Drury in 1979 used to slip information to the Liberals which he didn't give to the Conservative government. He was considerably embarrassed when Erik Nielsen, works minister in the Clark government, wrote to ask him for Commission documents which Drury had already given to Liberal MPs Jean-Robert Gauthier and Jean-Luc Pépin.)

Alongside the euphemism today is the word which has been given a completely new meaning to denote action where little exists or to give the civil service an aura of increased authority. "Affirmative action" means hiring women. "Agenda" is a list of items for a meeting, but its meaning has been changed to a program for action. The word "mandate", meaning authority, usually self-conferred, as in "I have a mandate ...," has been substituted for the word responsibility, which implied an obligation by the civil servant to do something on behalf of the public.

I have long been a collector of bafflegab and gobbledegook (when not practising them) and it is unnerving to find that expressions once scorned have come into everyday use: "financial disequilibrium" for budget deficit; "compensation" for MPs' and civil service pay; "disincentive" for a tax; "clients of Canada manpower centres" for the unemployed; "consumers of welfare" for the poor; "income maintenance programs" for pensions; "taxpayer service" for tax collection; "greater reward in the marketplace" for price increase; "instructional communicator" for teacher; "statistical breakout" for chart; "reverse upward trend" for decline; "resource allocation" for spending; "external environmental diseconomy" for pollution; "recreational complex" for park. I don't think this one ever caught on (thank heaven): "high-speed vertical transportation system" for elevator. The greatest single sentence of bafflegab I ever heard came from Liberal Herb Gray in the House of Commons on January 27, 1969 — "*Let me say at once, Mr. Speaker, this should not necessarily mean that ultimately on balance if it may appear that implementation of such a proposal is the best thing to do under the circumstances, that such a decision should not be made.*"

The government's Principles for the Management of the Public Service of Canada dictate that managers must ensure that titles of positions must be understandable within the civil service and to the public. I wonder what the public would make of this $30,920 job advertised by the RCMP at Regina in the summer of 1985: "Oral interaction assessor." Translation: a judge of the language ability of others. Here's a $37,279 job in the defence department: "Life cycle material manager, interface devices directorate of communications engineering and maintenance." The duties are officially defined: "Incumbent provides specialist services covering communications security and terminal interface, including design, development, acquisition, installation, project management and life cycle management activities."

15
___

"The Tap Is Still On and Running"

Canadians suffer, certainly, from multi-million-dollar bloopers. But they are also being nickeled and dimed to death by the civil service. For example:

The CBC is the biggest featherbedding operation in Canadian history. Many employees goof off during the week, then come in to work weekends at double and triple time. Auditor-General Kenneth Dye said that CBC technicians when at work stand around idle at least ten per cent of the time. Of the 8,500 employees who claimed overtime in 1982-83, a "significant number" made more in overtime than their base salaries and nearly 2,000 made between $5,000 and $40,000 in overtime. CBC reporters say one has to be pretty dumb not to pick up $30,000 or so overtime in a federal election campaign. The CBC's books were in such disarray in 1985-86 that Dye refused to endorse its annual report.

The Canadian Sports Pool Corp., a Liberal boondoggle shut down by the Conservatives, lost nearly $50 million. The severance pay arrangements called for as much as two years' full salary in event of dismissal of Liberal appointees on the staff.

In 1984, the government spent $60 million on long-distance telephone calls, $5 million worth of them personal calls by civil servants. That's 1,200 free long-distance calls a day or more than three million in a year. Free telephone service is provided for civil servants living near Ottawa in places where long-distance charges apply to everybody else. Thousands of civil servants receive free newspapers and magazines on the grounds that they must stay *au courant*; hundreds have television sets to follow, ostensibly, question period and important debates in the House of Commons.

Stealing by civil servants from their office buildings has become so prevalent that many departments now forbid removal of any equipment or material without written authorization. There are notices in washrooms asking users not to make off with paper towels and toilet paper.

The Public Service Commission sometimes awards no-cut contracts. I have one before me which says, "It is further agreed that, in the event a suitable position does not become available immediately upon completion of the [two-year] assignment, the Public Service Commission will guarantee Mr. V. continuous employment until such an opening occurs."

The government provides 21,000 free parking spaces for civil servants in Ottawa. It charges for its 7,000 other spaces, the top price (1986) being $2.30 a day for an underground spot in a heated downtown office building. By 1991, promises Treasury Board, the price will equal the going commercial rate.

Hundreds of civil servants run small businesses from their offices. A civil servant selling tennis balls from his office refused a promotion because the new position would reduce his time for private business. A civil servant who is also a licensed taxi driver has underground parking in his building.

Consultants are hired to do work which the civil service is supposed to do. A small example: In 1981-82, Canada Mortgage and Housing Corporation let a $29,500 contract to T.M. Douglas Enterprises Inc. of Sault Ste. Marie, Ontario, to "co-ordinate ministerial speeches, press relations, etc." The consultant didn't even have to write the speeches.

There are 9,439 civil servants in the social sciences, 60 per cent administrators and only 40 per cent researchers. The total number of employees dropped 14 per cent while the number of executives doubled in six years.

External affairs advertises on television that it sells passports. Does anybody else sell them?

Civil servants cash in personally on airline bonus schemes based on mileage though the travel is on government business. Often these civil servants are in a position to authorize their own trips.

A friend of mine accepted a new, higher-paying job within his department. He told his superior he could complete the first project handed him in three months. He was told to take a year. He said he would be wasting time: three months was plenty. He was again told to take a year; the branch didn't want to risk any staff cut. My friend went back to his old job, where he was busy.

Civil servants love to recommend expenditures. Here are just a few in 1978 by G. Hamilton Southam, then director-general of the National Arts Centre: extension of the Arts Centre into an adjacent park to include a bandshell for 5,400 persons, a 100-seat children's theatre, new offices for all employees of the Centre, four more rehearsal rooms, a 1,200-seat music recital hall, an elevated restaurant, another café beside the Rideau Canal, and an "open-air Greek theatre" (his words) on the front lawn of Parliament Hill. None of these things was done, thank heaven. The Arts Centre's three theatres now are mostly dark, partly because the man who hires acts refuses to fly. Like most amenities in the capital, such as parkways, bicycle paths, and the Rideau Canal's winter conversion to skating rink, the Arts Centre was built by civil servants for civil servants with your money.

In 1986, Treasury Board President Robert de Cotret announced that civil service managers will be awarded financial bonuses for meeting or exceeding spending reduction targets. One would think that was part of the job.

The heading "the tap is still on and running" is taken from the covering letter of an auditor of the National Capital Commission who had just looked into a Commission restoration-development project involving three adjacent properties on York Street in downtown Ottawa. Here's the introduction of his July 27, 1976, report to the Commission's general manager:

Approval in principle was received from Treasury Board (PC 1973-3/3192) for the reconstruction, restoration and development of these properties. The costs quoted were $75,000 for consultation fees and $910,000 for construction.

October 1974 we went forth with a submission for $335,000 for consultants at which time we stated that the reconstruction work was estimated to cost $2 million. To date, we have spent or have signed contracts for $3.5 million in construction costs, the architect has received $540,000, By-York Developments $190,000, and the interior design is not yet ready for us to go to tender. The fact that we do not have Treasury Board authority for some expenditures and other authorities have been exceeded does not appear to have any effect on the project. Another factor is that the original lease (which was never signed by By-York) had received Order-in-Council approval in 1974, was replaced by a management agreement (which was never authorized or signed by the Commission) which has now reverted to a lease that has not been signed by either party nor received Order-in-Council approval. A submission for extras on construction made in January 1976 stated the $5 million being spent is repayable over a 20-year period resulting in a $540,000 per annum payment to the Commission, whereas the latest draft lease calls for an annual rental of $200,000 per annum.

In order to legalize what we have done, certain authorities will be required, which are detailed in the various sections of the report.

In a time of constraint, we authorized the architect, By-York, and one of our people to go to England to purchase antiques. The architect's contract entitles him to a commission of 10 per cent of all purchases made on our behalf, and to act as our purchasing agent.

The antiques cost $60,000 and the travel expenses $4,500. The antiques were supposed to be for an English-style public house in the restored properties, but it has never been built. The antiques include a What the Butler Saw Machine, reconditioned bar billiard table, polyphon music box, church pews, portrait "The Vicars' Daughters," two Flemish tapestries, two British rail lamps, roast beef trolley, and six Trafalgar windows.

Eventually, a Mexican restaurant opened on the site, and a store which sells women's swim suits. Nobody knows where the antiques are; at least the auditor couldn't find out.

16
———

Keep It From the Public Forever

The influence which the civil service exerts on government communications policy is exemplified in this excerpt from a cabinet
paper in 1981 labelled *Government Communications: A Priority
Initiative* (the word initiative has replaced program):

> The Communications Policy Secretariat of the Privy Council
> Office is responsible for supporting the work of the Cabinet
> Committee on Communications in its development of the
> government's communications policy. More specifically, the
> secretariat is responsible for briefing the Chairman of the
> Cabinet Committee on Communications on the policy sub-
> stance of all proposals to Cabinet, so that he can better
> exercise his communications judgment as a member of the
> Cabinet Committee on Priorities and Planning and full
> Cabinet, where he makes a communications report each
> week.

Communications or, to use the old term, public relations,
occupy the minds of ministers and civil servants more than any
other subject. The more they think about press manipulation
the more ham-handed it becomes. The more they talk about
"open" government, the more secretive it is. In early 1984, the
Liberal government ordered that all inter-ministerial correspondence, no matter how trivial or mundane, be labelled "personal
and confidential," thereby exempting it under the *Privacy and
Access to Information Acts.* In early 1986, Prime Minister Mulroney ordered that no proposal to cabinet or to its powerful
priorities and planning committee would even be considered by
those bodies unless it contained a full-fledged public relations
plan for implementation approved by the cabinet committee on
communications. In short, public relations precedes policy. The
prime minister also gave instructions that the chairman of the
communications committee was to make a monthly presentation
to the priorities and planning committee on the progress of government public relations. Ministerial recommendations to cabinet

were to be separated out of the general analysis of ministers' proposals so that they could be withheld from the auditor-general. This meant a complete overhaul of the system for writing and handling cabinet papers.

Inger Hansen, information commissioner, said in her 1985 annual report to Parliament that the civil service keeps searching for ways to keep government information secret instead of finding avenues to release it. At the rate things were going, it would be at least the end of the century before there was freedom of information. Legitimate requests for information were being stonewalled by civil servants, sometimes for years. Hansen added: "Clearly, there is far too little support for freedom of information and far too much belief that something traditionally kept from the public should be kept from the public forever."

17
_____

Some Taxpayers Are More Equal than Others

One group which does not have much difficulty getting access to government information is lobbyists. I do not find anything sinister about them, though they seem to act that way on the supposition that the public so regards them. The regular lobbyists (the Canadian Federation of Agriculture is an example) are highly open, visible and straightforward. Some are far more effective than one might think. In early 1983, there were a least 200,000 illegal immigrants in Canada. They were vital to the low-wage hotel and restaurant industries and those industries did their best to protect the illegals. Indeed, they were highly successful. The immigration department once went so far as to recommend as a method of blocking illegal entry that nobody could draw unemployment insurance unless a Canadian citizen. Nothing was ever done about it. The most successful lobbyists of all, of course, are the biggest financial contributors to the party in power. You can imagine the philanthropic tortures they endure when a minority government is in temporary power.

My favorite lobby story concerns the sudden flurry of activity in a downtown Ottawa office building to remove a name from the directory in the lobby. Under British-American Oil Co. Ltd. there appeared: "Government representative — Hon. J.J. Connolly." Liberal Senator John J. Connolly was government leader in the Senate, a cabinet portfolio. A company couldn't hope for a much better-placed lobbyist than that.

Lobbying generally results in one taxpayer being treated more equally than another, and an account of such a case follows:

The wide disparity in the national revenue department's treatment of big and small taxpayers is illustrated in the concurrent cases of the giant Amway Corporation and some Newfoundland fishermen. While the department tip-toed around Amway, it thundered at the fishermen to pay up, and fast.

On February 6, 1979, Border Brokers Ltd. of Toronto blew the whistle on Amway Corp. of Ada, Michigan, and its wholly-owned subsidiary, Amway of Canada Ltd., London, Ontario, for dodging Customs duties and sales tax through undervaluation of goods by phoney invoices. By the end of 1986, not one cent of the original $148,018,478.48 owing to national revenue had been collected.

In early 1982, the revenue department descended on Newfoundland demanding payment from nearly 2,000 fishermen for what it claimed were unpaid taxes totalling some $8 million. This heavy hand was exercised by the deputy minister of national revenue for taxation, Bruce MacDonald, a good and honest man but afflicted with narrow vision. He put his campaign into effect despite the fact that Newfoundland's representative in the cabinet, William Rompkey, was minister of national revenue. Rompkey managed to ease the situation, after the event, and MacDonald was sent to deep obscurity in another department. But three years later, under a new Conservative government, and with a new deputy minister of national revenue for taxation, Harry Rogers, the department again went after 1,860 Newfoundland fishermen for alleged back taxes totalling $8.6 million — while the fishermen were experiencing their worst season in decades. In the meantime, the department had reduced its claim against Amway to $105 million.

Let's review the Amway case.

The investigations unit of the Customs and Excise division of the national revenue department moved swiftly after the accusations of irregularities against Amway made by Amway's own Canadian brokerage firm, Border Brokers. It quickly determined that Amway, a huge door-to-door salesman of soap and other household products, owed the Canadian government $148 million for the period January 7, 1977, to January 28, 1980. It filed its case in the Federal Court in Toronto in March, 1980. Nothing happened.

The Federal Court is one of those places where the press never runs regular checks. Furthermore, the Customs and Excise side of national revenue did not believe in tipping off the press to such cases. This was a holdover from the days of David Sim, a deputy minister in the department from 1930 to 1965 and a man with a terrifying command of detail. As a Canadian Press reporter, I once had occasion to put a question to national revenue and called an underling on the grounds that you don't waste a call to the brass for unimportant details when next time the brass might ignore you when the question is important. The underling said my call would be returned, and it was, a few minutes later, by Sim. "If you have a question about the department, you call me, and nobody else," he told me. "If I don't know the answer, I can get it damn quick." Officials in the department were understandably very shy about talking with reporters and this shyness persists, by and large, to this day. There is another reason, of course, as Sim explained to me many years later: the department is a tax collector and a tax collector seldom, if ever, has any good news for anybody. One does not court the press, he said, to issue bad news. Bad news finds its own way out quickly enough.

The $148 million Canadian government claim against Amway lay unreported in the Federal Court files for more than two years.

Meantime, back in the department, there was thought being given to criminal charges against Amway as well as the civil action. On December 5, 1981, J.C. Connell, deputy minister of national revenue for Customs and Excise, wrote to Revenue Minister Rompkey about the Amway case:

> As some time has transpired since Amway of Canada became the subject of a Customs investigation dealing with an alleged

undervaluation of imported goods, I wish to provide you with an update of the matter.

At the outset of this case, in view of the size of the alleged forfeiture, it was decided to immediately file Statements of Claim in the Federal Court. This action was taken to preclude the possibility of the Department becoming "statute barred" with respect to penalties by virtue of Section 265 of the Customs Act. The statements were filed with the Federal Court and duly served on Amway with the advice that a Statement of Defence was not required at that time.

Subsequently, I decided to refer the criminal prosecution aspects of this seizure to the R.C.M. Police. The R.C.M. Police after further investigation of their own, referred the file to the Crown Attorney for the Province of Ontario for prosecution. The Provincial Crown Attorney's Office was to determine whether the charges would be appropriate under the Criminal Code. It was agreed that this Department would not proceed with the civil adjudication of this case pending a determination of the charges, if any, which might be laid under the provisions of the Criminal Code. To date, despite numerous attempts to get a commitment, we have not been advised if the Crown intends to proceed with charges.

There follows mention of the possibility of Amway of Canada disposing of its corporate assets before the department could collect, and a discussion of going ahead with the civil suit "in view of the extremely large assessment alleged and the fact that the Province had not yet laid charges." Connell then presents to Rompkey varying amounts of duties, taxes and penalties which the department could exact from Amway under varying circumstances and conditions. Connell concluded his memorandum to Rompkey this way:

With your concurrence, I would like to proceed as follows:
— advise the Ontario Provincial Crown Attorney that we are proceeding forthwith with the civil adjudication of this case.
— advise Amway of Canada Limited that we are willing to accept any further representation they wish to make prior to decision.

> The course of action outlined above has been discussed with the Department of Justice legal advisors assigned to the Department and they are in agreement.

There was apparently no reply, or even acknowledgment, from Rompkey, and the office of the attorney-general of Ontario announced no action of any kind against Amway. Silence reigned.

On the taxation side of the national revenue department, however, plans were honed to go after Newfoundland fishermen for $8-million and early in 1982 departmental auditors swept into the outports and demanded that fishermen justify the tax-deductible expenses they had claimed. There were demands by the department that fishermen sell their houses to pay off assessments and threats to garnishee wages of fishplant workers.

Rompkey, apparently unaware of what his deputy minister for taxation, Bruce MacDonald, was up to before the blow struck, did his best to soften it after he found out. He appointed a St. John's lawyer, William Rowe, to look quickly into the situation and make some fast recommendations. Rowe had a preliminary report ready by May, 1982, and Rompkey promptly accepted his initial six recommendations. The main recommendation was that the portion of a fisherman's net income which could be garnisheed for back taxes be reduced from 50 to 25 per cent. That restriction remained in effect until October, 1985, when it was lifted by a new Conservative government with an Atlantic Provinces minister (Elmer MacKay of Nova Scotia) and a new deputy minister (Rogers).

Rowe in 1982 completed a final report, which was never published, and the abuses he outlined were not corrected by the revenue department. The Conservatives scented the growing public outrage with the department and, when the Liberals refused a special parliamentary inquiry, set up their own travelling committee at which citizens high and low unburdened themselves of pent-up fury at the revenuers. The chairman of the committee, Perrin Beatty, first elected to the Commons in 1972 at age twenty-two, made a hatful of publicity and ended up, with the Conservative election victory in 1984, as the minister of national revenue, where he issued a "charter of taxpayers' rights," which had no basis in law, before dancing on to his next portfolio eleven months later. All revenue ministers are on the way up or down. Beatty was on the way up. Twenty-four other ministers of national revenue since Confederation have held the office for less than a year.

Seven months after Connell's memorandum saying that the attorney-general's department of Ontario was not making any move and in the absence of any ministerial instruction to Connell to proceed with civil action, the Amway case was dormant. Amway in 1980 had put on its payroll Vernon Acree, former United States Customs commissioner rewarded with that job for using his previous job as U.S. internal revenue commissioner to draw the tax files on persons being forced into line by the Nixon administration to try to cover up Watergate. The millionaire owners of Amway, Jay VanAndel, chairman, and Richard DeVos, president, had close political ties with the Republicans. VanAndel is a personal friend of former U.S. President Gerald Ford and when the Ford presidential library at Grand Rapids, Michigan, was opened in 1981, Prime Minister Trudeau of Canada was among the guests. Premier John Buchanan of Nova Scotia had visited Amway headquarters at Ada, Michigan, also in 1981, Amway paying his way. Canadian ambassador Ken Taylor, hero of Iran, was given a medal on a VanAndel-DeVos yacht. VanAndel and DeVos were two of the five biggest individual financial supporters of the first Ronald Reagan presidential campaign (about $70,000 each) and in March, 1981, DeVos was made finance chairman of the Republican National Committee, a post from which he was fired August 12, 1982, for unstated reasons.

Within the Customs and Excise division of national revenue there was increasing frustration at the lack of any action, criminal or civil, against Amway, especially when it was known that the case against the company had been filed two years earlier in Federal Court where the documents were available to anyone who chose to look.

Finally, in the early summer of 1982, the *Windsor Star* began receiving small pieces of information about the case, but veiled and largely incomprehensible. They were enough, however, to prompt the newspaper to call Customs, where all kinds of officials were dying for such a call. Despite the old Sim rule, an official in the revenue department told the *Star* where to look — in the Federal Court in Toronto. One person on the *Star* knows the name of the informant. So do I, and I'm not telling, because it might hurt a promising career. The *Star* broke the story July 7, 1982.

Incredibly, nothing happened. It was obviously going to take a much bigger fire to smoke out the attorney-general of Ontario. The bigger fire was stoked up by the *Detroit Free Press*. On August 22, 1981, it reported that Amway had bilked the Canadian government of tens of millions of dollars in Customs duties. It had a sheaf of documents to back its charge. Amway the next day announced a $500 million libel suit against the *Free Press* but when the deadline came one year later for actually filing it, Amway took no action. Its public relations director, a man with a pure Amway name, Casey Wondergem, said the corporation couldn't fully air the facts in a libel suit because it was still involved in a "tariff dispute" with the Canadian revenue department.

The *Windsor Star* in its original story said possible criminal charges against Amway were pending, and the *Detroit Free Press*, not beating about the bush, had accused Amway of fraud. The *Star* kept up the pressure, with its own bundle of documents, and gradually more and more newspapers joined the hunt. Still, it was not until November 12, 1982, that the RCMP, acting for the attorney-general of Ontario (Roy McMurtry), laid criminal charges against Amway Corp. of the United States, Amway of Canada, and its top four executive officers: VanAndel, DeVos and William Halliday and C. Dale Discher, vice-presidents. The charges said they "unlawfully did, by deceit, falsehood or other fraudulent means, defraud" Canada of Customs duties in excess of $22 million. The question remains: would Amway have been charged if two newspapers, one Canadian and one American, had not uncovered the scam? The answer seems to be no, because no action had been taken in the previous two-and-half years.

Six days after the criminal charges were laid, VanAndel and DeVos held a press conference to say that the accusations stemmed from an anti-American bias in Canada, Canadian trade protectionism, and a vendetta by a former employee, Edward Engle, vice-president and business manager of the *Free Press*. Engle had worked for Amway from 1976 to 1979 and was kicked out when he confronted the executive with the company's deliberate fraud. Engel was not the chief informant from inside Amway, but he bravely made it appear so by telling reporters that he had talked with Canadian investigators.

To show how far and how fast Amway could reach politically, the Canadian embassy in Washington on November 22, 1982, received a gratuitous opinion from the U.S. State Department that the Amway executives could not be extradited, as Canada had sought, to face the criminal charges. Since extradition between the two countries is largely discretionary, the U.S. was in effect telling Canada that Canada could not get its hands on the four.

Another year went by, now almost five since the fraud investigation began and eighteen since the actual fraud had started. On November 10, 1983, Amway Corp. and Amway of Canada Ltd. pleaded guilty to fraud and were fined $25 million, the largest fine in Canadian history. In exchange, the crown dropped the charges against the four executives. The $25 million was paid to Ontario. The federal government still didn't have a dime from Amway of the $148 million originally sought.

One would think that Amway, having pleaded guilty to criminal fraud resulting in a record fine, would have paid the Customs duties, taxes and penalties owing. Instead, it managed through negotiation with national revenue to lower the amount owing for 1977-80 to $105 million, then defied the department to take the case to Federal Court to try to retrieve it.

And Amway applied more political pressure.

In early January, 1985, an official in Revenue Minister Perrin Beatty's office received a telephone call from the privy council office saying that Alexander Haig was coming to Ottawa to see Beatty on behalf of Amway. VanAndel and DeVos had called in another IOU.

The reason given by the official in the privy council office for a meeting with Haig, the former U.S. secretary of state, was that Prime Minister Mulroney did not want to do anything to hurt relations with President Reagan. A meeting had been requested and the request had been granted, period. Beatty was incensed at being put in such a position and did his best to try to get out of the meeting, attempting at one point to push it off onto Finance Minister Michael Wilson. Haig arrived secretly a couple of weeks later and Beatty did what he could under the circumstances; he refused to see Haig alone, as was apparently Haig's intention, and had a senior departmental official sit in as a witness.

The meeting came at a time when the lawyers for the crown and Amway were sparring over the preliminaries of civil court action. Later, Amway said publicly that even if the revenue department won a judgment and seized all the company's assets in Canada it wouldn't get back ten cents on the dollar. Furthermore, Amway could set up another company to carry on its Canadian business. From such statements, it is obvious (and no more so than to the officials of the revenue department) that Ottawa will never get $105 million out of Amway, or anything like that amount, ever. Indeed, authorities in national revenue had idly speculated on how much money Amway must have made by investing the $148 million (or $105 million) it saved by cheating the Canadian government. DeVos seemed to cap the affair in January, 1986, when he told the Michigan Press Association that Amway's "legal" problems with the Canadian government would have been quietly resolved if the press hadn't overplayed the story: "We, like others, have been the victims of poor reporting."

The Haig visit is one example of the under-the-counter pressure the Reagan administration has kept on the Mulroney government. Here's another, which will require some backgrounding.

18
―――――

Pakistan and the Bomb

It starts in the early 1950s (the date is imprecise because the records have been destroyed and the surviving principals will not talk for the record) when the Canadian Armament Research and Development Establishment at Valcartier, Quebec, a division of the Defence Research Board, built an atomic bomb.

The purpose was not a useable bomb itself, of course, but its mechanism to prove that Canadian scientists could produce one if the government ever decided to change its policy and enter the field of nuclear weaponry. Canada was already producing plutonium, the lethal ingredient of the bomb, for Britain and the United States. The intention was not to try to subvert the government's non-nuclear policy. (The Pearson and Trudeau governments later armed the Canadian military with American nuclear weapons, and allowed the Americans to store nuclear weapons in Canada for U.S. purposes, such as bombing Russia, but that is another story dealt with in the chapter on defence policy.)

The Valcartier bomb, as it turned out, was not difficult to build because Canadians already had a great deal of experience with atomic energy, including the atomic reactor at Chalk River, Ontario, developed during the Second World War, and the British nuclear arms program. Two of the men involved in construction of the Valcartier bomb had taken part in the British program (and were asked to leave when the British thought they knew too much). One was a scientist, the other an engineer. The Valcartier research unit did not broadcast its project, of course, but neither did it try to hide it from the government. Given its background and knowledge in the field, the unit did not even regard it as a stunning accomplishment but rather as a routine development of its gathered experience. In any event, the Defence Research Board, then but not now an important branch of the Canadian military, informed Prime Minister St. Laurent about the Valcartier bomb. He was taken aback, naturally enough, because the experiment flew in the face of announced and carefully nurtured non-nuclear policy. He ordered the bomb dismantled. This was done immediately, in 1954, and no more was ever heard of it, although a surprising number of officials came to know about it in a general way. In 1983, preparations were being made to write a short, official account of the Valcartier bomb, but the key man, Alex Longhair, was killed in a traffic accident while visiting England and the writing project was abandoned, temporarily at least.

I cite the Valcartier project to show that Canadians are no slouches in the field of atomic weaponry, even though the government gradually divested the Canadian armed forces of their American nuclear capability, thereby leaving them with far less firepower than they had in the Second World War.

In the late 1970s, Pakistan, among other countries, was working its scientific fingers to the bone trying to build an atomic bomb. It didn't have all the required parts and at first tried to obtain them surreptitiously in France and Britain. The French secret service allowed the Pakistani agents to assemble all the parts they were seeking in a warehouse at Marseilles for shipment. Then it tipped off Mossad, the Israeli secret service, which fired the warehouse. The British secret service was a little more subtle when Pakistan turned to the United Kingdom for the parts. Like its French counterpart, it permitted the Pakistani agents to collect the parts, then switched them for dud equipment. Presumably, the Pakistanis didn't find out until the fake parts reached the scientists at home.

It followed that Pakistan would try North America next, which it did, in Canada, in 1980. Our security service knew all about the clandestine operation, having been tipped off by French and British intelligence. At the time, Mark MacGuigan had been a nervous external affairs minister for only a few months and he was scared to death that he might make a mistake (he never did get over that). He dithered among several options: order the companies which made the parts Pakistan coveted not to sell to the Pakistani agents; deport the agents quietly; tell Pakistan privately but, if need be, publicly, to quit spying on us. MacGuigan couldn't bring himself to do any of the above, though officials pleaded with him to inform Pakistani President Zia ul-Haq that we were onto their game and to cease and desist before he was caused public embarrassment. Canada had special reason to take such action because it had supplied Pakistan with an atomic reactor which Trudeau had visited in 1971, receiving repeated Pakistani assurances that it had no nuclear arms intentions. But MacGuigan didn't want to harm relations with a Commonwealth country and, besides, he didn't believe that all the bomb parts Pakistan required could be acquired in Canada.

Pakistan set up two dummy companies in Montreal to acquire parts which had been made in the United States. Eleven shipments of electronic parts such as resistors and diodes were made to Pakistan in 1980 before Canada was forced to crack down. Two men were arrested in Montreal. In August, 1984, the two men and one company were fined $3,000 each for exporting restricted goods without a permit. The prosecution apparently used the soft pedal at the request of external affairs. One month before the conviction, President Zia said Pakistan has the capability to build a nuclear bomb but has neither the financial means nor the desire to do so.

The Mulroney government paid the price for MacGuigan's dithering. The Reagan administration insisted that Canada must bear down hard on exports of any nuclear-connected equipment, even parts for peaceful Canadian atomic reactors abroad. By the summer of 1985, an elaborate export controls system had been established and was in operation to detect illegal transfers of high-technology goods to the Eastern Bloc. In the first month, more than 140 shipments were detained pending proof that export was legal or otherwise or to await decision by external affairs, which meant checking with Washington. Canada even agreed to monitor exports to Nicaragua, and the United States objected to Canada sending CANDU reactor parts to Romania. Star Wars material and oil technology were put on the list of goods requiring export permits. There are American Customs agents in Canada to help oversee the Canadian export controls.

19

The Case of the Would-Be Defector

Another example of American pressure on the Mulroney government is the case of the Russian would-be defector, Miroslav Medvid.

The Soviet freighter *Konev* left New Orleans in early November, 1985, with crewman Medvid aboard despite alleged attempts by Medvid to jump ship and angry protestations by U.S. Congressmen that American authorities grab him in the cause of freedom.

The *Konev's* next port of call was Port Cartier, Quebec, in the federal riding of Prime Minister Mulroney. The United States, after bungling, probably deliberately, the attempt to free a defector who did not seem all that keen on defecting, suggested that Canada might play a hand in the affair. The *Konev* was due at Port Cartier November 18, the day before the start of the Geneva summit meeting of President Reagan and Secretary Gorbachev.

The prime minister's office, the external affairs department, the immigration department, and the RCMP, to name only a few, were thrown into a fit. What if something happened which would cause a ruckus at the summit, or even cancel it? Port Cartier was put on alert like no port in wartime. The place swarmed with RCMP and immigration officers. The instructions were that if Medvid really wanted to defect, grab him and hold him, but don't upset the Russians. How this double could be done, nobody seemed sure.

The nervousness rose another notch when the *Konev* couldn't berth on November 18 because of a gale and had to wait until the next morning, the very day the summit was to begin. Officials in Ottawa stood by their phones fearing the worst as immigration men clambered aboard the *Konev*, as they had every legal right to do, and asked about the crew and passenger list. The captain, they said later, appeared nervous. The manifest showed forty-two names but the captain said there were only forty-one aboard.

Ah ha, where was the forty-second?

Well, said the captain, that man had become sick and had been transferred at sea to another Soviet ship which carried a doctor. The sigh of relief in Ottawa caused a chinook in the Urals.